ALMOST A LIFETIME

To Cliff Dawe

April 26/96

Almost A Lifetime

John McMahon

Wishing you an abundance of happy and rewarding days in the years ahead

Sincerely,

John McMahon

oolichan books
Lantzville, British Columbia, Canada
1995

Acknowledgements

This work could not have been written without the help and the understanding of others, especially my wife Alice, who lost me for many hundreds of hours as I wrestled with the words that would tell my story.

My thanks to Barbara McMahon and her typewriter, without whose assistance and encouragement my manuscript would never have got off the ground. I appreciate her help and many suggestions. To Rachel DeCaria and her word processor, a big thanks. Her cooperation and tolerance regarding the many changes made it possible to complete this project. My sincere thanks to Jay Connolly of Oolichan Books, who has with patient dedication guided me through numerous editing excursions. And thanks to all the enthusiastic friends and others who, by continually asking, "When can I buy your book?" gave me the incentive to finish it.

Canadian Cataloguing in Publication Data

McMahon, John, 1921-
Almost a lifetime

ISBN 0-88982-144-5 (bound) — ISBN 0-88982-143-7 (pbk.)

1. McMahon, John, 1921- 2. World War, 1939-1945—Personal narratives, British. 3. World War, 1939-1945—Prisoners and prisons, German.
4. Prisoners of war—Canada—Biography. 5. Prisoners of war—Germany—Biography. I. Title

D811.M35 1995   940.54'7243'092   C95-910238-8

The publisher gratefully acknowledges the financial assistance of the Canada Council.

Published by
Oolichan Books
P.O. Box 10,
Lantzville, British Columbia
Canada, V0R 2H0

Printed in Canada by
Morriss Printing Company
Victoria, British Columbia

CONTENTS

*Dedicated to
my six aircrew comrades
who flew with me
and lost their lives
February 2, 1943*

FOREWORD

In this year of 1995, to a multitude of men growing old, memories remain vivid of the places and circumstances more than five decades distant. During World War II, these men were young airmen without wings —incarcerated behind barbed wire fences—and I was one of them.

I hope that as this story unfolds, it will turn back the clock for these men to days when their own strength of character, humour, and comradeship defeated the humiliation and restriction of confinement. My initial intention, in writing these chapters, was personal, but the story evolved into something that I felt must be shared. This isn't a war story in general terms, but a narrative about some of the people with whom I was privileged to share an extraordinary part of my life.

In Holland, early in 1943, a Dutch family gave me shelter and cared for my cuts and bruises (despite their knowledge of the severe penalties for helping Allied airmen) before German Military Police made me prisoner. Thirty-eight years after hostilities ceased, the names and location of the Dutch family were still unknown to me. I accepted the challenge of finding them. In May of 1983 I flew to Holland. My search ended when a tenacious Dutchman unearthed *one small scrap of paper* that led me to a remarkable reunion.

There was another person who played a fateful part in this narrative. Without his entry into the vagaries of life, most of this story could not have been written, because the events herein would not have occurred. As the only survivor of a shot-down British bomber, my search forty-one years later for the pilot of the aircraft that destroyed our plane and killed my six comrades was not a vengeful expedition, but one motivated more by curiosity to find out who and what kind of man was our enemy in the night sky of February 2, 1943.

— John McMahon, Saltspring Island, B.C., January 1995

CHAPTER 1

Joining the RAF

It was the spring of 1940 and a Wednesday afternoon as I peddled my old Rudge Whitworth cycle up Clifton Street, listening to the cycle chain creak and groan with the punishing strain of the gradient. The afternoon was warm for the time of year, and Belfast was enjoying bright sunshine.

I was a bright nineteen-year-old—5'7" and 145 pounds, with a fair complexion and good looks. Hard work in a grocery chain store helped promote my sturdy build, but being short in the leg irked me. I often kept the saddle of my bicycle higher than was comfortable, hoping that the constant stretching would in some manner assist leg growth. They never grew long enough to make me a six-footer, but in later years they endured a remarkable punishment and saved my life.

I had decided to open another door to a more exciting occupation. The war in Europe was seven months old.

I planned to join the Royal Air Force as a transport driver, and as I cycled up the street that day, other thoughts raced through my head. Joining the Air Force meant I would be leaving someone dear to me. Alice McAdam had been a big interest in my life since we met some four years before. Competing for Alice's hand was my good friend, Alexander Campbell, a store employee and workmate who went by the nickname of Sandy. He often returned late from lunch and caught a tongue-lashing from old Tom, the manager. "I missed the trolley," he'd protest; or "The roads were plugged by an accident."

I knew the real reason. My information came from Alice. Whenever possible, Sandy waited for the trolley car that carried Alice to work, and if he spied an empty seat beside her, down he would plop, smiling and congenial, his eyes twinkling with delight at his own accomplishment. This, for me, was definitely competition.

Another friend and store employee was Andrew Duke, a couple of years our senior. The three of us made up a good team, and we spent many pleasant working hours together. Tom delighted in calling this third staff member "Andrew the Duke." Shortly after the outbreak of war, Andrew joined the Royal Marine Commandos.

I'd kept secret my journey to the recruiting offices. I had some misgivings about my decision to join up. I would be leaving home comforts, friends, my job and girlfriend, but I had to prove something to myself and take the chance that I'd live to return.

At my destination I hopped off my old cycle and propped it against the wall. A moment later I was hailed by none other than a grinning Sandy Campbell. "It'll be headlines in the German papers when they get to know. Won't Hitler be worried now?" he exclaimed. "What are you talking about?" I queried.

"Me!" he laughed. "I've joined aircrew and passed my medical. I'm going as air gunner." His exuberance was fascinating. "I'm going to phone old Tom and tell him to stick his job."

So this was his reason for taking the day off work.

"Don't think they'll take you in the Air Force," he grinned. "Better try the Army!"

He sprinted after the trolley car that was slowly gathering speed up the incline. His legs flying like pistons at full throttle, he overtook the trolley and flung himself aboard. Grasping the upright pole on the platform, and with one foot on the step, the other swinging in space, he leaned out and waved a mock farewell.

I made my way down a dark hallway. At the end, a big blue arrow on a white background pointed the way to a door with "RAF Recruiter" stencilled clearly on the glass panel.

A voice from behind said, "Go right in, sir." I turned and came face-to-face with two rows of World War I ribbons vivid on the left breast of an Air Force uniform. Above the black tie and starched blue collar, I beheld a round, weather-beaten face, quizzical blue eyes, and a crown of close-cropped grey hair.

"Can I help you select which branch of the Air Force you desire to serve with?" Off guard, I found myself minutes later sitting with him discussing my future, which resulted in my signature for ground-crew training.

Ninety minutes passed before I was again out in the sunshine, retrieving my bicycle from two ragged little kids who were taking turns riding it up and down the sidewalk.

Pushing up the hill towards home, I considered the afternoon's events. To see the other side of life and play a little part in the war was something that had been gnawing at my conscience for many weeks. Was it the chance for adventure, an excuse to get away from home, or "the poignant call of King and Country"?

✈

I had a date with Alice that night at 7:00, and I did not want to be late. I took advantage of a lull in the family chatter to drop a bombshell by saying: "I joined the Royal Air Force this afternoon."

Father, stepmother, my older brother Fred, and my young sister Kay looked at me in consternation.

There was a moment of hushed silence. Then Kay clapped her hands with delight: "I love Air Force uniforms," she chanted.

Father's face took on a worried look. "Will you be flying?"

"No, at least not for now." I was surprised with my answer, as aircrew was not in my plans.

✈

After the show that evening, we ate fish and chips at our usual cosy restaurant, and I told Alice my plans.

Her blue eyes saddened for a moment and then brightened. "I'm glad you did this. I'll be very proud of you."

"Sandy Campbell was at the recruiting office," I went on, "and he joined aircrew as a gunner."

"I know. We were on the same trolley car yesterday at lunch time."

Sandy had been up to his trolley-car tricks. Maybe it was better this way. At least it did not appear I was joining up because Sandy had decided to do so.

We lingered longer than usual saying good night. "Don't come in," she said. I knew she didn't want her father to argue with me because I had kept her out after 10:30.

Walking home, I felt a little frightened at the prospect of the uncertain future, signed and sealed by my own hand.

✈

Seven weeks later the "On His Majesty's Service" envelope arrived. I was ordered to report to the Recruiting Centre in three days.

My last evening was not a happy one. As I walked the deserted streets towards home, my morale was low. Close to midnight I opened the iron gate and closed it gently, so not to wake father. My brother Fred had not drawn our bedroom drapes. He was sound asleep, so I slipped quietly into my side of the big bed. Outside, the gas-burning street lamp shed warm slivers of yellow light into the small room, and soon I drifted off to a dreamless sleep.

Next morning I woke early and stared for a while at the slanted ceiling of the attic bedroom I'd shared with my brother for the last fourteen years. He was still asleep. I got out of bed and moved to the open window. Looking southward across the slate rooftops of the city on this clear June morning, I could see, away beyond the city outskirts, Scrabo Tower glistening in the early sunlight, tall and slim as a new school pencil. East, away across the Irish Sea off Scotland's Ayrshire Coast, the big rock called "Paddy's Milestone" loomed clear.

On the dresser below the window sat the gold Hunter pocket watch an uncle had given me. I took it in my hands and pressed the release catch. The cover sprang open, and the old face seemed to smile at me through the cracked glass: six o'clock.

A trolley car rattled past the corner of our street. Across the road, from his horse-drawn wagon, the Windsor Bakery salesman filled a big rectangular basket with fresh bread, rolls, and confections for the grocery store. The horse's feedbag had come loose and hung only by the horse's ear. The animal was annoyed because the bag opening had closed and he could not eat. He threw his head up and down, and each time the feedbag swung outwards it spilled oats, much to the delight of pigeons and sparrows that had gathered for an unexpected early morning breakfast.

The salesman about to enter the store noticed what was happening and put down his basket of bread and baked goods. Quickly he rectified the problem, but first decided to give the horse a couple of hard smacks on the side of his mouth—chastising him for wasting oats.

I chuckled as the salesman picked up the basket. He had not seen the youngster in bare feet taking advantage of the unattended basket to steal a few goodies. I thought, Good—the salesman deserves to lose. If he hadn't spent those moments beating his horse he might have caught the little boy in the act. And there was a question in my mind. Was it the penny custards and currant squares or the two-penny cream-filled buns the barefooted urchin got away with? I knew about these things because my father was also a bread salesman. Each morning, he left the house at 5:00 a.m. to pack his bread wagon at the bakery. He'd then harness and hitch the horse to his wagon before heading home for an 8:00 a.m. breakfast.

Going down to the bathroom, I washed and shaved, then made my way upstairs and changed into grey slacks, white shirt, and brown tie.

I sat down to breakfast with my brother Fred and my stepmother. At ten to eight, Kay came downstairs in her housecoat and volunteered to watch for our father. "Here he is," she said after a minute.

I picked up my bag of essentials and met Dad in the hallway.

"Sorry I'm late," he said.

"Got to get going, Dad." Knowing how sentimental he was, I wanted to leave quickly.

"Good luck, son. We'll be praying for your safety." I grabbed my jacket. After a quick goodbye, I bounded down the steps and out the garden gate. At the street corner, I turned and waved. The four of them waved their own farewells.

When I arrived at the recruiting office, several men stood outside with small parcels or suitcases.

By nine the complement of recruits for that day's transportation had arrived. We hustled to our transport and scrambled aboard.

At our destination, the London Midland and Scottish Railway station, the first spatter of rain mottled the dry pavement. The Boat Train that made connection with the ferry service to Scotland was crammed with troops and almost ready to depart on its short twenty-four-mile journey north to Larne.

I followed my twelve companions.

An Air Force Service Police sergeant took charge. "Okay, you people, board this rail car quickly." We obeyed his command and were to hear the term "you people" many times before our official induction into the Air Force.

Soon the train clanked and puffed out of the station onto the main line North as rain clouds let go a steady downpour.

I could see through the rain Harland and Wolffe Shipyard, with its giant gantries.

Across the Lough on the County Down side there was no rain, and sunlight spread shimmering light on the green slopes above Holywood and glinted off white sails in the bay as one of the yacht clubs had set out for a few hours' sailing.

I wondered what this new life would hold for me, and what would the "cost" be for my return fare? A lost leg, arm, or some other disablement? Would I return at all? Sure, there was the possibility of being killed; this was wartime. But at nineteen one feels indestructible, and I felt certain I would survive.

A tall, good-looking pipe smoker in our group produced a pack of cards, introduced himself as Tom O'Donovan, and asked, "Who wants to gamble?" The card game survived the boat trip, plus two train journeys, and was still going when we arrived at our destination.

At the induction centre we were relegated to quarters, all commands preceded by the words, "You people." There was little talk that first night.

Six o'clock next morning I opened my eyes to the cry of "Rise and shine!"

"We people" washed, shaved, and ate. Next we were sworn in and provided with clothing. Suddenly, "You people" became "You airmen."

I would not be a truck driver, I discovered; I would be trained as an airframe mechanic.

The journey to training camp was monotonous. We were the pioneers in this new camp—the first recruits—and it was here we were introduced to our disciplinarian, Warrant Officer Mulcaughey, or "the Mighty Atom," as he was ultimately christened.

I claimed a bed in one corner of the hut. On the opposite side were three people: Vincent Devenny, Frank Wilson, and Harry McNeill. These three had become firm companions and were nicknamed "the Three Musketeers."

✈

A weekend leave was granted—Friday 1600 hours until Sunday 2359 hours? We didn't know anyone in England. We had no friends to visit, and no extra money to pay hotel bills. After a brainstorm session, six of us put in for weekend passes, with destination Northern Ireland, knowing if the passes were processed without question we would be at least a day late returning to base. All six were unexpectedly processed. Some of us accepted the consequences of being away one extra day or more without permission: the Three Musketeers (Wilson, McNeill and Devenny), plus George McKay, Tom O'Donovan, and me.

It was a fine, warm Saturday morning when we arrived in Larne. The journey to Belfast was hot. Tom O'Donovan made arrangements for meeting again on Monday morning.

At York Street I left the group and dodged into the ladies wear store where Alice worked. When I went in, she was serving a customer. Suddenly she looked up and in shocked surprise exclaimed, "Why didn't you tell me?" Then added, "You look good in uniform."

Sandy Campbell, it turned out, had already been home on leave. He had passed his training and was returning to a Bomber Squadron in Lincolnshire, England. Alice said it was now Sergeant Campbell and he wore his air gunner badge and three stripes with great pride. I knew from the way she spoke that here indeed was real opposition.

"I'll explain at lunch time. We've only forty-eight hours leave. See you at noon." I exited quickly to visit old Tom at the grocery store, and he gave me a hero's welcome.

"Come in, come in," he crooned. "Boy, you look good. Have some tea," and he fussed around, opening a package of cookies and firing up the gas ring under the old blue enamel teapot.

He wanted to know everything that had happened to me since I'd left. Exhausting his queries, he turned to me with a sly look. "How about the girl in the ladies wear store? That's what you're here for, not to see me. They close for lunch at noon and you're just putting in time." He elbowed me playfully and, laughing, pushed me out of the store.

Alice and I ate at a small café on Royal Avenue and arranged to meet again later.

On the Number Six trolley home, I wondered what surprised and shocked greeting was ahead.

✈

That night, after a wonderful evening with Alice, I returned again to my childhood bedroom. My brother was snoring gently when I entered the attic room. I slipped into bed and thought about Sandy Campbell and his sergeant's stripes. I was still lowly Aircraftman Second Class John McMahon, which didn't come close to the sound of "Sergeant Alexander Campbell, Air Gunner Bomber Command." I lay awake and thought of the last time we'd met and the exuberant joy bottled in his laughing brown eyes. "I've joined aircrew and passed my medical. I'm going as air gunner."

✈

On Sunday evening—the last precious hours of the weekend—I walked with Alice toward her home. Our footsteps slowed until in the dusk at her street corner we stood searching for comfort.

When we stepped inside the house, her mother quickly poured us cups of tea. I knew something was wrong. Her father asked, "Did you see last night's paper?"

"No," I said. "Didn't have time to read much this weekend or listen to the news." I smiled at Alice.

Alice's father handed us the Saturday night edition of the *Belfast Telegraph*. Alice whispered, "No." But there it was—on the same page with half a dozen others—above the heading MISSING AIR OFFICER. The caption of another bereavement read, DIED WHILE WAR PRISONER. There was a farewell letter from a young airman who, like many others in wartime, had had a premonition of his own impending death. This was not a mistake—in print was the notification to those who knew him and to all who read these Saturday night sad columns. The heading read, BELFAST YOUTH OF 19 MADE SUPREME SACRIFICE, followed by, NOTIFICATION HAS BEEN RECEIVED THAT SERGEANT ALEXANDER CAMPBELL HAS BEEN KILLED ON ACTIVE SERVICE.

We read the report several times, trying to absorb the reality.

A few weeks earlier my parents had mailed me a newspaper clipping with the same quarter-inch capital letters: ROYAL MARINES COMMANDO KILLED IN ACTION. A similar announcement, this time from different heartbroken parents, explained that "Andrew the Duke" had paid war's full price. And now Sandy. My two friends from the grocery-store days were dead.

MADE SUPREME SACRIFICE.

BELFAST YOUTH OF 19.

Notification has been received by Mr. and Mrs. James Campbell, of Wheatfield Crescent, Belfast, that their son, Sergt. Alexander Campbell, has been killed on active service.

The deceased, who was 19 years of age, joined the R.A.F. in December, 1939, as a wireless operator-air gunner, and had participated in several operations over enemy territory.

A brother, James Campbell, is serving with the Canadian Active Service Force.

Early in the war, I lost three friends. I had worked with Andrew Duke and Sandy Campbell and had been to school with Robert McClure.

ROYAL MARINES COMMANDO

KILLED IN ACTION.

Andrew Duke, Royal Marine Commandos, son of Mr. and Mrs. John Duke, 141 Alliance Road, Belfast, killed in action. He was a former member of 3rd Belfast Company, Boys' Brigade. Two brothers are serving, William in the R.A.F. and John in the Royal Navy.

YOUNG AIRMAN'S LAST FLIGHT.

FAREWELL LETTER
TO BELFAST SISTER.

Before taking off on an operational flight over enemy territory from which he did not return Flight - Engineer Robt. M. M'Clure, R.A.F.V.R., left a farewell letter addressed to his sister, Mrs. R. Wright, 2 Comber Road, Dundonald, Belfast. Aged 20, he is now reported killed.

"I should like this letter to be forwarded on to my sister if I should not return from this operation. I have written many letters in my life, but in writing this one I find it much more difficult than any yet attempted," he wrote.

"First of all let me say I don't want you to grieve over my loss. This is the life I chose myself and the job which I am very proud to undertake. In this life I have learnt how to be grateful, because the crew in which I serve are the finest bunch of young men in the world. They are all willing to give their lives for the just cause.

"It's my hope that those whom I have left behind will make good the cause for which we gave our lives. This was a poor world before the war began—a quarrelsome and selfish world. I hope the horrors of war will have taught all a lesson and give justice to all.

"I have always thought how lucky you people have been to live so far away from a battlefield and to continue the quiet life which we have now learned to cherish.

"In conclusion let me say God is with me and all will be well in the end. Goodbye, but not for ever.—Robert."

An only brother of the late Sergt. Flight-Engineer M'Clure is serving with the Royal Navy.

CHAPTER 2

Volunteering for Aircrew

I spent two years doing ground crew duties on various airbases. Mostly this involved servicing aircraft and repairing damage caused by German anti-aircraft guns and enemy night fighter cannon shells.

Volunteering for aircrew had often crossed my mind. One day after our airbase chores were completed, I was drinking tea with Harry McNeill and Frank Wilson when Harry suddenly announced, "I'm going to volunteer for aircrew. I'm tired of getting pushed around by these sprog[†] corporals and jumped-up sergeants. Soon I'll be a sergeant and then in a few months an officer."

"That's okay," replied Frank. "Think that way if you like, Harry, but if you're dead it doesn't matter if you're wearing sergeant's stripes or an officer's uniform. You're still dead."

Harry said, "You just have to take the chance, Frank. What say the three of us volunteer together?"

It surprised us how swiftly these requests were processed. We were quickly ordered to the base hospital for medicals. As it turned out, both Harry and Frank failed the aircrew medical. Only I passed.

In August, after my training, I went home on a week's leave. I was

---

[†] "Sprog." A new pilot with little experience, or any recently promoted commissioned and non-commissioned ranks were called "sprogs." The term was used mostly in a derogatory manner, but sometimes in jest.

toasted by many and invited to numerous homes. My reception everywhere was a happy one. I wore sergeant's stripes and aircrew insignia, but as yet I had no stories to tell of bombing missions "over there."

When the leave ended, I crossed the Irish Sea once again and journeyed east by train, then south through the English countryside towards my new base in Lincolnshire. At every stop I saw familiar faces. One belonged to a big six-foot Scot, Jock Martin, who had been in my aircrew training class.

"Paddy McMahon," he grinned as he boarded the train at Dumfries. "Thought you might stay in Ireland—decide not to risk the training." He was referring to stories we'd heard about the Air Force losing more planes and men in training crashes than on operational flights.

"You can't believe everything you hear."

"And only half of what you read." The voice was Canadian and came from a bright-eyed individual in RCAF pilot's wings and sergeant stripes. He stood in the doorway, his only kit a leather hold-all slung casually over his shoulder. With a broad grin, he held out his hand.

"Peter Chadwick, sprog pilot, transferred for training on big stuff. I've been spending my leave up in Scotland hunting for haggis, but I'm told it's their time to hibernate."

"You've spent too much of your leave in Scotland's pubs," laughed Jock, as he grasped the Canadian's hand. "If we get another leave, I'll take you home and catch one for you."

"I'll keep you to that," chuckled the Canadian.

The crowded coaches and corridors were alive with youthful laughter and jostling crowds of young men and women in uniform. Eventually we arrived at our destination, and with a number of others bound for the same unit, converged on the exit, where transport waited. The driver stood lazily leaning against the door, the glow of his cigarette showing clearly in the inky blackness.

An aircraft roared overhead at a low altitude. Its silhouette glowed in the exhaust of its four merlin engines. As the aircraft's black shadow disappeared from sight, our driver, still leaning in a nonchalant manner against the door, looked up at the sky and remarked, "That goddamned pilot is too low. He won't make it unless..." Before he could finish, there came a sound like a great thump, and the whoosh of an explosion shuddered through the ground, shaking the truck before wasting its energy amongst the railroad station's buildings and beyond. Then a great sheet of flame streaked skyward while all of us looked aghast at this sudden death of a Lancaster crew.

The truck driver volunteered, "That's the thirteenth crew to go for a burton† this month. These sprog pilots sure make a mess around here."

Later that morning, we stood before a large bulletin board and a checklist of new crews. This was the coming together of bomber crews for the first time. Here among this turbulent chattering crowd of young men were those I would be flying with and depending on for survival. Already there were a few little groups of seven standing aside from the mob, eagerly finding out about each other. Jock Martin and I pushed through, and Peter Chadwick, the haggis-hunting Canadian, hollered as he struggled his way towards us, "Wait for me."

Jock was first to see the names and turned to the Canadian. "Now I'll have to tell my folks to prepare for a big haggis hunt because next leave I'll be bringing home my Canadian pilot." Jock and Peter Chadwick had been crewed together and were shaking each other's hands in great delight when a young man wearing the insignia of a navigator came on the scene.

"Peter Chadwick?" The accent was unmistakably Welsh.

"Yep," replied the Canadian, "and I bet you're my navigator."

"That's what the board says," came the reply. "My name is Bill McKeown."

"Now we have three," said Jock. "Let's find out what the other four look like."

Quickly they were gone.

I found my name on a crew list, under Flying Officer R.A. Jackson. Our wireless operator was Flying Officer E. Dunand and the bomb aimer was Pilot Officer W. Lane. The remaining ranks were sergeants like me: E.M. Magder (navigator), A. Clover (upper gunner), and L.G. Alexander (tail gunner).

Ten minutes later I found Alexander, Clover, and Magder sitting together.

"Knew you would find us if we sat together." Lionel Alexander stood up first and introduced himself. He was a short, small-framed twenty-three-year-old (the correct size to squeeze into a Lancaster's rear gun turret), with fair hair and a moustache. He was English like his coun-

---

‡ Crew who are killed in crashes or do not return from operations. They have "gone for a burton." It was reported in the October, 1986 issue of the Ex-Airforce P.O.W. Association Magazine *The Camp*, that of sixteen thousand Canadian aircrew killed in WW II, three thousand were killed in training.

terpart, Alan Clover, who would operate the upper gun turret. Clover was nineteen, two years younger than me. It wasn't necessary for our navigator to inform me he was Canadian. The letters were clearly visible on his uniform. Murray Magder was from Toronto, Canada, and just past his twentieth birthday. So of the four sergeants in the crew, we now had two Englishmen, one Canadian, and an Irishman.

"Have you met our pilot?" asked Lionel Alexander.

"No, Lionel, not yet," I replied.

"Call me Alex, that's what stuck with me since school days."

"Okay, Alex," I replied, "that sounds a good name for a rear gunner."

Our foursome trudged out towards the hangars in search of Jackson.

Number Two hangar doors were open and a twin-motor Manchester stood halfway out with its engine cowlings removed. Working from tubular scaffolding, busy mechanics made repairs or adjustments on the big Vulture motors.

"These Manchesters are death traps," volunteered Clover. "They won't stay airborne when a motor packs up. There's a lot of problems with the Vultures—problems with the coolant system and oil circulation. My uncle believes it is a despicable act asking us to fly in these devils."

We entered the hangar. Three aircrew officers stood talking beside the aircraft's tail unit.

"That's him," volunteered Alex, "the short one in the middle."

Jackson approached us and, smiling, introduced himself. "I'm Robert Jackson, been in the service since 1938. Most people call me Jaco."

He looked at Alex, "We've already been introduced, and now I know my navigator and mid upper." His blue eyes were friendly as he shook my hand. "You must be Johnny McMahon, our bonus of an Irishman for luck. You and I will share the up front view from the flight deck. They say it's the best spot to see the fireworks display."

He introduced his officer companions as Emile Dunand, our radio man from the wild prairies of Canada, and Bill Lane, another Londoner, who was supposed to set the bombs down on the correct spot once the rest of us got him there.

Then we gathered beneath the nose of the Lancaster, and Jaco set out the rules. We were to train on Manchesters, almost identical aircraft to the Lancaster, but they had those two notorious Vulture engines instead of the Lancaster's four Rolls Royce Merlins.

Jaco spoke quietly but with conviction. "We are now a crew," he said, "and a Bomber Command crew is seven men working together in harmony, each man doing the job he was trained for, and doing it under all circumstances to the best of his ability. To a certain degree, we work individually, but we must never for a moment forget that our lives will depend on each other. One error by one crew member—and it doesn't have to be a major one—could kill us all. It's the *Luftwaffe* and ground defences that will be our enemy. Get to know each other and you'll find that confidence in your flying comrades is a great state of mind."

He paused for a moment and looked thoughtfully at his hands. "I believe in two things: friendly communication and respect for each other. Over Germany or anywhere we fly, we are a team—a bomber crew—and we're going to be a good one. In future I think we'll all feel at ease if we use first names, or nicknames. Mine is Jaco. Alexander, I hear your friends calling you Alex, so Alex it is." Looking whimsically at me he said, "And what else for you but Paddy Mac, even if you do come from the British part of Ireland."

Arrangements had been made for a first training flight in a Manchester the next morning at 0900 hours. Seeing the apprehensive looks on our faces he said, "I know there are a lot of rumours going around about treacherous aircraft, but it's all Air Ministry has to give us, and I've already flown a few of them, so I'm sure Paddy Mac and I can handle the beast. We'll get through this part of the training as quickly as possible, and then we'll be on Lancasters. See you in the morning at 8:30."

Then he was gone, accompanied by Bill Lane, the tobacco smell from his pipe leaving a comfortable fragrance around us.

First Flight in the "Problem Child"

The next morning, with nervous anticipation, our little group waited. At 8:35 the bus rattled to a stop. In the front seats were Jaco, Dunand and Lane.

It was a short ride out to dispersal. We were the first crew to get off and there it was—a Manchester. The two ugly Vulture engines gave it a sulky, mean look that seemed to say there were good grounds for all the complaints.

We gathered ourselves together in preparation for boarding this "problem child" aircraft. The pilot instructor saluted us from the flight deck. Ground crews were busy preparing for start-up.

Jaco was about to precede us up the ladder into the aircraft when a strong south-of-Ireland voice silenced our chatter. "Jesus, Mary and Joseph, if it isn't the Orangeman from Belfast. What the hell are you doing on flying crew duty?"

It was Vincent Devenny of the Three Musketeers, now Corporal Devenny. He was Corporal in charge of this aircraft and its ground crew.

"Where did you leave my buddies?" he asked.

"Back in Ireland's green and pleasant land, probably sleeping off a night out on the town."

"I should have stayed there," he replied.

"You wanted stripes, now you're a corporal."

"I still want to live." He eyed the aircraft. "Looks like you don't." As he moved away, he shouted above the splutter of a motor his ground crew were trying to start, "Good luck you Orange bastard, but remember—I'm in charge of this kite. It'll take off okay and you'll climb up there among the clouds, but I won't tell you how it's going to come down."

The motor refused to start and fell silent. I called out, "Vincent, you Southern rebel, you haven't learned a thing. Why don't you do something about getting this 'kite' of yours airborne? We can't take it up if it won't start."

I turned to find that Jaco and the others had not moved. He looked at Vincent, then spoke to me. His English accent was strong and angry: "Did you hear what that man said? He should not be permitted within one mile of an aircraft. I'm going to report his remarks when we return."

"He's okay, Skipper," I replied. "We served many months together on ground staff. That's just his way. Come on, let's get these motors going, and then it'll be up to you and the instructor to get us up and down again safely."

My little speech broke up the group and soon we were clambering inside and taking our flying positions. The instructor did a quick run-through of the instrument panels, with great emphasis on motor temperatures. In a very casual way he said, "Keep your eyes on the temperature needles. When they get into the red, shout out."

"Okay," I replied, but thought danger red must be a regular occurrence.

It was an uneventful flight, except the temperature needle showed that the sulky starboard motor ran close to red at all times. Jaco took over the controls shortly after we were airborne and accomplished three landings and takeoffs with the precision of a born pilot; then the instructor very casually said, "Let me out and you guys take her up again by yourselves. Make one circuit and then come in."

As we neared the pad, our 'teacher' put his hand on Jaco's shoulder. "I'll be off now," he said, "you have the feel of this old gal. Make sure you return her all in one piece." Turning to me he grinned and pointed his finger at the temperature gauges, "She's a hot number. Watch out for her." And he was gone.

With the okay for take-off crackling in our ears, Jaco swung the beast onto the runway. Without hesitation he throttled forward and committed us to those two hot motors. I called out the speed as we lumbered down the runway and those two Rolls Royce Vulture motors, each 1845 horsepower, at 90 m.p.h., lifted us off the deck. Jaco eased back the throttles; I adjusted the flap lever and we laboured to 1,000 feet. Instead of one circuit we did three, and those damned temperature gauge needles for both motors edged themselves into the red several times before Jaco called for flaps and we made our descent. I thought of an engine seizing up and stopping dead before touchdown—that would be curtains for another crew—our crew.

There were no crashes, no one killed this day, so that was a bonus in itself, and we delivered back to Vincent Devenny his big brute, all in one piece. In fact, within a few days, Jaco's proficiency as a pilot was so good a Lancaster was entrusted to his care.

Before hopping aboard the crew bus after that first flight, I called out to Vince. "Remember the old days on Coastal Command when you were always looking for a hot lady? Now you've got one, and her motors are really hot. See if you're good enough to cool them down."

Who was Reginald Mitchell?

Today, fifty years after World War II, many people in Britain would shake their heads and perhaps look up at the sky and say, "Sorry I don't know," or "I've heard of him but can't remember what he did." In Canada, too, the majority would have no idea.

During the second half of August 1940, especially in the south-east region of England, the population strained their neck muscles by looking up for long periods of time at the myriad contrails in the sky, as pilots of Spitfires and Hurricane fighter planes of the Royal Air Force fought air battles with the German *Luftwaffe* above their embattled island.

The Spitfire—ah! yes, it was the famous British Fighter with its youthful pilots who decimated the German *Luftwaffe*, thus turning the tide against Hitler's attempt to destroy Britain's air defences before his invasion of England. It was Churchill who, in speaking about this victory, said of the young Spitfire and Hurricane pilots who fought, "Never in the field of human conflict was so much owed by so many to so few."

Reginald J. Mitchell never watched those air battles in the summer August skies. He never witnessed enemy aircraft diving to earth in flames. He never felt the fear when a maimed out-of-control Spitfire hurtled earthwards, and he never heard the great shout of joy as a small figure fell from the plane and the multitude of civilians shaded their eyes from the sun to see another Spitfire pilot and his parachute descend safely to earth.

Reginald J. Mitchell never witnessed the thrill of seeing a Spitfire do a victory roll after shooting down an enemy, because he died of cancer two years before the war, when he was in his early forties. But what a legacy he left behind. It was Reginald J. Mitchell who designed and developed the famous Spitfire fighter plane. Mitchell died in 1937— one year after the Spitfire made its first flight and three years before his dream aircraft became the most prominent weapon for downing German aircraft.

Had he lived, it is possible that bomber command's air war could have been changed by the introduction of a new four-engined aircraft that was designed to fly much faster than the Lancaster. Mitchell had this new aircraft design on his drawing board.

Soon we were posted to our new squadrons and I lost my good friends Peter Chadwick, Big Jock Martin, Bill McLean and crew. There was no opportunity for a farewell party, but we promised to keep in contact. We wished everyone good luck and safe returns, then parted to find new friends, new surroundings and more new Lancasters on our new Squadron at Scampton, Lincolnshire.

Scampton was a peacetime air base, well built and comfortable. Murray Magder and I were relegated to comfortable living quarters where we shared a room; Alex and Clover shared another.

We were airborne as much as possible and worked together as a crew without friction. Our confidence in each other grew. Winter days and winter nights rushed by, and we continued, often in rotten weather, to fly many hours over Britain—preparing for the "okay" to make our first bombing trip into Germany.

At Christmas we ate turkey and all the trimmings, and later, danced or simply listened to the station band play dance music until early hours. There were no operational flights this festive day of 1942, and we made many toasts to Christmas '43.

Of course, there were those who squeezed out the last dregs of this day, and long after the band had ceased, a piano player wearing new aircrew insignia caressed the ivory keys as young airmen and airwomen gathered around him. Many of those aircrew would die long before the next Christmas, but now they sang their hearts out with the "Whiffenpoof Song." Their young voices echoed around the high ceiling:

> *We are poor little lambs who have lost our way*
> *Baa, baa, baa*
> *We are little black sheep who have gone astray*
> *Baa, baa, baa*
>
> *Gentlemen songsters off on a spree*
> *Doomed from here to eternity*
> *Lord have mercy on such as we*
> *Baa, baa, baa*

Many of the young women in uniform had tears in their eyes; some shed those tears for the airmen standing close to them, and others for the ones who had already gone, never to return. Then, as everyone joined hands for another rendering of this favourite song, a young woman next to the piano player broke down and wept uncontrollably, but stood her ground. Her boyfriend had been killed in a crash landing the week before.

I heard a fine tenor voice to my right and realized it was young Clover. Alex was sitting on the piano, his deep voice out of tune, trying to keep time with an empty beer mug and crying for what, or for whom, he probably did not know. It was the third rendering of this song so meaningful to aircrew, and as the final "Lord have mercy on such as we" echoed and faded into the night, I looked around at this group of youth. We were taking our great courage from one another, pushing away our fears, holding hands and not wanting to let go. Each of us hoped and prayed that the good Lord would permit him to survive this war. I saw smiles on faces still wet with tears and I quietly walked towards the exit.

Outside, the crisp winter air made me realize that I had tears of my own to wipe away.

John McMahon "Paddy Mac" in 1943, aged 21 years.

Flight Lieutenant R.A. "Jaco" Jackson in 1943, aged 27 years. Jaco was our skipper and the unifying force of the crew.

CHAPTER 3

First Operational Flight

On Tuesday, February 2, before lunch, we joined other crews around the operations board. The day had arrived: We would take part in a bombing force going somewhere tonight.

I wrote a letter to Alice and approached a friend whose crew was not flying. "Will you mail this for me if we don't return tonight?"

"Sure, Paddy, sure, just throw it on my bed." It was a common thing for special letters to be left for mailing in case crews failed to return.

After our Pre-ops meal it was back to the billets. We tidied our own bedspace areas. Placing my polished going-out boots neatly on the floor at the end of my bed (I was wearing my flying boots), I tucked in my blankets, straightened the pillow, then stood back to admire my handiwork. I guess it was the religious upbringing plus my own inner feelings that took over as I stood looking at the neat and tidy bed. The time capsule in my memory rolled back and I saw myself as a child, kneeling in prayer at my bedside, a nightly ritual with our family. As other aircrew prepared for the night's ordeal, I knelt beside my bed and prayed for a safe return. Slowly rising to my feet, I noticed a number of my friends lowered their eyes when I looked their way.

Alex's voice broke the silence, "Are we all ready to go, Paddy?"

"I'm all set."

"Good luck!" shouted the airman I'd given the letter to. I looked down and saw half a dozen letters on his bed.

The night's operational crews assembled; doors were closed and locked. Wing Commander Slee uncovered the big map. A silence replaced the hubbub of voices. "It's the railroad marshalling yards at Cologne tonight, lads," and he jabbed his pointer at the cathedral city.

There were navigation courses to and from the target, ETAs on target, takeoff times, a warning of expected night fighter activity at 17,000 feet, a few hints from the gunnery officer, and a cheer for the weatherman: rain expected before takeoff, clear above clouds and over the Channel.

We collected our escape kits and walked to the Crew Room, which was a hive of industry, cluttered with all sorts of flying equipment. I strapped on my "Mae West" floatation gear and parachute harness. Except for my flying helmet, oxygen mask, parachute, gloves, and a few odds and sods, I was ready. Others had more cumbersome equipment.

Gunners were testing their heated suits by plugging into electrical outlets. In my position on the Flight Deck, the hot air from the motors would keep me warm. Alex put on a pair of his wife's nylons—either for luck or for extra warmth. "Look at that leg," someone jibed.

"Saw better hanging out of a bird cage," added another.

Skipper approached looking quite happy. "You chaps ready? The wagon's waiting." We boarded the station bus, my parachute in one hand, the yellow box containing our homing pigeons—used for emergency messages—in the other, and my engineer's log sheets held tightly under my arm.

The WAAF (Women's Auxiliary Air Force) driver stopped on the perimeter track, midway between two aircraft.

We clambered out. The other crew trudged towards their aircraft and we to ours. As the bus turned, its dimmed headlights picked up seven pairs of flying boots, one with flopping unbuckled straps. It seemed for a moment that one pair of marching flying boots dragged a little, hesitated, and almost stopped. Then a clear voice echoed back through the darkness, "See you over Cologne." The headlights swept on, the driver changed gears, and almost immediately the red tail lights were swallowed up by darkness. We seven gathered underneath our aircraft. The bomb doors were open and the barrel-like four-thousand-pound bomb seemed to nestle comfortably up there, surrounded by gleaming trays of incendiaries.

Skipper talked for a moment with the NCO in charge, then picked up his parachute and other paraphernalia, and walked to the starboard side of the aircraft, where the short ladder and open doorway invited us aboard.

Quickly he proceeded up the few rungs, feet encased in those black peacetime leather flying boots he was so proud of. Murray was next and seemed eager to get started on his navigational data. Our bomb aimer, Bill Lane, was number three. He had to scramble up front to his position in the nose compartment.

Dinny, who had been enjoying a last pre-raid smoke while sheltering under the wing away from the fine drizzle of rain, stubbed his cigarette as if he had suddenly made some drastic decision. Grabbing his chute, he bounded up the ladder and was gone.

Alex, Clover, and I lingered for another moment, hesitant about leaving terra firma. I was next to climb aboard, the two gunners right on my heels. On my way forward, I half turned and glimpsed Alex with the turret doors open, about to wedge himself into those cramped quarters.

As usual when negotiating across the main spar, I hit my knee and grimaced. We jokingly called these knocks, "main spar bruises." Clover, climbing into the upper turret, saw me and made a mock painful face and then a big grin. After depositing the pigeons, I proceeded to the flight deck and closed the armour-plated doors behind me.

We were flying in aircraft L for London, a fairly new machine. Our Squadron letters were E.A., so for communication with the control tower the letter designated to a particular aircraft was always used for identification. The large letters on each side of the fuselage read E. A.-L.

With ground crew gone, we were alone. Jaco and I did our cockpit drill, running up each motor, checking oil pressures, temperature gauges, oxygen supply, and so on. He called each crew member on the intercom. Everyone answered loud and clear.

We signalled our ground crew to pull away the chocks, and we moved slowly out of our dispersal circle, lumbering towards take-off position with the slow, rhythmic bounce that reminded us of the full bomb weight we were carrying.

Squadron Leader Cracknell's aircraft was already airborne at 1824 hours. Close behind was Flying Officer Armstrong's at 1827 hours, and five minutes later Flight Sergeant Millar had boosted his Lancaster and crew into the night sky. Minutes crawled by. With rain blurring my vision, I watched Flight Sergeant Webster's "Lanc" #452 take the full length of the runway before it was airborne at 1840 hours. Now aircraft #467, V for Victor, piloted by Flying Officer Fawkes, was the only one ahead of us. We could hear the scream of her props over the sound of our own motors.

Then Fawkes released his brakes. Hesitating for a moment, not sure of its freedom, "Victor" rolled slowly forward, gathered momentum, and sped off down the runway, spewing in its wake a spray of Lincolnshire rain water before disappearing into the darkness. It was 1847 hours.

Then we received clearance. We slithered around to take-off position on No. 2 runway and straightened out where V for Victor had been a few moments before. Behind us, another Lancaster waited for us to vacate our position. With brakes on, the paralysed seconds ticked by, and as we waited, the drizzling rain made the flare path flicker. I looked down the runway and wondered just what lay beyond.

"Okay, Skipper, ready," I said. I looked quickly at the engine temperatures, oil pressure, and the rest of the gauges. My hand shook a little as I adjusted the flap control to the right degree for take-off. From the control tower a GREEN was flashed by Aldis lamp. With throttles open, revs 3,000 and boost gauge needles hovering at plus twelve, the four propellers screamed. A final word to control, then brakes off. The four Rolls Royce Merlins pulled us down the lighted path at ever-increasing speed. Careful, ease port throttle back a little. Check that swing, steady now, that's it Skipper, right rudder—end of runway drawing near. Was that speed never going to reach 100?—90, five more: hear those engines sing! One hundred at last, and another ten. Good show! Now, lift her up. Gently does it. Wheels up, trim her back a little. Height 1,000 feet, flaps up and Lancaster ED 440 with 49 Squadron letters of E.A.-L. was safely airborne at 1851 hours. Below, two lines of flares faded.

We climbed smoothly through the drizzle to clearer weather above the Lincolnshire rain. In the eerie darkness of our cockpit the multitude of luminous dials seemed like so many watching eyes. On the raised seat to my left, Skipper Jaco sat motionless and seemed at ease, his hands holding ever so lightly on the control column, his feet, in their shiny black flying boots, caressed the rudder bar.

"Oxygen, please." Jaco's request was always very formal and he never forgot the "please."

Ensuring that everyone was receiving oxygen, I checked my gas gauges, temperatures and oil pressures, took the readings, and made the necessary entries on my log sheet. We reached the coast at 17,000 feet, then set course for enemy territory on the second leg. Peering down through the blister, I could see the dark outline of the English coast receding far below us. The English Channel was as black as the sky.

We sped on, still climbing, and it took little time, cruising at 200 m.p.h., to cross that dark expanse of water. Soon we would reach the enemy coastal defences, the *ack-ack* and those dreaded German night fighters, who had already welcomed the crews ahead of us.

Skipper warned Alex and Clover that the Dutch coast was coming up fast. "Watch for fighters." Already the defences had picked us up, and at 20,000 feet the flashes looked so puny and harmless—until the puff of shells burst around us.

The first human impulse was to run away from it all. But where could one run to on the narrow, darkened flight deck of a Lancaster at 20,000 feet above enemy occupied territory? Behind the blackout curtains sat Dinny and Murray, concentrating on the work that kept them from seeing what was happening outside.

Searchlights wavered back and forth, seeking us in the darkness. *Ack-ack* fire thickened; more and more searchlights blinked on, and suddenly Skipper's voice cracked over the intercom, "We're off track. That must be Rotterdam down there."

A searchlight beam lit the cockpit for a moment, lost us, and wavered away, crossing two other beams in its dash across the sky. The night was alive with snaky beams of light, and with the bursting *ack-ack* shells around us, it was as if a great giant was trying to shake us to pieces. Back came that ribbon of light. Relentlessly it followed, lighting up first our starboard wing tip, then the spinning prop of No. 4 motor. It lost us for a moment, then back it came and held us. One, two, three—almost instantaneously the lights came like hungry ghosts in the night. All seemed to swing onto us at once. Completely blinded, we flew through the hell of shell bursts that now erupted.

Forward went the control column as Skipper dipped the nose, taking us down in a 300 m.p.h. dive, cork-screwing as we went. I held onto a hand grip in the cockpit and braced myself. Being the only crew member standing, I was almost knocked off my feet by the sudden downward plunge.

The bright lights held us, lost us, held us, and I could see Skipper trying to pull back the control column. He was having difficulty. The pressure was too great—he couldn't get an answer from the elevators. "Trimmers." I heard the soft English accent as he murmured this urgent request to me over the intercom. Holding tight with one hand, almost swinging off my feet, I reached over and pulled back a little on the wheel that activated the elevator trimmers, and out she came in a shuddering, protesting swoop—back to level flight and the wonderful darkness of the Dutch country sky.

Being the lone aircraft over the city of Rotterdam, we had drawn the wrath of its defences. The escape from being coned by searchlights was luck in itself. (Being 'coned' was one of the dreaded experiences of aircrews and more often than not meant the end of a flying crew.)

Now we were out of range and speeding across Holland. The dive had cost us 3,000 feet in altitude, which meant we were not at our correct 20,000 feet, but at the warned-off fighters' zone of 17,000 feet. We were off track and south of our flight plan.

My gauges showed everything normal. Skipper and Navigator made quick decisions and came up with a new heading plus exact time to our target. Skipper repeated the course as we edged slightly to port and I adjusted the throttles to requested speed.

"Keep a sharp eye for fighters," crackled the voice in my earphones.

Every nerve a-tingle, I swept the black expanse outside the cockpit, straining my eyes to the utmost, trying to penetrate the inky blackness to whatever enemy lurked, even beyond the scope of my vision. Glancing down through the perspex blister on the starboard side, I saw far below the T-shaped flare path of a fighter 'drome. "Fighter 'drome flare path below to starboard." I spoke the message quietly into the mouthpiece. "Okay, Paddy, I see it." It was Alex's voice, replying from 60 feet away in the rear turret. I felt he had answered just to give himself the sense of belonging to those far away up front. Tail-end Charlie is a lonely fellow. In 1943, his life expectancy was not much more than six weeks.

Ice began to form on the cockpit windshield, making it more and more difficult to see, and the de-icers were not sufficient to clear it. The outside temperature was 40 degrees below F, but the side windows were still clear and I continued my intense watch.

"Target should be coming up in five minutes," reported Murray. "See anything?" "Nothing yet," came the crisp reply from Bill, who had been so very quiet and was now lying on the cushions covering the escape hatch and peering through the clear perspex of the bomb aimer's window.

I made my check once again on the instruments in my care. We were at 19,000 feet, still 1,000 feet below our flight plan.

A few minutes passed, then suddenly the intercom crackled. "Green flare about 2,000 feet below at nine o'clock." It was Alex's voice from the rear turret. "Bomb burst on the ground," he added. I looked down through the blister. A flash of bomb bursts dotted the area below. "We're here now," returned Bill, as he lay peering through his bomb-sight. The aircraft shuddered. A wall of flak bursts seemed to blanket the sky to starboard and directly ahead. Jaco banked the aircraft to port, and I could see a green flare hanging limply in the sky about 2,000 feet below. Instructions were to bomb on the path finder's green flares and our second choice the red ones. "Bomb doors open," came the request.

As we made our run on this flare, it went out. Oddly, the flak barrage was only to starboard. "Red flare coming up," came Bill's voice, and simultaneously I saw it hanging there like a great ball of fire. "Steady, left, a little left. Hold it." I was sure my heartbeats could be heard above the roar of those four Merlins. A few seconds passed as we waited for the "Bombs gone," but it never came. Instead there was a rending, tearing series of thumps in quick succession along the belly and fuselage. Our aircraft shuddered like a bird mortally wounded but instinctively trying to remain airborne.

"Hello, gunners," comes the Skipper's urgent voice, but there is no reply. "Hello, Alex, Alex, can you hear me?" Still no reply from the rear turret. Fear-filled seconds tick by and only silence from the gunners. Then it comes, a faint voice filled with fear. It's Clover. "Alex must be dead, Skipper, looks like there's no rear turret; it's a mess of twisted metal." The shocked voice dies away and then comes back loud and clear, filling the intercom with "Fire, fire, the aircraft's on fire!" Instinctively, I half turn towards the curtain and the armour-plated doors separating us from Clover's voice.

For a second of time there is silence as the heavy thought that already one of our crew is dead or dying penetrates our thinking.

"Open the escape hatch," comes the quiet, matter-of-fact order, as if it were the door to the mess. It is Jaco's last order, for hardly are the words out than down goes the nose—slowly at first, as if one of the control surfaces is damaged and breaking off. Skipper has the stick right back, and as I grab for my 'chute, the blackout curtains separating us from the navigator's bench tear aside and the shocked face of Murray emerges, a look of horror on his face. The deck under my feet cants to a 45 degree angle. Hydraulic fluid spews quickly along the deck. Below me, Bill Lane batters on the escape hatch with one foot, trying to break it loose from the ice that has frozen it shut.

Grabbing my parachute with one hand, holding to the side of the aircraft with the other, I am thrown to my knees but succeed in attaching one harness clip. The aircraft takes a nose-down plunge that throws me headlong into the bomb aimer's compartment. I have the presence of mind not to use hands to protect my face, but to concentrate on attaching the other clip to my harness as I fall, and this is one of the factors that saves my life. With a crash, I land against the butt ends of the front guns. Bill is gone, so I reckon he bailed out before the aircraft went out of control.

We somersault earthwards with only the bomb aimer's compartment, where I am, and the flight deck free of flames. The rest of the aircraft is a fiery furnace, and inside the fuselage there are explosions from pyrotechnics and ammunition belts. I feel sure Clover is dead. We fall in a crazy circle, with motors screaming full power as we tumble over and over.

I lose all sense of direction, fighting to keep from being knocked unconscious. For a time, I find myself wedged by my buttocks between the front guns, only to be thrown back with crushing force against the bomb bay bulkhead as the plane somersaults once again. Time and time again I try in agonizing frustration to grab hold of the many hydraulic pipelines, but it seems so very hopeless, and every second I wait for this hurtling mass of flames to explode or hit the ground and blow us all to pieces.

The heat is intense. I catch a glimpse of the bomb bay through an inspection window. It is a white-hot glare of incendiary flames (we had thirteen cases of incendiary bombs on board, plus the 4,000-pound bomb usually known as the 'cookie'). I expect all of this and the loaded fuel tanks to explode, but miracles happen every day. I think Bill Lane must have jettisoned the 4,000 pounder, or surely it would have exploded and blown 'the works' to pieces.

With the awful knowledge of my impending death, and the unexplainable feeling of helplessness to prevent it, fear clutches my stomach. Panic takes control, devastating my nervous system as our aircraft plunges uncontrollably earthward. It is uncertain what minutes or seconds are left but life is too precious, at 21, and the survival instinct too strong to give up the struggle, even if it is enemy soil we are falling to.

I make one more desperate effort, and with a mad lunge, finally grip a pipeline. My back is to it, arms stretched sideways, holding on with the strength of desperation. My arms feel as if they will be *pulled from their sockets as my body arches with legs flying free in the air and knees tight against my parachute pack with every somersault.*

How he got there I don't know, but clinging hopelessly in a similar position to mine is Murray. His eyes meet mine. "What happens when we explode on the ground?" they say. "What is this thing called death?" I know the escape hatch must be there between us, but to let go my grip will mean being dashed back and forth again and probably this time knocked unconscious.

I can see black polished flying boots on the rudder bar up there and know that Skipper is trying the impossible.

Those of us who are still alive know there is no hope. Any moment this twenty-eight tons of aeroplane and war equipment will plough into the ground and explode with such force that our bodies will never be found—only the charred pieces. It will be instantaneous death.

For moments I feel certain I am not in my body. From somewhere outside I can see myself trapped before dying and I hear people talking about my death. Perhaps my soul has already departed from its earthly body ahead of time.

Either I let go, or my numbed fingers lose hold on the lines. Thrown forward, I half turn on my side to protect my face, but instead of being smashed against bruising equipment, I fall backwards with head and shoulders through the small rectangular open escape hatch. A rush of sucking air takes my breath away, my right flying boot catches on something and rips off. Then I am outside, falling alongside the blazing aircraft, amid scorching pieces of flaming materials. I can feel their great heat, but I am unscathed. In seconds I am alone, hurtling head over heels down through the black night, gulping fresh air.

My ripcord! As I think of it I pull the pin and get a terrific crack on my forehead from a harness clip as the opening 'chute swings it high above. The crazy headlong rush through the February night sky towards oblivion stops abruptly and I am left gasping for breath and swinging slowly under the silk canopy. I look down, and almost immediately below is the aircraft, a blazing mass on the ground. The feeling of hanging motionless following the opening of my parachute is such a contrast to the turmoil of my horrific earthward plunge. I descend silently from the sky to land with a thud in a ploughed field, twisting my bootless ankle on the uneven ground. I lie for a few moments before my billowing parachute brings me to reality. I pull it into a crumpled heap around me, and it flattens to the contours of the furrows under the heavy rain. It is impossible to foretell one's thoughts and reactions when faced with a desperate situation. I had knelt and prayed for protection on this bombing mission. Now once again I kneel, this time in the soggy wet ground that is enemy soil. My words are lost in the roar of the holocaust close by as our aircraft burns furiously with intermittent explosions. Great flames leap to the heavens and my eyes follow their towering path of light as I thank the 'pilot' of our destiny for my deliverance.

Excited voices echo across the field. The crashing aircraft has brought people out to investigate. This is certainly not the city of Cologne or Cologne's railroad marshalling yards.

The time between my exit through the escape hatch to contacting terra firma *was only seconds, hardly enough to realize what a parachute descent was like, so close had we been to the ground when I was thrown clear. It must have been only six or seven hundred feet. I had been trapped in the aircraft for almost all of that four-mile plunge, and it is difficult to realize that I am alive.*

Staggering painfully to my feet, I undo my Mae West, wrap it and parachute together as another great explosion rocks the aircraft and my shadow dances across the furrows like a demented giant who seems angry at the miracle of my deliverance. The whole crash area is brightly lit by burning incendiary bombs and over a thousand gallons of flaming high-octane fuel.

Fear had not yet penetrated my thoughts, but as I painfully dragged myself across the wet earth to a ditch on one side of the field, from somewhere in my fogged senses came a message. *This is Germany, this is enemy country. You were on a bombing mission to destroy railroad yards—if caught you will probably be killed by angry civilians or shot by a furious soldier.* I dug a hole with my hands, buried my parachute and harness along with the Mae West floatation gear, and wondered if, by some miracle, other crew members got out.

Bill Lane was out, but he would be miles away from here. Could Murray or one of the others be crouching in some nearby field, burrowing holes for their chutes too? Suddenly I realized home base was a long, long way off, and here I was, alone inside enemy territory.

"Get as far away from the crash as quickly as possible" was the advice we had always been given. Germans would be speeding to this very spot on a search for survivors. I half scrambled and half crawled across the remainder of the field, which was skirted by a cart track. My right leg ached and gave way every few steps, and having only one flying boot made walking difficult. I decided to make as much time and distance westward as possible. On the cart track, I hobbled along, stopping now and then to listen for other footsteps.

The rain drove into my face, and little rivulets ran across the track. I could hear a stream gaining momentum as it was fed, probably by the drainage from nearby fields. It seemed a lifetime since I had looked down that wet runway in Lincolnshire, but this was all too real to be a dream, and my head was throbbing. I discovered a deep gash on my forehead. Blood and rain wet my face, but in the dark I could not see how much I was bleeding. I looked up at the night sky as a high-flying aircraft sped homeward. Soon the crew would be drinking hot cocoa and making out their reports. OH, IF ONLY I HAD WINGS! As the healthy drone of those engines faded away, I stumbled along a narrow road.

I must have been walking in a dazed condition, for I'd no recollection of ever turning off the cart track. I was about to take to the fields when three cyclists rounded a corner, dropped their bicycles by the roadside, and ran to me.

"You RAF?" one asked in broken English. I nodded, wondering what was next. "Friends," said the first speaker, and all three shook my hand. "Friends,"—I couldn't understand. This was German territory; any civilians would be antagonistic towards British Air Force, but here were these three saying were friends. I couldn't think properly. Strong arms on each side half carried me to a nearby house. We entered and turned right, down into a stone-floored kitchen, where they sat me in a chair at a well-scrubbed table.

An oil stove, light blue in colour, was at the far end of the room and beside it sat a man with a white beard and steady blue eyes. He smoked a continental pipe with a water cooler at the firing end. A woman in her late fifties, looking very frightened, left the room as I entered. Numerous people had gathered by this time—three or four middle-aged men and about half a dozen in their twenties. One poured me a cup of cold ersatz coffee that a young woman had brought.

The young woman returned with a basin of hot water and some cotton. The older lady bathed the gash on my forehead and washed the congealing blood from my face. Another newcomer spoke to me in perfect English, telling me they were sorry, but to help me was impossible at the moment, I was in Holland, close to the German border. "Give me your name and service number," he said. "We will do our best to get word to your home." I did so. He bade me goodbye and good luck and left, his pals going with him, leaving my first three helpers and another, who looked like a policeman. There was a telephone on the wall behind me and to one side of it was a large sculpture of Christ.

These Dutch people, with a brave glow of hope in their eyes, wanted so much to help further, but feared the consequences. This was 1943, and already they had served three years as prisoners in their own land—ruled, murdered, and tortured by the enemy. They asked me, with hopeful looks, when the second front would be opened—as if I, a single member of the RAF, could answer such a great question.

"It will come," I said.

The Tragedy of Youth on Bomber Command

Some very frightening statistics reveal the tragedy of the youth who flew on bomber command during World War II.

From the beginning of the war in September 1939 until it ended May 1945, of any given 100 of these young aircrew flying on operational duties, 60 would be killed (51 on operational flights and 9 in accidental crashes in Britain). Three would be seriously injured, and twelve would become prisoners of war. Twenty-five would survive the ordeal 'unharmed.'

Twenty-five out of the 100 survived 'unharmed.' Physically unharmed, perhaps. I haven't seen printed statistics regarding the postwar mental condition of those twenty-five out of each hundred who survived 'unharmed' or the twelve who became prisoners of war.

Not very good odds.

In bomber command alone, over 55,000 young aircrew—most between the ages of 19 and 25—were killed. Sufficient to make up the population of a small city.

There was the swirl of gravel as a car screeched to a halt outside. Heavy boots crunched nearer, and then the door flew open. Before anyone could move, in ran *Luftwaffe* Military Police.

I said, half to myself, "It will come." It had to come, for now I was about to join the band of those who waited with faith in the promise that liberation troops would some day land and sweep across Europe to victory.

Often I'd wondered how I'd react if ever I was taken prisoner—would I show my fear? Now that it was a reality, I eyed these two young giants with calm interest. They were both over six feet, in their early twenties. Dressed in winter greatcoats and armed to the teeth, they looked masters of any situation, but how did they know so quickly that I was in this house?

They sat down on each side of me and began a thorough interrogation of my hosts, frisked me for weapons, and indicated I was to go with them. I hobbled to the kitchen door, turned, and saluted my late hosts. They looked unhappy and forlorn, as if it was all their fault I was being led away a prisoner.

Indicating I was to take the rear seat, one guard sat beside me. The night temperature had dropped and my rear seat companion took off his greatcoat and gave it to me to cover my legs, a very friendly gesture from the enemy Air Force.

We finally made an S-turn, climbed a gradient, and were halted by a sentry. He poked his head in the window, looked at me quizzically, spoke to my companions, then raised the barrier. We stopped a few yards inside at the foot of concrete steps.

My back seat companion helped me from the car, but once outside I came face to face with a German officer, who screamed a command. My captors indicated I walk up the steps to what appeared to be the guardhouse. On my first attempt my leg gave way and I fell. My back seat companion jumped to assist, but his superior shouted at him and immediately he stepped back.

Under my own steam I stumbled up the steps to a brilliantly lighted doorway. Inside was so much like a guardhouse on any air base in Britain: orders pinned on the wall, the duty corporal sitting behind a desk with phone at hand.

I was searched again, then taken down a corridor with cells on each side, some occupied by *Luftwaffe* personnel. My allotted cell was halfway. The guard asked for my suspenders, explaining in sign language that I might use them to hang myself. I looked at him in amazement. "Hang myself after such a miraculous escape? I'm not that crazy!" The cell door was securely locked. I was alone.

The cell was about 6' x 10'; it had a wooden bench for a bed with an adjustable board pillow, and a tiny wooden table.

There was a small barred window close to the high ceiling and the cell was lighted by one 25-watt bulb. I lay down on my bench, just as I was—no bedding or blankets, so exhausted I went off to sleep immediately and did not wake until the jailer aroused me next morning. The third of February, my first full day as a prisoner of war, had begun.

The guards had changed. This guard had a jovial face and dark, twinkling eyes. He was short and tubby in appearance, his uniform neat, clean, and well-pressed. He said, "Come," and flashed an encouraging smile. I followed him to the guard room where to my surprise they issued me a Gillette razor complete with Gillette blade, a toothbrush and Maclean's toothpaste, face cloth, towel, and my first bar of German soap—that small, square bar that just wouldn't lather.

I was shown to the ablution area. *Luftwaffe* offenders were also having their morning wash and shave. I took off my battle-dress jacket and aircrew sweater. A shave and wash helped my morale. Those *Luftwaffe* personnel deliberately slowed up and watched me with interest.

Donning my sweater and jacket, I straightened up smartly for the benefit of those watching eyes, took my time to tighten the buckle of my jacket, and flicked an invisible object off my shoulder. "Damn! Wish I had two flying boots—can't walk in a military fashion with one foot encased only in an Air Force issue sock."

I was served breakfast of white bread, jam and black coffee. I ate sitting at a table by the guard room window that overlooked flat countryside. Midday came and once again more food—this time mashed potatoes, butter and cold meat.

Immediately after lunch I was taken to my cell. I thought of home. Today they would get that telegram, "Missing on operations, regret to inform you, etc." The small barred window shed little light, as the guardhouse had been built into the face of what looked like a wall of earth.

Suddenly, the bolt rattled back and my cell door opened. My guard stood there with a tall, high ranking Luftwaffe officer accompanied by two junior officers. He looked at the bench and surveyed the cell, then gave orders to my guard, who scurried off. The officer smiled, raised his arm in a half salute, turned sharply, and with his entourage of two they were gone, leaving my cell door wide open. Almost immediately my guard returned with a helper carrying a straw-filled mattress, a blanket and a pillow.

I was interested in knowing who my benefactor was, so I asked my guard and learned by sign language that the visitor was a high-ranking night fighter pilot. I immediately realized he could be the pilot who had shot us down, but it was now too late to ask him, and I'd never know.

Around 7:00 p.m. I ate again, then locked up for another night. Next morning I was awake and waiting when my jailer opened the cell door for the beginning of my second full day in captivity.

My guard brought four pairs of German boots and signalled I should try them for size. The third pair were correct size so away he went, humming a tune. Later he returned to inform me I would be seeing the Adjutant today. It was after midday when two young guards arrived. They were about my height and age. Both carried rifles and fixed bayonets. With a guard on either side of me, I was marched up a gradient to the right of the guard room.

We came to a long and low building. It was the air base's administration offices. Entering to a centre corridor, one of my guards knocked on a door and went in. A minute or two later he reappeared and beckoned us to enter. Behind a desk sat a middle-aged *Luftwaffe* officer. In a well-cultured English accent he said, "Sergeant McMahon, I would like you to check these few belongings of yours and confirm they are correct. You will get them back upon your arrival at permanent camp."

After verifying that everything was in order, he dismissed us. We went back to the guardhouse for the remainder of the afternoon.

The phone rang and the sallow-faced corporal in charge held it up and pointed to me. A phone call for me, a prisoner? It seemed crazy. I shakily took the phone from him and said "Hello." "Remember your interview with me this afternoon?" came that well-cultured voice. "Yes," I replied, wondering what was coming next.

"I want to congratulate you on your very lucky escape. You are the only survivor of your crew."

I listened dazedly as that cool voice went on to explain how three charred remains were inside the wreckage, two outside, and one two kilometres away. He asked if everyone aboard had a parachute, because the body found some distance away was not burned and it appeared this crew member got out of the aircraft from a high altitude without a parachute. Into my mind flashed the picture of Bill struggling with the escape hatch. The ice that had formed around the escape hatch must have suddenly given way. He'd gone through without his chute at approximately 19,000 feet.

"We have six remains and only four names," the voice went on, "as two were not wearing dog tags." Slowly he read their names, "Flight Sergeant Magder, Sergeant Alexander, Sergeant Clover, Flying Officer

Jackson." I thought, for a moment, that maybe he was only bluffing, but then I remembered the great sheets of flame and my impossible struggle before I was thrown out moments before the aircraft slammed into the ground. I knew they would have had no hope of escape.

I breathed the other two names softly into the telephone and dazedly handed it back to the pale-faced individual behind the desk, who seemed to have the ghost of a smile on his lips. Asking that I be taken to my cell, I dejectedly preceded my jailer down the corridor. As the door clanged shut behind me, I lay down in the quietness, stunned and shocked by this information. A great feeling of utter loneliness dispelled my previous cheerfulness. My six pals, who a few hours before had been full of life and hope for the future, would probably be buried in the same grave. It was a long time before I fell into a troubled sleep.

"A wet February night in 1943." This cartoon, like many
of the others that documented our lives in prison camp,
was drawn by my friend Bill "Toad" Hughes.

43

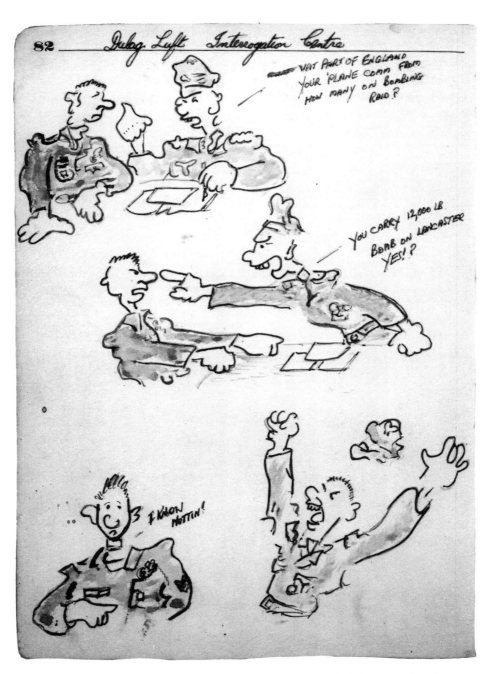

Captured aircrew were usually interrogated at the Dulag Luft Interrogation Centre.

CHAPTER 4

To Prison Camp

Two *Luftwaffe* Military Police arrived, armed with sub-machine guns and stick-type hand grenades. "We are taking you to Amsterdam," one volunteered. They escorted me to a car and we drove to a railroad station.

My journey to Amsterdam was interesting, although for most of it I was wedged between my new guards. For a time I felt like a celebrity, for at each stop Dutch passengers who alighted gathered on the platform right outside the window of our coach, and in absolute defiance of the *Luftwaffe* guards, they waved and gave the V for Victory sign as the train pulled away. Eventually my guards solved the problem by pulling down the window shades before each stop.

It was dark and raining when we reached Amsterdam. On the crowded station platform, with the pressure of a guard on each side of me, we approached the exit that led down a flight of concrete steps to a wet street. At the bottom of the steps stood half a dozen armed German soldiers and a bus. I was delivered into the custody of this antagonistic group and their sadistic-looking *Unteroffizier.*

A number of Allied Air Force prisoners were already seated, some looking dejected, others quite cheerful. My *Luftwaffe* guardians pushed aside the *Unteroffizier* guarding the door and entered the bus. Each shook my hand and wished me good luck. So I said goodbye to my first captors, the German *Luftwaffe*, who had treated me well and with respect.

A burly looking individual with officer's shoulder tabs walked to the centre of the bus aisle and snapped, in perfect English, "You are going to a receiving barracks and then you will go to Germany. I want no talking. You—will—*not*—talk—to—one—another." He delivered this last sentence in a slow, menacing tone.

The journey was full of forebodings.

The bus swung into a barrack square. Rudely we were ejected and marched into the dingy hallway of a large building—one of Amsterdam's jails—where we were quickly separated and taken to solitary confinement. My cell was up one flight of stairs.

I spent three days in solitary. During that time I had one thin slice of rye bread and ersatz coffee for breakfast each morning, a sour, thin soup for lunch, and a similar issue of bread and coffee in the evening. On the fourth day, I was transferred to a cell-like room at a higher level with three other prisoners, two English and the other Welsh. A coal heater warmed us, and we had a view from a small window overlooking the barrack square far below. Beyond the square were a canal and busy streets. Numerous German military vehicles moved amid the mixture of civilian transport—mostly bicycles and crowds of Dutch citizens.

The next morning I was grouped with twelve other aircrew prisoners assembled on the barrack square in readiness for the military bus that would take us to Amsterdam railroad station.

On the train a special coach had been reserved for us, the wooden seat type. As we clanked our way out of Amsterdam, heading east, I felt a terrible irony: a few miles west across the sea lay England and freedom; we were heading the opposite way.

Our next stop was Dulag Luft. On arrival I was again put into solitary confinement. A steam-heated radiator, bench, table, water jug, and chair furnished the cell. The heat was turned off. I was made to strip. A guard took my clothes, and a shivery hour passed while they were searched. I was taken under guard to the toilet, and when we returned, I lay down on my cot and fell asleep, still wondering what fate had in store for me here.

I was wakened by a guard bearing breakfast: two thin slices of that horrible-tasting rye bread and a mug of tea made from mint leaves. About ten o'clock a bemedalled German officer came into my cell. He was all smiles and pleasant, and carried a large official-looking book under his arm. I thought to myself, here is my first real interrogation. Slowly he opened a package of English cigarettes, withdrew one, lighted it and inhaled with much satisfaction. He threw the almost-full pack on the table and beamed, "Help yourself."

"I don't smoke," I said with a touch of triumph in my voice.

"Lucky man," he replied, but picked up the package and placed it closer, with one cigarette protruding invitingly. Apparently he didn't believe me.

We had been well briefed on the squadron as to what we could expect at the Dulag Luft and about how we should answer any questions.

"What squadron were you flying with?"

"I don't know."

"What air base did you take off from?"

"I don't know."

"What new equipment did you see in your aircraft?"

"I don't know."

"What was your target?"

"I don't know."

"Is your squadron fully equipped with Lancasters?"

"I don't know."

"What was your bomb load?

"I don't know."

My interrogator was unperturbed, but I suppose he was used to the same answer from hundreds of shot-down airmen. I had the feeling that this gentlemanly attitude would soon change and the rough stuff begin. On the third morning I was escorted to a large hut where I met once again the men I'd arrived with. Apparently we were being shipped out to make room for new arrivals.

In a few days we were mobile again—on a train, under guard, and travelling eastward across Germany. It was still early evening, but we heard RAF bombers overhead and saw bomb bursts in the distance. A few hours later, as the train crawled to a stop in Cologne station, the air raid sirens wailed and we were led by the guards to shelters below the platform. It seemed the irony of fate that our crews had set out to bomb the railyards in this city, and I was now finishing the journey by train, crouched in an air raid shelter while our own bombers roared overhead.

This was the beginning of a long and seemingly endless struggle to survive.

Yes, I had reached Cologne, but it was going to be a long way home. I was a prisoner of war and would remain so until some army or miracle liberated me. And if that didn't happen, I'd probably end my days looking west, with home still in my heart. But already a deep-rooted assurance was forming, taking hold of my thoughts: I was the only survivor, so I must one day see home again.

The shrill note of the all clear siren echoed through the shelter and we marched back to the train. The station had sprung to life again with bustling civilians and uniformed members of a variety of German forces. Apparently no bombs had been dropped in the immediate area and this was probably lucky for us, considering the mood of the German public regarding Air Force types.

As we walked those few yards along the dimly lighted platform, a large group of civilian spectators crowded around us. There were menacing looks and shouts of "*Luft* Gangsters." A good-looking woman with a gentle face spat at my feet as I passed, and the crowd pressed menacingly closer. This was Cologne, one of the most often bombed cities in the country, and as members of the enemy Air Force, we were reprehensible to them, and thankful for once to have German soldiers guarding us.

Soon we were clattering eastward toward Leipzig and Dresden. From time to time we were shunted to side tracks to permit priority trains to pass, but eventually we picked our way through the myriad of rail lines entering Dresden Station.

At Dresden we pulled alongside a platform, where we saw a large company of SS troops decked out in their Russian Front gear—white covers on their steel helmets and other equipment. Everywhere it was hustle and bustle, preparing for a train journey to meet their enemy in the East.

It was of great interest to watch these soldiers. We were deep in the heart of Germany, a country we'd been fighting for almost three and one-half years, and here was a sort of behind-the-scenes view of Germans preparing for battle. This was the enemy, the elite German troops preparing for the front. Sweethearts and wives bade farewell to their menfolk. Officers barked orders; subordinate ranks clicked their heels and did as they were commanded. One could feel the tension in this land. The dark railroad station cast its own blanket of gloom.

Soon we were puffing eastward again, with driving snow racing past the windows as high winds whisked it in eddying circles. The next stop, our guards informed us, would be Breslau.

"Sure's going to be a long walk home," someone remarked.

"Hope it's summertime when we do," I replied.

It was dark when we arrived in Breslau. The swirling snow and bitter chilling wind had not abated. What looked like the same trainload of soldiers we'd left in Dresden was pulling away from the opposite platform, leaving more civilian well-wishers. Some women wistfully looked down the empty rails after the departed coaches, wondering, I'm sure, if they'd ever see their menfolk again.

Two German Red Cross women boarded our train and served vegetable soup that tasted delicious after the long hours of cold and hunger. It looked like leavings from the troop train, but who cared? It was warm and helped to bring new life to everyone.

The train's clattering wheels had barely faded away into the white, windswept night before the uniformed and civilian figures of those left behind disappeared through platform exits or down dark stairways. Across those two sets of shining rails was the darkened and deserted platform. Now it was a very quiet night in Breslau Station, with no sign of men going off to war or the hustle-bustle that had just taken place.

Our locomotive was disconnected and taken elsewhere.

There was no heat in the coaches. Another hour passed. The temperature dipped and the warm soup no longer fanned our internal warmth. I curled up, shivering in a corner, sometimes trying to sleep, other times watching out the window for something interesting to happen.

I must have dozed off for a while, for I was awakened suddenly by the shrill note of a train whistle. Almost immediately another troop train thundered through the station without stopping. This one was pulling an additional line of flatbeds loaded with armoured vehicles. Most of these were covered, but we noticed a few tanks without their protective tarpaulins. As the train raced through Breslau's darkened station, snow swirled and flew in the rushing slipstream of air, splashing and plopping to the tracks near us in great blobs of white. The ghostlike train, its coaches filled with shadowy military figures, its cars loaded with their white-covered war machines, flashed before our eyes and was gone in a swirl of snow, the last of its rolling stock shuddering eastward.

The noise and rush of wind roused the others from their shivering siesta, and we all pressed close to the cold glass windows. But the scene ended as suddenly as it had started, and apart from one shadowy railway worker, already sweeping away the great globs of snow and ice that had found their way onto the platform, the station had returned to its darkened, deserted state. I was cold, miserable and dejected.

"Maybe they are taking us to the Russian Front," some bright spark joked.

"Can't be any colder than here."

"I sure as hell don't want to find out," came a voice from the far side of the coach.

There was silence after that. For at least two hours we huddled together for warmth. The banging of the couplings brought us to life. Another locomotive was attached to our coaches. Apparently no more priority trains were due, so we could move on to the main track. The outskirts of Breslau passed quickly, and then, once again, the monotonous white expanse of countryside.

The snow had stopped but the wind continued. For a time, the lights of a convoy of army trucks wound their way almost on a course parallel to ours, then suddenly the road twisted away from the railroad track and their red tail-lights disappeared into the night's whiteness. It was after 3:30 a.m. and everything seemed to be moving east. We made little attempt to sleep, for we were getting worried about where they were taking us. Our guards would say only, "We tell you soon."

The train rattled through a station with its name obliterated by black paint. Then, about an hour after leaving Breslau, we moved slowly through a station with the name "Brieg" still discernible, although an attempt had been made to cover up the sign. After Brieg, the train seemed to gain more speed than before, and clickety-clacked its way to a stop at a place named Oppeln, where no attempt had been made to blank out the name.

"Is this it?" asked Ken Morgan, whose jokes and bright spirit had helped to lift our morale on this journey to the unknown.

"*Nein! Nein!*" was the guards' reply, and that was all the info we could get.

Once again we heard the sounds of our locomotive being uncoupled and watched as it passed slowly towards the rear. Surely we were not going to shiver here for more hours! People disembarked with their bags, cases, and parcels, among them a few soldiers, a number of Air Force personnel, and a couple of sailors.

There was no one getting on, and Ken, with his indomitable spirit, asked, "Know why there's no one getting on?" We expected a funny answer, but he said, "This train is going to a place called 'Nowhere'!" Perhaps he was right, and "Nowhere" was the end of our line, too. A serious and quiet mood prevailed among us after that.

The locomotive was coupled once again, this time to the rear coach. "We're going back to Breslau," someone offered. Another said, "We should have got off at Brieg when the train slowed to a crawl; somebody made a mistake. We're going to switch to another spur line." We decided Brieg was the most likely probability.

With a shrill whistle, spinning wheels and hissing steam, we clanged our way out of Oppeln station, back the way we had come, but only for a short distance. Soon we veered left.

Forty minutes later, our guards told us to get ready—we were nearing our prison camp. After another ten minutes, we were hustled, stiff and cold, onto the platform of a small railway station with a sign that read "Annahof."

"We're close to Stalag VIIIB," a guard volunteered.

"Let's hope there's food in there," grinned our still-cheerful Welshman, Ken Morgan, though he looked as if he'd already frozen to death.

When the guards were satisfied that no one had disappeared or died on the way, the short march to camp began. We passed through a village, still dark at 6:30 a.m. A villager out to start the day's chores eyed us with indifference. We trudged along a winding, rutted road that skirted the edge of a pine forest. The snow had stopped but lay fairly deep as we made our way, breathing in the crisp air and with each breath expelling a small cloud of steam.

Word from the guards came along the line of men: "This Stalag VIIIB, the camp we're going to, is mostly army POWs. The village we passed through is called Lamsdorf."

At the edge of a small clearing we had our first view of the camp. Machine guns protruded over the edge of guard boxes standing high around the perimeter. Searchlight beams crawled along the wire and across the camp, and as the beams of light passed by, double barbed wire fences glinted in the glare.

The big double main gates stood open as our column approached. Passing through, we entered the outermost compound where the guards had their billets. A welcoming committee of three German officers and a number of camp guards stood eying our weary dozen. We stood to attention in the best military order possible. It was a defiant little group that stood in the snow, waiting for the unknown.

Ken Morgan and Scotty McPhee stood in silence—no wisecracks. Ken looked down at his foot and made a little mound of snow with the toe of his boot. McPhee stared blankly at the foreboding entanglement of wire—or maybe over and away westward to the bonnie hills of Scotland with their smell of heather after rain.

"*Achtung!*" The sharp German command brought everyone back to reality, and a new figure emerged. The Camp Commandant was a naval officer of retirement age. Taking a position in the centre and forward of his officers, he gave us his welcome speech in English:

"Welcome to Stalag VIIIB. You airmen are the lucky survivors. If you behave yourselves and obey orders like good military men and don't try to escape, you have a very good chance of surviving the rest of the war. You will be taken to your barracks shortly. Prior to that you will be showered and deloused, then it will be past roll call, but you may still be in time for hot tea. Remember to salute any German officer you meet, as you would do with officers back on your own squadrons. Your barrack commanders will fill you in on all daily orders and camp requirements. Good luck to you."

Quickly we were shepherded to a large building and ordered to strip. Our clothing was placed in separate boxes. Each man was given a number to claim it later. The shower room was warm. The floor was concrete with numerous drains to equal the shower heads above. We were issued one bar of rough sandy soap between four men, but we did appreciate standing beneath that warm water.

Our clothing, when we collected it, smelled of disinfectant. Now we were deloused and acceptable as Stalag VIIIB prisoners. Quickly our small band was ousted from the warmth of the shower room, and the bitter cold wind felt more acute after the hot water.

"*Achtung!* March!" We headed, shivering, towards the menacing compounds of barbed wire and more double gates, trudging wearily past the guard who stood rigidly outside the striped sentry box, his long winter greatcoat buttoned up to his throat. The wind threw the heavy fabric around the contours of his black jack boots.

We had passed through three massive double-wide gates of wire and now stood inside prison camp proper. The inmates were already very much awake, and with roll call finished, the camp had come to life for another day. We were surrounded on each side by a mass of curious faces. In the first compound on our right were prisoners taken at Dunkirk, mostly the BEF (British Expeditionary Force), who had been here since 1940. Of course, we didn't know any of this until later; at that moment we saw only what we knew were British soldiers behind the wire.

The air was full of a chorus of shouts asking about home towns. "Who's from London?"

"Anyone from Bradford?"

"Glasgow?"

"Notts?"

"Any 'Brommies' with your lot?"

I didn't hear a single question about Belfast or Ireland, and recognized no one, but of course most of these men were peace-time army personnel who had been captured about the time I joined up. To us they looked old—many in their 30s and 40s. Two years or more in POW camp had not helped to rejuvenate any of them.

As our group of weary airmen trudged up the grade, I realized there was silence among us, each man with his own thoughts: Is this it? Is this where I will spend the rest of the war? Or my life?

It was damned cold and my white choker sweater and cloth battle-dress jacket were no match for the Obersilesian winter day. I searched the hundreds of faces behind the wire, hoping to recognize a face I knew or hear a voice with an accent from home.

My teeth chattered as we approached two more compounds. More army personnel, much younger looking than the soldiers in those other compounds, lined the one on the right. "Canadians?" someone shouted, and then immediately the word, "Dieppe." So these were the survivors of that tragic misadventure where the Germans almost wiped out the whole Canadian contingent. That 19th of August, 1942 was a black day for these men, but the Dieppe Compound was buoyant with humour and defiance.

Immediately to our left was a group that, even in these dire circumstances, was a somewhat uplifting sight. Lining the wire were hundreds and hundreds of "boys in blue," young men of nineteen, twenty—twenty-five, perhaps, at the oldest. This was the Air Force Compound. They looked like a bunch of school boys out in the yard for a break. Uniforms sported pilot's wings, the insignias of air gunners, navigators, wireless operators, flight engineers, and so on.

There were a dozen excited shouts of recognition. "Hi, Clarke!" "Hi, Joe!" "Jimmy Moore!" "Walt Butcher!" "Tubby Brown!" Someone screamed over the babble of voices, "Morgan!"

Ken said, "Indeed to goodness, it's old Jeff!" Old Jeff was about 21 and doing his best to get the message over that he would have a place for Ken in his barrack room. This bunch of healthy looking young flying crews were the survivors of clashes with German night fighters, anti-aircraft fire, mechanical failure, or other catastrophes. I recognized some wearing the dark colour of the Australian Air Force uniform, a contrast to the blue of our RAF, RCAF, and New Zealand Air Forces.

The guards who had marched us into camp were unmoved by this sudden hubbub of recognition by old friends. Their faces remained solemn and stern, their rifles at the ready.

A voice with a Scottish accent shouted, "Paddy Mac!" I looked in the direction of the voice and saw Big Jock Martin waving frantically.

"I've been waiting for you," he yelled. "Got an extra corner bunk—a middle one, too." I waved back to confirm I heard, and shouted, "Okay!"

"Where's Jaco, Magder and the gang?" Jock yelled.

I raised my hand and gave the thumbs down sign.

"All of them?"

I nodded the reply.

"Look for me," he shouted, and disappeared from the throng. I could see him running towards the double gates at the top end of the compound.

The gates were opened by an *Unteroffizier* with square-set jaw and stern-looking appearance. We were shepherded into an area surrounded by barbed wire. It was one of the inner compounds, and it housed approximately a thousand aircrew. With so many pilots and navigators, the Germans thought it best to keep those who would have a knowledge of navigation as far away from the perimeter wire as possible, making it that much harder to escape.

It was luck that after another line-up and head count, I was relegated with five others to Hut 15A. Big Jock was delighted. Pushing me into the barrack room, he guided me halfway down the room past tiers of bunks three high.

On the opposite side were a dozen tables spaced at intervals, and in the centre of the room there was a large rectangular heater. Here Jock turned left down a sort of corridor between bunks. There was a dirty window at the end. Jock pointed and said, "Grab that middle bunk next to the window and to the right, and hurry!" He blocked a couple of other people from getting past until I had deposited myself on the bunk's seven bedboards.

Then standing beside me he asked, "What happened, Paddy? We've been looking for you in every new batch that came in. We knew you'd be here, or dead."

I told him the story.

Almost as an afterthought, he said, "Peter is around somewhere." How quickly one can grow up during wartime! Jock told me they had been posted to a squadron at Waddington and immediately on operations. They had completed five ops in the short time between leaving Conversion Unit, and their exit from Bomber Command. After being hit over Hamburg by very accurate anti-aircraft fire they headed for the Dutch coast but had to bail out over Holland. All survived except the upper gunner.

When Peter arrived he immediately asked, "Where's the gang?" meaning my crew.

Jock stepped in and said, "Peter, I'll tell you about it later."

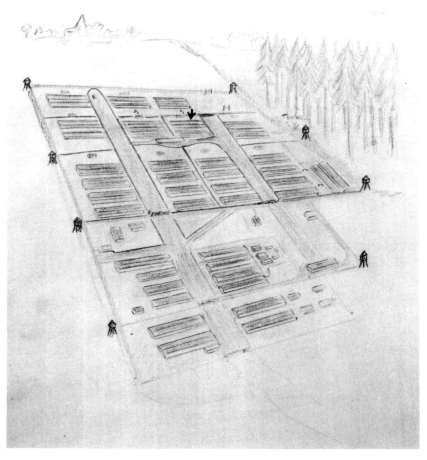

A drawing of Stalag VIIIB. The mark in the second row indicates Hut 15B, where I lived.

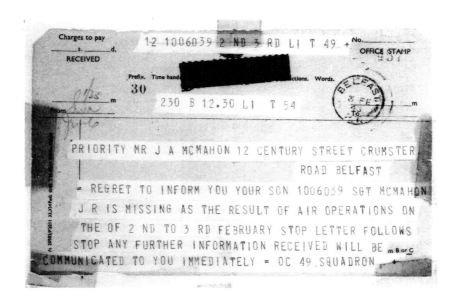

The telegram above was received by my family when I was shot down.
The one below came when it was discovered that I had been captured and
taken to Stalag VIIIB.

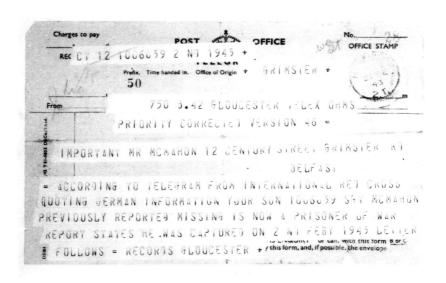

56

CHAPTER 5

Initiation

The barrack Senior Man called for the new men to come forward. The job of this man (whom the Germans called the Barrack Commander) was to inform all new prisoners of rules and regulations laid down by our captors and to mediate any disputes. He was responsible for keeping his barrack clean and the men under control. A vote by those in the barrack could see him evicted and a new Senior Man elected.

Senior Man Alec MacKinlay told us we had missed a parcel parade four days ago, but arrangements were being made that one Red Cross food parcel would be issued between two men, so each of us should choose a partner (or a "mucker," as he called it) to share with. The German army issue blanket, the straw-filled palliasse, and the seven bunk boards comprised each man's sleeping arrangements, plus an issue of wooden clogs. He warned us that any man caught burning his bedboards or clogs to fire up a cookstove would have to answer to "Ukraine Joe," the German officer in charge, and suffer the consequences.

"What's the consequences?" someone asked.

"Don't burn your boards or clogs and you won't have to find out," said Alec MacKinlay.

I had to pick a "mucker" from among the new arrivals, but who? I looked at the men standing almost dejectedly, looking at each other. It was suggested we put our names on separate pieces of paper and have Mackinlay pick out of a hat the first two 'muckers.' The remaining four would also be paired. (I learned later that even small pieces of paper were at a premium.)

My name came out first, and then that of Arnold Hobbs. I put on my most hospitable Irish face and suggested we wait together to see what materialized in regard to our parcels. Today's parcels would be English Red Cross issue, a two-man food ration for one week.

The next issue would be from the Canadian Red Cross. Apparently those were classed by prisoners as Top Notch food parcels containing an assortment of items that were far superior to the English issue.

Beggars can't be choosers, and no one refused food, English or Canadian. The sour dark German bread issue, one-seventh of a loaf per day for each of us was difficult to relish. One had to get used to it. Daily there would be watery soup at midday, an issue of approximately four potatoes, and the odd issue of a small piece of German sausage, plus something called Prima margarine.

This made up the complete food ration. To make a food parcel last seven days took difficult manipulating, plus a lot of trust by the two people involved. This was made particularly difficult by the fact that each can in the parcel was punctured by our captors prior to issue (a deterrent against storing food for escape).

I was not too enthused about the "draw" result. Arnold's first remark—"I'll take care of the rations"—brought my defences on the alert. I didn't show my feelings but made a mental note to be careful. I didn't like the way he promoted himself to take charge of rations that were yet to be issued.

I saw Jock Martin beckoning me, so excusing myself, I hastened to his table. He motioned me to sit down. We were divided into sections of eight to ten men, organized in this way for easier distribution of rations, especially the German issue such as bread, potatoes, soup, and anything else that had to be equally divided.

In front of Jock was a round aluminum "dixie" of hot porridge covered in milk. It looked scrumptious. "Sit ye down, Paddy," he commanded, "and enjoy some good Midlothian oats."

"That's not my rations," I started to say, but he cut me off in the middle of my sentence.

"Let's say it's a welcoming gift, and a little repayment for all the times ye found me in the blackout on Shifnell Station." Those nights returning to base in the blackout helping Jock on to the train when he'd had a few too many seemed so far away in a dim and distant past life.

When I said, "Sure glad I didn't leave you in the blackout," he chuckled.

"Well," he said, "I guess I'd still have to look after ye."

The porridge was delicious. As I supped the warm cereal, Peter said softly, "Sorry, Paddy, about Jaco and the gang. Your Irish luck must have been riding with you."

"Guess so," I replied, and the conversation was dropped as Arnold Hobbs passed by. He didn't stop but made his way to the barrack commander's private corner.

While I ate my porridge, Peter and Jock tried to fill me in on camp procedures. Half past six was reveille and "wakie-wakie" call. Check parade was at 7:00 a.m. Each day began outside, regardless of the weather. Winter and summer, we must stand and be counted. After parade, an issue of mint tea; then around 10:00 a.m. the potato and bread ration, sometimes with a little margarine. About that time there should be a ration of hot water from the "copper"—a large boiler set inside a brick surround, with a fire underneath, situated out in the washroom area.

There would be a soup issue every day. It could be sauerkraut, cabbage, a cattle-feed turnip soup called "Swede," "bird seed soup" (made from boiled millet), or "surprise soup," which was made from whatever the German cookhouse had available at the moment. Peter claimed they never washed anything they put in it. Apparently the German POW rations were completely inadequate for a man to survive on in any healthy condition, so we would depend on the Red Cross parcels to augment the camp food. Having a good mucker was therefore an absolute necessity.

"Cigarettes are camp currency," Peter said, and suggested when I wrote home I should ask for cigarette parcels.

"What about mail?" I asked.

Jock volunteered the information. Letters could only be one short page, and each postcard a seven- or eight-liner. Peter was convinced most of the mail never left the camp.

The black market could be a bit tricky. As is the case in any army, some individuals were always on the lookout for a deal, no matter if it was with the enemy. The German army cigarette ration was two or three per day, and it surprised even the POWs that cigarette parcels were permitted through the camp postal facilities.

I had no cigarettes and it seemed unlikely I'd receive a personal parcel containing cigarettes any time soon. Chocolate and soap were two items that were very scarce in Germany and brought a good exchange.

After check parade at 5:00 p.m. it was usual to cook up whatever sort of meal you planned, with whatever food you had from any source. This could mean a long wait for a turn on the section's home-made stove.

Peter emphasized it would be very foolhardy to leave anything on the stove without keeping at least one eye on it. In a place where people were always hungry, the temptation to steal food was high.

"By the way, I almost forgot," declared Peter, "the person in charge of the Air Force Compound is *Unteroffizier* Kussel, a stickler for discipline. Looks tough and belligerent," explained Peter, "but his bark is worse than his bite. He has rules. No one to lie on their bunk, except between the hours of 12:00 noon and 2:00 p.m., and after five o'clock parade. He takes pride in keeping these Air Force barracks clean and feels he has a superior job looking after aircrew prisoners.

"Now, for instance," Peter went on, "this *Unteroffizier* Kussel is from the Ukraine. His Christian name is Joseph, so naturally we named him 'Ukraine Joe.' He will not permit army personnel to use our latrines and virtually kicks them out of the Old Forty Seater."

"The Old Forty Seater?" I said. It was the second time I'd heard someone mention that. "What's that?"

"Ye haven't visited the can yet?" Jock asked in amazement.

"No, but I've got to go there pretty soon," I answered.

"What a treat's in store for ye," he laughed. "Come on, I'll show ye, if y've finished licking that spoon. Let's go—but before we do, a personal question: Are ye gonna be sitting down for a while? And if so, I dinna' think ye have any 'bumf'."

Another predicament, I thought to myself. Even on the train we were able to get the rough German product that served as toilet paper, but here in prison camp, where could one get such a thing?

"Ye scrounge paper," Jock said. "Now here I've been reading some of this propaganda junk they give us occasionally, so let's share a page." With that, he ripped a sheet from a German weekly written in English, then tore it in two again and presented me with one half.

"That's all ye get," he joked, "and if ye need more, it's just too bad."

"When you come back I'll give you a copy of our daily routine as I see it," volunteered Peter. "I've written a few copies, and I usually sell them for five cigarettes, but I'll give you one if you promise not to use it for bumf."

I thanked Peter for the porridge and said I'd be delighted to have a copy of his Daily Camp Routine. Then I followed Jock in the cold morning air towards a rectangular building across the parade square.

Entering this edifice and using its facilities for the first time was an experience to remember. On each side of the building were smooth broad wooden benches, each with ten holes. Down the centre were two more benches, back to back, with ten holes in each. So this was the Old Forty Seater, or Forty Holer as some people called it.

"Sit beside me," said Jock, "and do as I do." He walked to the bench that was closest to the barrack side. "We will take these two." Before sitting down he kicked the supporting wall below the bench a few times and told me to do likewise.

"Why do you do that?" I asked.

"Rats," he replied. "Lots of them. And remember, this is the safest side to sit on. There's more rats over on the other side, near the cess-pool's opening. Always give a good kick to the front before sitting down, and don't sit too long without knocking hard with yer heels to keep the rats away. After getting out of that Lancaster alive, ye don't want to lose yer manhood to some Kraut rat." Not wanting to lose any endowment at all, I did as I was told.

Sitting there, I noticed that the two supporting beams in the centre were being used for advertising. What better place? Enterprising individuals promoted to their captive audience an amazing variety of services. "Will wash your laundry," somebody had written, and he had included a list of items with prices in cigarettes for each.

"Pair of Army boots, size 8," read another. "Good condition. Ask for Big Harry, Hut 20B. Cheap."

"Will repair holes in socks." "For sale: mugs, plates. Top class workmanship."

"Very enterprising," I said, as I crumpled the shiny paper in an effort to soften it. Thinking I'd heard a noise underneath, I kicked the wall hard with my heel.

Jock heard me. "The rats run along a few inches from yer nearest part, on a little ledge on the wall underneath ye. Sometimes if ye hit hard enough just as they pass ye can knock them off and they have to swim in that stuff or drown. What a death, eh Paddy?" At that he crumpled his piece of paper, smoothed it out again, and as we both finished the paper work, he chuckled, "Now do ye think ye can go to the can by yerself?"

I screwed my face into a thoughtful look. "Think I can manage. If I need any more lessons I'll call you."

When we emerged, there were a number of people walking briskly around the compound in twos, threes, fours and more.

"A daily occurrence," Jock volunteered. "Peter and I usually go for our walk after lunch time or before it gets dark. Try to keep fit, Paddy.

Some day we may have to walk or run to save our lives. That's why ye see all these guys walking the compound. I think it's twenty times around makes a mile. I'll give ye a shout when Peter and I go."

It was nearing 11:00 a.m. when we re-entered the barracks. The windows were open and the cold fresh air had chased out the smoke and the smell of cooking, the cigarette smoke, and most of the other odours made by one hundred men closed in one room for the night. There wasn't much glass in the window frames and the empty spaces had been replaced with cardboard from Red Cross food parcels. Not very good insulation against the Obersilesian winter winds!

Peter was sitting at their table, writing with a pencil that was so short it was hard to hold.

"Just finishing a new 'Chadwick's Daily Routine' or 'A Day in Stalag VIIIB,' or whatever you want to call it," he said.

Thanking Peter for his masterpiece on daily routine and Jock for his help, I said, "I'd better find my mucker and see what's happening."

I was concerned that Hobbs must be hungry. I had the porridge and it was eleven o'clock. I was sure he'd had nothing since the soup from German Red Cross workers at Dresden Station. I hadn't been very congenial, partly because I'd found two good friends.

I found Hobbs walking alone in the yard. I was about to speak to him when the call came for the parcel issue. At the food parcel warehouse we lined up at a shuttered "hatch" and waited our turn. We were given our English Red Cross food parcel, and it was disturbing to look at the triangular hole punctured in each can.

"I'll take this to my bedspace and we can sort things out later," Arnold said, indicating the parcel. I didn't like his enthusiasm for taking possession of our food, but I guessed it had to go to somebody's bedspace for safekeeping.

He disappeared quickly, returned a few minutes later, and remarked, "It's in a good safe place." Hoping that he was right and my half would be as safe under Arnold's bed as his portion, we collected our bedding.

The blanket was a poor excuse to keep one warm. The mattress looked like an oversized net potato sack full of straw. Jock came on the scene and helped carry the bundle to my bed space. We heaved the mattress onto the bunk and covered it with the blanket. Now I had really staked my claim to this particular bedspace. I laughed as I held up my wooden clogs, but Jock said, "Dinna laugh, they're warm on your feet."

Next was introduction to the man who occupied the bunk above me and the two men across the narrow space between my bunk and the next tier. Above me was an Australian named Eddy Anderson and across the narrow dividing space, on the top bunk, a New Zealander named Giddens. He had been nicknamed "Nabber" because of all the things he was able to scrounge—nails, pieces of metal, screws, cloth materials, wire—anything. He was forever on the lookout, and the bottom storage space was crammed with all sorts of junk.

In the space below Nabber—on the middle bunk next to mine—the occupant was a chubby little Englishman named Markellie, the son of an English farmer.

Jock Martin's bunk was three tiers away. The middle bunk was his, and Peter Chadwick occupied the top one.

"Better find your 'mucker' with the rations," said Jock, and I detected a warning note in his voice.

I found Hobbs relaxing on a top bunk.

"How's it going? Where are we keeping our rations?" I hung heavily onto the plural "we" and "our" rations. I felt my half of the rations were too far away from my bedspace for comfort, but at the moment I was helpless to make any changes in the situation.

"Tea up!" came a cry from the barrack entrance. I expected to see a big rush, but only a few people casually wandered towards where the duty prisoners had deposited a large wooden "kubel" with steam rising from it.

"How do we get tea? Are there mugs?" I queried a pleasant looking lad in the top bunk next to Hobbs.

"You'll get an issue of a 'dixie,' a sort of army issue pan for all uses, but if you want a mug see Nabber Giddens. He makes them from tin cans, and that's the only kind of mug you'll get around here." As an afterthought, he said, "It'll cost you 20 cigarettes. He makes plates, too."

Having no cigarettes and no "dixie," it would be useless even to line up, but there was Jock looking down the aisle and beckoning to me. "Paddy," he said, "you can borrow my tin mug if you want, but unless you are completely out of Red Cross tea or coffee, don't bother. This German tea is supposed to be mint, but it is horrible, and if I'd just received a parcel with English tea in it, I'd tell the Jerrys what to do with their mint tea. We use it as shaving water!" He pointed at my face. "Speaking of which...you look like you could use a shave. Then again, you don't have a razor or blades. That's another hurdle I'll have to show you how to get over." He gestured to a small shelf. "Go ahead anyway—take my mug and get some tea. We all try it once. I think they mop out the Jerry cook house with the water first."

At that, he took off, saying, "I have to visit an old friend."

The mug was a 16-ounce tin, coloured blue, with "T. Eaton" written across it in white lettering. The handle was neatly made from material taken from another can and riveted to the sides, a very expert job. Just a little touch of rust showed down the seam of the can. I lined up, got my murky mint tea, and with the first sip realized what Jock meant when he'd said, "We use it for shaving water."

With the mug of hot liquid in my hand I looked for Jock. I found him and asked, "Where do I get a razor and blades?" Again my good friend came to the rescue and produced a Gillette razor complete with German blade, a shaving stick of soap, and a funny looking stubble of a shaving brush.

"Go and shave, Paddy, out to the washroom between the two barracks." He handed me a square of cloth to use as a towel and another tin with no handle. "I dinna' want you to use my tea mug to shave in. We will get you set up with shaving gear tomorrow."

Transferring the warm tea into this receptacle, I thanked Jock, gave him back his tea mug, then made my way to the washrooms and had my first of many shaves using mint tea, then returned Jock's shaving gear.

Approximately 100 men lived in this Barrack 15A. The same number were housed in the other end. Dividing the building in two was a washroom consisting of long concrete troughs, and at intervals, water taps. This is where we washed ourselves, our clothes, and anything else. Often there was no water, so it was a good thing to always be prepared with soap and a towel at hand. When someone shouted, "Water's on!" immediately there would be a stampede. Dozens and dozens of prisoners would scurry to the troughs to wash themselves, their clothes, or their eating utensils—all in the same concrete trough.

I had just returned to my bunk when there was a rush of activity and shouts of "soup's up."

"Come on, Mac," said Giddens, jumping off his bunk. And so, with a dozen others, I made my way to the front of the barrack. Arnold Hobbs was there with two dixies.

"Got you a dixie," he said. "Do you want the round one or the square one?"

"Any one," I replied.

"Okay. I'll put my hands behind my back, and you pick which hand yours is in."

"That's fair enough," I said. "I'll take the right hand."

He handed me a fairly clean, square dixie, which for the next two years would contain an amazing assortment of prison camp recipes. In ordinary times, some of these would have made me throw up, but to a starving "Kriegy," they tasted scrumptious.

"We're in number eleven section," Arnold said. "I had a talk with the Barrack Commander and there was room for two more in that section. It's the last table but one."

"By the way," I said, "where did you get the dixies?"

"From the Barrack Commander." He eyed me cautiously. "I'm hungry. I saw you eating at your friends' table."

"Yes," I said, feeling a little guilty. "It was good of them to give up some of their rations."

Ignoring my reply, he continued, "It's an English parcel we got. So we'll have to go through its contents and make up menus. There will be another issue in three days, so we're ahead of the game. We'll have a bit of a food buffer when the next parcel is issued."

As we neared the *kubel*—the soup container—the smell of the "Swede soup" was anything but appetizing. We held out our dixies. If there was soup left after everyone had their ration, seconds would be given on a rotating basis.

I watched as the man dishing out the rations carefully dipped into the soup, extracted the can, and emptied the contents into my dixie. He looked up and said, "New, eh? Your stomach gets used to it—after about a month."

With dixies of the foul smelling liquid in our hands, we faced two problems: where would we sit (as yet we hadn't been designated a place at our table), and how would we eat the meal? To our rescue on the second part of the dilemma came Nabber Giddens, the "tinsmith."

"I made a couple of spoons yesterday," he said. They're for sale. If you wish, I can give you one each on credit." He paused and grinned. "I don't think you'll run out on me."

"How much?" Arnold and I asked, almost together.

"My usual charge is five cigarettes per spoon."

"Okay by me," I said. "I'll pay you when I get cigarettes."

Arnold also agreed. Nabber rushed off and returned seconds later with two good-looking spoons, very well made.

"Tell you what, guys," said our benefactor, "just give me a big smile, keep some of your empty cans for me, and we'll call it square. Now go and sup your lousy soup before it's cold."

We thanked him and sat down at our designated table, and with difficulty swallowed our first Stalag Soup.

"Tastes better as the weeks go by," volunteered a young pilot with dark curly hair, whose name was Mark Watson.

At least the soup was filling, and still hot. We finished every spoonful.

"Where do we clean our dixies?" Arnold asked.

"If there's water on, you might manage a few drops," said Watson. "If not, just use it for whatever, and in the morning you can use the mint tea ration to shave with or to swill out your dixie."

The other prisoners at the table made no comment.

One of the men sorting out a food parcel asked, "What the hell happened to our potatoes today? They're late!"

"The carriers went for them before soup ration," said a serious looking navigator wearing the old original navigator's Observer Wing. He wore glasses and was reading a book entitled *Your Career in Banking*.

There was the cry, "Spuds up!"

"How do we get our potatoes?" I asked the man close to me.

"Same as we do," he replied with a solemn face. "You'll find out we cut the cards for a lot of things."

Our section leader appeared with a Red Cross box full of cooked potatoes—all different sizes, and all cooked in their jackets. Putting the box down, he introduced himself: Sam Warnock from Cardiff, Wales. "Hope you guys are making out okay," Sam said. "If I can help, just shout."

"Okay, you guys, clear one end of the table and let's see how many rotten spuds we have today. Or are you all willing to gamble again?" asked Sam.

"Put them out according to size and let's gamble as usual," suggested a young New Zealander who had his name, Tim, embroidered below his air gunner insignia.

Sam looked at his box of potatoes and appeared to be talking to himself. "With the two new men, that makes ten of us. We were supposed to have two extra rations, but it sure doesn't look like there's any more spuds than we got yesterday." He looked pensively into the box.

"Better make out two new cards, Kiwi," said Sam, looking directly at Tim.

"Okay," replied Tim. From a box under the table he brought out a number of old, dirty, dog-eared playing cards and took eight cards off the top. Then he put two more on the table, and with a poised pencil in his hand, looked up inquiringly.

"Don't know your handles, guys. But for sure," he said, pointing at me, "you are a Paddy and from the North. My grandfather came from some place in the state of Antrim. You talk like him."

I introduced myself and told him he was 99 percent correct, but we didn't call them states—that was American. It would be the County of Antrim that his grandfather had left. So "Paddy Mac" was written on one card, and "A/H" on the other, for Arnold Hobbs.

As Tim was writing our names on the faces of the cards, Sam set out ten rows of potatoes, with the biggest ones first. When he finished, there were ten short lines—some with five and others with four potatoes, none of them looking too healthy.

Then Sam picked up the ten cards, shuffled them, and asked Arnold to cut, then placed a card face up above each row of spuds.

"There you go, me boys," he said. "Pick up your Kartoffels and say thanks to your *führer* who giveth all things."

Arnold and I picked up eight potatoes between us and made off with our loot to his bedspace. Looking at them, I said, "Arnold, two of these are rotten."

"Well, ain't you guys lucky! Only two rotters in your ration. They're being kind to you, seeing it's your first day. It's usual for half the spuds to be rotten, and you'll find most of the bread ration is covered in mould—and the mould tastes better than the bread."

This little sermon came from the top bunk above Hobbs' bedspace. A round, cherubic face with laughing blue eyes looked down at us, and the barrage of words continued.

"I'm Archie Vickers. Got here in time for the Christmas dinner that wasn't. It's not bad if you keep yourself occupied. I told my girlfriend I'd buy her an engagement ring for Christmas, so Hitler saved me that expense. If you guys don't smoke, you might be able to get enough to eat by trading with the Jerry guards."

Archie continued his chatter unabated while Arnold and I decided that with our potatoes and the can of meat and vegetables from the parcel, we could make up something hot on the stove for supper.

"The Army working parties who go out to work on the farms say that for a chocolate bar and a cake of scented soap, you can have a woman and get change back in German marks?"

We made no comment on that story, and there was silence for about half a minute. Then Archie came back loud and clear, as though someone had turned up the volume on a radio once more. "I hear you're Irish. I had an Irish mucker once. But he got transferred to Stalag *Luft* III, the officers' camp." He eyed me for a moment. If you have the guts to slip past the guards and under the wire to the cookhouse, then you might want to know that there's an Irish potato racket in camp. You can get a lot of extra potatoes. You will probably be approached very soon."

"How does it work?" I wanted to know.

"There are two Irish guardsmen who work in the Stalag kitchen. You get an old haversack—there's an old army one in the compound—in Hut 16A, I think—and you take it to the back of the kitchen. When one of these guys gives you the signal, you throw it in the open window, you will get it passed out full of hot, cooked potatoes. Then the fun begins. It's easier getting there with an empty bag, but trying to hide that bag full of hot spuds and get it back through the wire and past the guards is tricky business, especially on a cold day when the steam rises from the potatoes. One guy got caught. The Germans were going to charge him with stealing from the stores. At other places they've shot people for that, I hear. It was a guy named Paddy O'Leary that got caught. He's in Barrack 21B. The compound commander and the padre went to bat for him, and all he got was fourteen days in the clink. He was lucky. It didn't stop the potato racket because he wouldn't tell how he got the spuds. So the Irishmen inside the kitchen are still there."

This encyclopedia of camp knowledge continued his barrage of chatter. "You'll find a hole under the wire at the third post from the corner on the other side of Barrack 18A. That's the way out to the lane if our compound gates are locked. It can't be seen because the wire is just broken at the post and can be peeled back enough for a man and a sack of potatoes to crawl through. I know because I did it once when my mucker was sick. Boy, was I scared. But I managed it."

Archie continued his prattle and seemed to be just warming up. "If you should get in on the extra potato racket, make sure you close that wire after you crawl through. If you don't, then when you come back with that haversack of spuds, you might find a Jerry guard and his rifle and bayonet waiting for you this side of the hole."

There was a pause in Archie's torrent of information, and I took advantage of it and asked a question. Still not being conversant with the camp layout, I asked, "When you go through that wire for the extra potatoes, is that still inside the camp?"

"Oh, sure," he said, "Don't think anyone would risk crossing the trip wire and going outside for a few extra potatoes. If you ever got through the perimeter's double wire and the tangle of barbed wire in the middle, you'd be heading west and thinking of wine, women and song—not potatoes. But Obersilesia is a long, long way from home." He paused and thought for a second. "Switzerland or north to Stettin and the chance of a ship to Sweden would be your best bet, if you ever did get out.

"Now about the escape committee . . . "

At this point we both decided we should move back to the table, so we excused ourselves, thanked Archie for his information, and on second thought took our rations to my bedspace, where we had no one wishing to give us all the information he had about camp life in a single lesson.

Big Jock Martin introduced me to the "forty holer" and instructed me on how to kick the wall to knock the rats away.

Imperial War Museum Photo HU 47156

Above: The day of the Red Cross food parcel issue was always an important one. Note the expressions on the faces of the prisoners.
Below: The inside of a typical barrack— home to 100 men. Note the homemade cookstove to the centre left of the photo.

Imperial War Museum Photo 47107

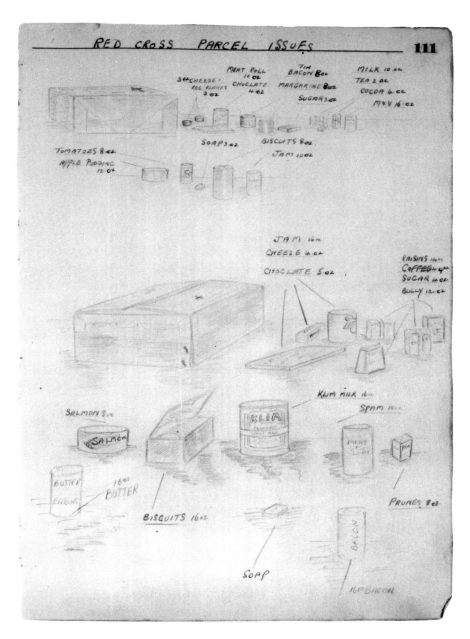

A comparison between the contents of English (above) vs. Canadian (below) Red Cross Parcels. One parcel had to last two men for a full week.

CHAPTER 6

Settling In—Day 1

We laid out the contents of our parcel on my bed and immediately ate the chocolate bar. It tasted wonderful! Next the tin of hard tack biscuits. We borrowed a tiny can opener from Nabber Giddens to open the strawberry jam and the biscuits. We smothered them in jam and devoured every single one.

Nabber, in the process of putting a handle on a new mug, had been watching us finish the chocolate, our can of biscuits, plus a large portion of the jam. "I know how you feel," he said, "my mucker and me ate all of our Red Cross parcel the first two days, then we had to live on Jerry rations for five days. Remember, there's always tomorrow, and you'll want to eat a little bit of Red Cross every day. Over time your stomach will shrink and the hunger pains ease." With these words of wisdom, he patted his stomach and continued with his tinsmithing.

"Will the two new men in Section Eleven pick up their bread ration!"

Hobbs immediately volunteered to get the bread ration.

"What one do you pick?" he asked when he returned. Once again he hid the bread behind his back.

"Left," I said, and was awarded a portion of bread—an end piece that smelled horrible, had a number of mould spots, and looked like it was impregnated with sawdust. It was supposed to be a one-seventh portion of a whole loaf, but as yet I had not seen a whole loaf. Looking at the bread with disgust, I picked off a few tiny pieces of what looked like tiny wood chips. Without raising his head from his work on the new mug, Nabber said, "It *is* sawdust; they roll the dough in it after the loaf is formed. This bread started off for the Russian Front and came back again because the Sixth Army surrendered to the Russians. They decided to feed the prison camps with it." As an afterthought, he added, "The mould won't hurt you; it's good for rheumatism." He chuckled at this remark, looked up with a twinkle in his eye, and said, "Can't you see us all here at 80, fighting for mouldy bread to ease our rheumatic pains?" He jumped off his bunk, held up the new mug, and said, "I think I'll charge 30 cigarettes for this one. It's a beauty!"

"Should we eat our bread now?" I asked Hobbs.

"Go ahead, but I'm keeping mine until later."

Apparently this was one part of our rations that would not be communal. Looking at his bread, which he held half hidden at his side, I saw that it was not an end. It also looked bigger.

Hoping to get a better look, I said, "Is there much sawdust and mould on yours?"

"About the same as you have," came the reply, but he made no attempt to move his hand and show me.

"I see," I said quietly.

The bread was sour and my taste buds rebelled against the horrible flavour. The colour was a dark, uneven brown, and in no way resembled the rye bread that could be purchased back home. If anything, the mould softened the sour taste.

Leaving out our tin of meat loaf and the potatoes, Arnold Hobbs began to repack our parcel. "I'll return this to my bedspace," he said. "Bedspace" referred to the area each prisoner claimed as his territory.

"What about a cup of tea later?" I asked.

"Might be an idea," Arnold said without enthusiasm. "There will be hot water about eight o'clock."

"Okay," I replied. "Tea, bread, and more jam—something to look forward to in the evening." I said this lightly and with a laugh, but got only a sombre look from Arnold. I thought, I've got to change muckers somehow. I didn't want to go through whatever lay ahead with this dull and distant character. Arnold was as sour as the German bread ration.

I was standing surveying the window at the bottom of my bedspace, with its broken glass and cardboard repair and a few pieces of rag stuffed in here and there, when Nabber returned.

"It's one of the best in the room," he said, indicating the window. "There are three whole panes of glass out of six. Fifty percent. That's the best average in the barrack!" He sat down and eyed his new mug. "I think there's a depression in these here parts. No one will give me even 20 cigarettes for this mug." He looked up at me. "Might as well give you this masterpiece now." He handed me the mug with a manner one would use to present a coveted award. "Now you can have a mug of tea when the brew does comes up." "Brew," of course, was hot water from the copper. I thanked the friendly New Zealander.

Following Nabber's example, I clambered onto my bunk, rolled up my jacket to make a pillow, and pulled the thin blanket up to my chin.

I suppose there was the disadvantage of a lower bunk; top ones were warmer in winter, being closer to the ceiling. But smoke from the tin cookstoves left the hotter air with less oxygen and I wouldn't want a top bunk during midsummer's heat.

There'd be no summer flowers for me this year. I was here in the hands of the enemy, and as Winston Churchill once wrote when he was a prisoner in East Africa in 1899, "It is a melancholy state. You are in the power of the enemy. You owe your life to his humanity, your daily bread to his compassion. You must obey his orders, await his pleasure, possess your soul in his patience. The days are very long and the hours crawl like paralyzed centipedes."

A beat-up looking calendar above Nabber's bunk read February 21. In 48 hours it would be my 22nd birthday. With that thought in mind I dozed off. Then, suddenly, Markellie was shaking my arm. "Better get up and tidy your bed. Ukraine Joe's on the warpath. Listen!"

I didn't have to listen for long. I heard the gruff voice shouting, "*Raus, raus, raus!*" and the banging of a stick or rifle against bunks. It was ten after two. No one could lie on his bunk unless he possessed a "chit" from our POW medical officer.

Joe had come through from the other barrack via the washroom and caught a lot of people unaware. Now there was a scramble as he inspected bed areas for neatness.

"Joe treats us like we were in his army," said Markellie, "but I guess it keeps us on our toes."

I quickly tidied my bedspace, made the blanket look as neat as possible, and put on my jacket. I was standing with Nabber and Markellie when the big *Unteroffizier* came storming down the aisle, rattling a heavy stick along the bunks. Everyone in our aisle was up and standing by his bed; Joe had no complaints. He was gone only a couple of minutes when we heard a rumpus at the far end of the barrack. Someone was asleep and Joe was raising Cain.

"Probably it's Montrose again," volunteered Nabber.

"Who's Montrose?" I asked.

Nabber said, "George Montrose. He's always late for parade, always sleeping when he shouldn't be, and Joe usually makes a beeline right to George's bunk. If we're short on our count, especially in the mornings, the first question is, 'Where's Montrose?' His mates try to make sure he is awake."

I excused myself to get fresh air. Skirting the cracks and holes in the concrete floor, I made my way outside. Buttoning my jacket against the cold, I continued around the compound, keeping on the well-worn path close to the wire. I felt lonely and scared, but thankful for the old friends who had received me so warmly and shared what they had with me. I had a good feeling about the new friends in my bedspace area—Nabber with his wholesome New Zealand accent and warmth of character, and Markellie, with his swinging gait and chubby face, made this scary scene so much easier. Eddy Anderson I'd find out about as time went by.

I watched the cobbled path, with its uneven rocks and many holes, but still I slipped on an icy piece of ground and almost fell. I regained my balance in time to hear a Welsh accent close by: "Indeed to goodness, Paddy, where did you get the drink? They didn't tell me there was a pub in the compound." And there was Ken Morgan, our train-journey morale booster, with a blue knit scarf wrapped around his neck and a woollen hat pulled down over his ears.

"What hut are you in?" I asked.

"Seventeen-B, right there," and he pointed behind him. "I found a pilot from my home town of Cardiff. He's been here six months and got two sets of knitwear, so he gave me one. He says this is the safest place on Bomber Command. Apparently 'Jerry' is knocking down a lot of our bombers! I'll walk with you. I was just starting, so let's go. It's getting cold."

I fell in beside Ken. His 5'3" frame made my 5'7" feel much taller.

"Did you hear about the chains?" Ken's voice took on a serious tone.

"What chains?" I asked.

"The chains you'll be wearing around your wrists tomorrow."

"What are you talking about?"

"Well, it's like this," Ken volunteered. "My mucker says that during the Dieppe raid last August, the Canadians took some prisoners and tied their hands behind their backs. Rumour is that some German prisoners fell over the edge of the cliffs. How they fell is open to question."

"What's that got to do with us?"

"For some time now," Ken went on, "the prisoners in the Dieppe

Compound and the Air Force Compound have had their hands tied together with Red Cross string every day from 8:00 a.m. till 4:00 p.m., as a reprisal. Then the Germans brought in short chains with handcuffs on each end."

"I didn't see anyone chained up," I replied. "Are you sure your friends aren't pulling your leg?"

"You haven't seen chains because the Geneva people from Switzerland were here yesterday. The Swiss Red Cross come the odd time to inspect prison camps. It's a farce, really. They're shown only the best camps. Yesterday the potato ration was all good spuds—no rotten ones—and no chains to be seen. That's the reason we got a nice hot shower and disinfected before entering camp. The Geneva inspectors were here when we came in."

I wondered why Nabber, Jock Martin, or Peter had not told me about the business of the chains.

It started to snow—that gritty fine stuff like so many tiny hailstones. Ken ducked into the doorway of Barrack 17B. "Come and have a hot brew sometime," he shouted.

"Thanks," I called out. "You, too," and I wondered what my mucker Hobbs would say if I entertained another prisoner with a mug of tea.

When I returned to 15A, there was activity around the big heater. It had been fired up and people were putting dixies into a sort of oven above the firebox. They fueled the tin stove with small bits and pieces of wood chips, empty cigarette packets, and other assorted pieces of paper. Two "kriegies" were trying to fry sliced meat loaf and sliced potatoes in their dixie.

I decide to find Hobbs and see what was happening to that precious Red Cross parcel. As I approached his bedspace, I could see him getting something together.

"Where have you been?" he asked sullenly.

"Went for a walk with Ken Morgan," I explained.

He nodded indifferently.

"Looks like we're sticking to our menu," I said. "I see you have the meat loaf sliced already, and the potatoes. Good. I'll cook tomorrow's supper," I volunteered, hoping to gain some control over our rations. I paused for a moment, but he said nothing. Finally I said, "Do you know that we'll be chained up tomorrow—handcuffed?"

"Yes," Arnold said, "I heard," and continued to slice the ration of potatoes into the dixie.

"How are we going to heat this?"

"The oven's full," came the reply. "We might have to wait until after roll call."

"Okay with me." I looked at the sliced meat loaf and counted seven thin slices. "Not a very big meat loaf?" I said it as a question.

"Those tins are not full to the top," Arnold said.

"Where did you get the can opener?" I asked.

"Borrowed."

Hobbs wasn't volunteering any information as to who loaned it, and wasn't interested in conversation. I couldn't help but stack those seven slices of meat loaf in my mind and gauge them against the height of the empty can.

"It might be better if we waited until after check parade to cook supper. By the time we get on the stove or in the oven, it will be almost five."

"I'd like to try now," Arnold said sullenly. Then, with the potatoes and sliced meat in the dixie, he was off to the cooking area. I followed a few minutes later and arrived in time to hear a big redheaded pilot say, "Listen, chum, if your name's not on the list now, you haven't a snowball's chance in hell of getting on the stove or in the oven 'till after roll call, unless you have fuel for this bloody stove. If not, just take off and come back later—much later!"

Standing with the dixie of food in his hand, Arnold Hobbs was a pathetic figure. He looked up at the big Canadian and asked almost pleadingly, "Isn't there anywhere else we can cook our food? Where is the list of names? How many before us?"

These questions were blurted out in a childish voice, and I noticed a slight tremble in his speech. Arnold sounded as though he was about to break down and cry.

"This is where it's at. There's no other place to cook in the barrack, and tonight I'm in charge. Here, write your name below McCabe's." The redhead was gruff in his reply as he held out a dirty scrap of Red Cross parcel cardboard with about twenty names written on it. Almost half were scored off as being finished or in the process of cooking. Arnold picked up the stub of pencil and shakily added our names to the list. It was 4:30 p.m.

I touched Arnold's arm and quietly indicated that we should go back to his bedspace. Without hesitation, he preceded me away from the turmoil of assorted menu preparation. The mixture of sickly odours was enough to give us second thoughts about trying to gain a place where there was sufficient heat to cook. Certainly we had no fuel to offer and no idea of how to obtain such a precious commodity.

Arnold marched in front of me, his arm fully outstretched, holding the dixie of food as if he were pointing it at something. He was distraught and turned down the aisle to his bedspace as though sleepwalking. I took the dixie from his tight grip. He did not protest. The sliced potatoes had turned a dark colour but the slices of meat loaf looked all right.

Sitting on his bunk, Arnold stared straight ahead. He whispered, "Will we have to do this for years?"

"No," I volunteered softly. "Maybe six months." And then, to break his doleful outlook, I said, "Let's eat this the way it is—cold."

He looked at the dixie of food. With something like relief in his eyes, he said, "Would you?"

"Sure," I replied, "I'm starving."

We devoured the cold potatoes and sliced meat loaf, dividing them as equally as possible—except for the seventh slice of meat loaf, which seemed to stick in Arnold's dixie. I used the tin spoon Nabber had given me to cut the potatoes and meat into small pieces to make them last. As I scraped the remains from the edges of my dixie, I checked Hobbs' to see if that odd slice of meat loaf was still intact. He had eaten his ration but had left the last slice alone. He looked at me, and for a moment I thought he would eat it. Then, without hesitation, he divided it equally and gave me half.

Earlier, when I had counted those seven slices, I was sure I had come on the scene too soon and that Arnold's intentions were to eat that extra slice himself. But now here he was, for the moment beaten down by a gruff Canadian pilot, and allowing his own pent-up emotions to get the best of him.

Our scattered thoughts were interrupted by the cry, "Outside on parade!"

With twenty days of constant wear, my choker sweater was no longer white and my other clothing was badly in need of washing. For the first time I wondered how the majority of these men got Air Force greatcoats—they sure weren't part of an aircrew's flying gear!

Eddy Anderson was lying on his bunk wearing a greatcoat and a woollen balaclava covering his head and face; only his eyes, nose and mouth were visible. Markellie was standing dressed and ready for parade but finishing the remains of his evening meal. Nabber was already on his way outside.

Markellie gobbled down the last remnants of his food, reached to a homemade tin shelf, picked up his mug, and quickly drank the remaining steaming hot liquid. Then he said, "Come on, Eddy, don't go to sleep or Ukraine Joe will have your head, balaclava and all."

I joined him as we made our way with the stream of men, leaving Eddy Anderson well behind.

There was little light in the barrack room—only a few 25-watt electric bulbs to light the twelve tables and no official lights close to the bunks—not a very bright picture. I buttoned my battle dress jacket as I was "poured" out the door with the mass of bodies and into the bitter cold evening. I turned up the turtle-neck part of my sweater to cover my mouth and nose. The cold air seemed to be warmed a little through the wool.

Barracks 15A and B were closest to the piece of ground that was termed parade square. We lined up as quickly as possible in rows of five (always the count was in fives) and waited on this very cold February evening for the masters of our destiny to find out how many bodies were on parade, satisfy themselves that all were present, and dismiss us to the sparse warmth of our barrack.

Standing there shivering, I felt helpless, but at least I had the comfort of knowing that here on this small tract of white-carpeted German soil were about a thousand fellow aircrew who had been spared their lives. If our luck held, we would return home. Having so many in the same boat, so to speak, gave all of us a sort of solid front against our captors.

Unteroffizier Kussel started his count and continued down the line of men. He did not get the correct result, so back he came to the first row, and in his broken English, commanded everyone to "Kommer off, Mistas" (cover off, men) meaning that we were to line up properly in straight rows of five so that he wouldn't make another counting error.

Slowly and meticulously he counted, row by row, assisted by our Senior Man repeating the count in German. After three attempts, someone discovered that Joe's count was incorrect because he had forgotten to add six new prisoners to our barrack's total. The error extended our check parade time by ten minutes. During that time there were many derisive cries from the populations of other barracks already checked as correct, but unable to leave the square because of our uncertain numbers. Thinking that we might purposely be throwing the count, someone shouted, "Smarten up, you guys. It's too cold tonight to mess things up!"

Other remarks were directed at the big *Unteroffizier*: "Hi, Joe, count in English!"

"Joe, my kartoffels are burning!"

"Hey, Joe—what school did you go to?"

Ignoring the jibes from other barracks, Joe turned toward the exit gates and marched away, throwing both arms up as he went, as if to say, "So what, I goofed. But I don't care!" His black jack boots threw up a small flurry of snow with each step. Then, suddenly, he stopped and turned around; he'd forgotten to dismiss us. With a grin he shouted, "Dismiss!"

I brushed damp snow from my clothes and returned to my bedspace. I shook my jacket well before hanging it on a nail at the end of the top bunk. This was probably Eddy Anderson's substitute for a real coat hanger. I made a mental note to ask Nabber if he had a spare nail that I could use for a similar purpose. But how would I hammer a nail in the wood? A hammer was a destructive weapon and no way permitted to be in the hands of a prisoner! Feeling quite sure that Nabber would have some novel substitute for a hammer, I removed my German issue boots. Surprisingly, I had been permitted to keep them.

I lay down. I didn't have material to make a pillow. My jacket was wet but later it would be dry enough to roll up as a substitute pillow.

The barrack had wooden shutters that closed over the windows. They were in disrepair but would keep out some cold. The bunk above me and the two beside me were empty. Markellie, Anderson and Giddens were off, each doing what was important to him at the moment. Little light filtered through the smoke haze of the barrack, but being close to the window provided the extra bonus (if the shutters were open) of brightness from the light of the prison camp itself.

I could see the bright circle from one of the lights on the path separating us from the Dieppe Compound. Beyond was the double perimeter wire, and between these fences, the entanglement of barbed wire. I made a mental note to take a close look at this in daylight—maybe tomorrow. I would need to remember not to touch or cross the tripwire strung six feet away from the double wire. To cross that wire, Peter said, could mean a burst of machine gun fire from the nearest guard box, high up on those stilt-like structures. He had warned me to be very careful and always to give that trip wire every consideration when out walking "the wire trail." "See it as a threat to your life," he said. "Just pretend it's got high voltage running through it."

Apparently, the guards in the sentry box at times became trigger-happy, especially if they had received word that some friend or family member had been killed in an allied bombing raid. Right below them were scores of "Luft Gangsters," as their daily newspapers liked to call aircrew, and revenge was sometimes a high priority.

The snow had turned to sleet. The searchlights had been switched on, and in the guard box outside the wire and behind the Dieppe Compound, the German on duty was slowly and methodically swinging the big beam along the perimeter wire. It would disappear from my view and then return, and for a number of seconds I could see its strong rays as the light swung slowly to meet its opposite number coming from the next sentry box.

I dozed off, but a little later I was wakened by the sound of someone close by. I opened my eyes in time to see a pair of bootless feet and two long legs disappearing to the top bunk. Then came the heavy *plump* as the body that was attached to those legs and feet sank into the straw mattress above me and sent down a shower of small pieces of straw, accompanied by minute particles like so much dust.

I sat up in my bunk, shook dust from my hair, and brushed straw off my sweater and blanket. The occupant up top must have heard me. A face appeared, but it was upside down. Eddy Anderson leaned precariously from his top bunk and apologized profusely for the shower he had caused.

"Sorry about the straw," he said. "I'll have to get used to someone underneath." As he spoke, his lips curled in a funny way that didn't seem right, even though he was upside down.

"It's okay," I volunteered. I looked at this character's head, hanging there in space, his sparse hair straggling down from the sides of his head. In the middle he wasn't bald, just covered with light fuzz. I had a feeling that things were not right with him. He grinned and showed a row of very small yellow teeth.

I hadn't noticed this when first introduced, but now the upside down version looked more than just funny; he seemed a little odd. Perhaps the reason this enviable bedspace of mine had been vacant.

Markellie returned with Nabber a few paces behind him. When Nabber saw Anderson's head hanging over the edge he said, "Eddy, all your blood will run to your head if you keep that position too long, and then you'll go crazy again. If you want to visit, why don't you come down from your perch and do it like a gentleman?" With that, Anderson recoiled back into his straw mattress, saying he was tired and wanted to rest.

Nabber looked at me, and just loud enough so I could hear, whispered, "He's lost some of his marbles." Later, I would hear prison camp inmates say of someone on the verge of a nervous breakdown (or gone a little strange because he couldn't cope 100 percent with life behind the wire) that he was "Stalag Happy." If you were Stalag Happy it could be anything from a minor problem to a complete mental breakdown caused by stresses and strains under abnormal conditions. There was no sliding scale, so to speak. You were either Stalag Happy or normal, whatever "normal" was.

Quite often it was the strongest, toughest-looking individuals who would sit on their bunks and cry like little children, and that was no shame, no crime—just a release from the awful uncertainty of an existence in which every move you made came under the enemy's watchful eye. I think this was the most destructive part of prison camp: We were in the hands of the enemy, humiliated and restricted, in an atmosphere that pushed men toward despair. To cry was a release that helped many, I believe, not to go Stalag Happy. So the big and the small, the weak and the strong, the Stalag Happies and the Normals all had to help each other to survive and return to their families, God willing, when the stupidity ended.

Markellie was curled up reading a book. It was all tattered and torn and I couldn't see the title. Nabber was about to hoist himself to his top bunk when I asked, "Would you happen to have an extra nail?" With his foot on Markellie's wooden bed rail and one hand on his own, ready to spring up, he looked down at me and said in a shocked voice, "A *nail*? Now where do you think, Paddy, I'd get a nail? Don't you know nails and all other sharp instruments are classed as lethal weapons in this here Stalag? Don't you realize that you can be killed with a nail?"

I went along. "Sorry, Nabber, but I noticed the nail my jacket is hanging on and thought it belonged to Anderson, and I see you have one, and so does Markellie. Thought I'd ask to make sure I hadn't missed a nail issue."

"What a load of Irish blarney!" Nabber bellowed. "You know damned well I have nails; you probably looked under my bunk." He gave up the idea of vaulting to his "straw bed" and got on his knees below Markellie's bunk and began rummaging through a Red Cross box half full of rectangular sheets of metal he'd salvaged from Red Cross cans. He found a large nail that looked strong enough to hold a heavy coat. Then, pulling down his blanket, he put his hand into the straw mattress and produced a short thick piece of metal.

"Where did you get that?" I asked, and immediately knew it was the wrong question.

Nabber looked at me, shook his head and remarked, "You'll learn as the weeks go by."

He placed the nail against the aisle side of the wooden support for the top bunk, about six feet from the floor.

"Is this about the right height?" he asked.

"Yes, okay, just great," I replied. He drove the nail in sufficiently so it would hold a coat.

"One coat hanger—five cigarettes," he said laughingly. "You're sure getting into debt," he jibed, as he returned his "hammer" to its hiding place and vaulted onto his bunk. I said my thanks and assured him that one day his good deeds would be rewarded.

Markellie looked up casually from his book to say, "Maybe the Führer will decorate him with the Iron Cross First Class."

There was no comment from Nabber to this remark. He had already picked up a piece of paper and was writing. It looked like it could be one of those letters or cards that Peter had told me we were permitted to send, and although my curiosity was aroused, I didn't think I should press my luck by asking if it was a Stalag letter.

Peter's masterpiece on daily routine was tucked in my battle dress pocket. There was a little less than an hour to wait before water rations and the cry of "Brew's up!" If I got hold of Arnold Hobbs, we could make tea and have the remainder of our bread ration.

Suddenly I remembered my own bread ration remnant in the unwashed dixie. I lifted up the green sacking-type material surrounding the storage space, half expecting my meagre bread ration would be gone. But there it was, and it seemed to have grown a little more mould. I was hungry and tried to remember what I'd had to eat that day. Looking up, I saw Nabber peering over his piece of writing paper at me.

"You okay, Paddy? You look like you're somewhere else."

"I'm fine," I replied. "Just cooking up in my mind a few scrumptious recipes from Red Cross rations. Tell me, Nabber, what's in the small cans in those English parcels?"

"Egg flakes—2 ounces; cheese—3 ounces; a tin of lousy white oleo margarine; a tin of 'condemned' milk, and a can of bacon." He rhymed these items off as though he were answering a school teacher's question.

"I remembered the bacon and the condensed milk." I recalled that we used the "condemned milk" terminology in Old Sam's grocery store, but that was in some other lifetime.

Markellie had heard my question and volunteered from behind his book, "Soap, sugar and apple pudding."

"Soap, sugar and apple pudding," Nabber repeated. "You're right, but I don't think they'd mix too well together." Then with a smirk and a jerk of his head, he said, "Might be a good recipe for constipation."

Offering my thanks to both of them, I picked up my Eaton's tin mug and my mouldy bread ration, and went in search of Hobbs.

During the conversation with Nabber and Markellie, I had seen something that wasn't in keeping with the usual semi-darkness that reigned away from those official 25-watt bulbs. There was a certain brightness around their bedspaces that had not been there before. I spied electric wires strung to a beam and across the V supports. They disappeared across the barrack ceiling to some sort of power source. Ingeniously, a fairly large piece of broken mirror was attached by Red Cross string behind the light at an angle to throw enough reading light onto Markellie' pillow area so both could read at the same time.

"A special privilege?" I asked, pointing to the light.

"Only for special people," Nabber grinned, and made no attempt to explain further.

When I got to Arnold's bedspace, I found our Red Cross parcel sitting on his bunk, closed. There was no sign of Arnold. For a moment I was tempted to open it, but didn't, although I reckoned he must have been once again checking its contents. The "information expert," whose accommodation was above Arnold's bunk, was nowhere in sight, which was a relief. I didn't wish to hear his chatter. I looked at the cardboard box with the Red Cross on it, and thought to myself, half of this is mine—even half the cardboard if I want to use it. So why am I standing here waiting for Hobbs to return?

I quickly turned it around and lifted the lid. Then suddenly, like a young monkey jumping from branch to branch, came the "information expert," Archie Vickers. He must have been a number of top bunks away, visiting a friend. Seeing someone pick up the food parcel, he had come bounding across the empty bunks with great agility.

"Oh, it's only you, Paddy!" he exclaimed. "Wish I'd known. I was left in charge of protecting your food. Your mucker went to wash his dixie. You're having cocoa when the brew is ready. And by the way, there will be no chains tomorrow because the Swiss Red Cross Inspectors are staying another day... Where's your bedspace? You're not anywhere around here? The hot water will be ready in about five minutes. We got an extra ration of briquettes. I think Zellbad paid off the German in charge of fuel. It's good to have Zellbad in our barrack. He's in all the rackets and gets this barrack extra wood for the copper, so we are sure of hot water. Have you met him yet? He's just a little guy."

With that, he peered through Hobbs' bunk and pointed to a table that was in line with our vision. "That's him, sitting at the far end of the table."

I looked to where he pointed and saw a small dark-skinned man playing cards. So this was the great man able to extract all these extra things over and above normal rations. According to Archie he could get almost anything.

Without waiting for answers to all the questions he'd already asked, Archie continued his barrage until I felt like saying, "Hold it, Archie. Pick two questions you'd like me to answer."

Arnold Hobbs came to my rescue, and as he approached, Archie took off across the top bunks again to continue his visit.

Hobbs seemed puzzled and a little upset. In silence he looked at the bared contents of our parcel.

"I hear we are having hot cocoa tonight," I said. "That'll be okay with me. I brought my bread ration, so maybe we can have bread, margarine, jam and cocoa. What do you think?"

"We'll have to line up for hot water," was his only comment.

"I'll do that if you look after getting everything ready," I said, "like jam on your bread. Let's mix the cocoa in a little water first, put some in each mug, and break in a piece of that square of sugar. Maybe we could add condensed milk to the cocoa and mix it that way."

I was enthusiastic about the thought of hot cocoa laced with condensed milk and sugar added for sweetness.

"Come on, Arnold," I said, picking up the tin of cocoa and the milk. I knew Arnold wasn't pleased at me helping myself to our rations, but I took the lid off the cocoa, emptied what I thought would be sufficient into my tin mug, and poured in a portion of condensed milk.

"Where's your mug?" I asked. "How strong do you like your cocoa, and how much milk?" It felt good to take control of the rations. I knew my mucker didn't like it, but I wasn't happy with his attitude, and this was the first opportunity to show that ours was supposed to be a fifty-fifty deal.

In both tin mugs I mixed the milk and cocoa, using a small piece of wood about the size of a pencil. Suddenly "Brew's up!" echoed throughout the barrack.

Like a startled stag, I made the distance to the copper in a few bounds. There were only six people in front of me. The wooden lid was off, the fire was glowing red underneath in the fire box, and the water was boiling. I watched it bubbling, clean and hot, as if to say, "Welcome! I'll give you of my warmth!"

I held out the two mugs. When boiling water hit the mixture of cocoa, a delicious aroma drifted up almost immediately. It gave me a sort of buoyancy as I struggled through the crowd. I was going to have a hot drink to warm my insides!

I returned to Hobbs' bedspace and gave him his mug of hot cocoa. Again I stirred the mixture in my own mug and handed the stick to Hobbs. Then I put the mug to my lips and swallowed my first swig. It tasted sweet and full and warm.

I set my mug on a small shelf joining the two bunks, broke my bread in two pieces, and used the stir stick to spread the jam.

"Well, what do you think, Arnold?" I said.

"It's okay," he admitted.

"It's delicious!" I said, "the bestest cocoa I've ever tasted, or ever will! What are we having for tomorrow's dinner?" I put forward a suggestion, but there was no enthusiastic reply from my mucker, no counter-suggestion, just silence.

"Okay," I said, "I'll make out a menu for the next two days and we'll talk about it tomorrow morning."

For the next five minutes I tried unsuccessfully to make conversation with Arnold. Eventually, I gave up, and said, "See you on parade in the morning."

I made my way to a more congenial area, my own bedspace. Nabber and Markellie were sitting together on the bottom bunk. Each of them held a mug of hot brew. Their hands were wrapped around the warm tin mugs. The *verboten* light was out and the situation actually looked quite cozy.

"Hi, Paddy Mac!" said Nabber. "Your Canadian friend was here looking for you, a pilot named Peter Chadwick."

Sitting facing these friendly people, I felt a new warmth of comradeship. These two were genuine, outgoing young men, real morale boosters, and once again my thoughts went to the possibility of changing muckers.

"Do you two muck in together?" I queried.

"No way!" said Markellie. "We live together. We don't want to eat together!"

On a more serious note, Nabber remarked, "I heard the Russians have retaken Rostov. Jerry's Second Army is surrounded in Southern Russia. I'll bet the Russians will liberate us. How would you like a victory parade in Red Square? Wouldn't that be something? I hear there's free love in Russia, and there'd be a scarcity of men. I might never go back to Auckland. They could send me my back pay in rubles, and I'd spend it on vodka, women and song. Hi! What about that?"

"Where did you get the war news?" I asked, ignoring Nabber's fantasies.

"Oh, one of the Army boys came in from a work party. He'd heard the BBC news in some farm house, secret-like."

As we were talking, Peter Chadwick had quietly returned for a visit.

"Hi, Peter," I said. "I think you've already met these two bandits."

"Yes," he replied. "Carry on and bring me up to date."

Turning to Peter, I said, "Nabber here tells me he knows the Russians have taken Rostov and the Germans got clobbered at Stalingrad and von Paulus' Sixth Army had to surrender. And Manstein's Second Army is almost trapped in the southern area. He knows more about what's happening than the people back home!"

"He's got a red telephone direct to New Zealand's War Office," Markellie jibed. "He keeps it in one of his tins under the bunk."

"Wouldn't surprise me," I said.

I asked if they knew Roosevelt and Churchill had a big meeting together. They didn't, so I told them what I remembered: that it took place around the middle of January at Casablanca—Roosevelt, Churchill, and their Chiefs of Staff. Stalin was to be there but didn't turn up, supposedly because of the big battles that were going on, or because he wanted to be ornery and independent.

"Hope they talked about getting us out of here," remarked Nabber.

"Now I'm sure, Nabber," I said, "that very first thing on the agenda would be, 'How can we get Nabber Giddens out of Stalag VIIIB?' You'd better pack up your nails and mugs."

With the four of us sitting on opposite bunks and bantering back and forth with good-natured jibes, a half hour passed quickly. Four countries were represented here—Northern Ireland, England, Canada, and New Zealand.

Peter jumped down from the bunk. "Twenty minutes till lights out, Paddy. Come to our table and we can yak for a while."

We sat down at the unoccupied end of the table and, at his request, I told Peter the story of our tragedy from take-off until we were shot down. He asked questions as I talked, and being a Lancaster pilot, he was interested in every phase of the operation.

With great sincerity, Peter looked at me and said, "I guess some of those Irish Little People must have been riding down all that way with you, or else the 'Sky Boss' has earmarked you for some greatness when we get out of this damned place." I promised when that greatness came, I would not forget him.

The lights had gone out while we talked, so I bid him good night and then went back to my bedspace. There was a fair amount of light coming through the windows that had not been shuttered, and it seemed the guard's searchlight beams were moving with more alacrity than usual, maybe hoping to find a hardy prisoner trying to escape. I didn't think there was anyone dumb enough to try on such a cold, snowy night.

Anderson was in bed. I guessed he must be asleep. Nabber, in his top bunk, raised a hand in a good-night gesture. My jacket, hanging on a new coat hanger nail, was now dry. Taking care that the buttons were turned inside, I folded it carefully into a pillow. I took off my German-issue boots, placed them in the storage area beside my clogs, and without taking my clothing off, climbed on to my straw mattress. I wrapped the German Army issue blanket around me as tightly as possible and lay down for my first night in permanent prison camp.

An English voice from Markellie's direction said, "Are you okay, Paddy?"

"Fine," I said, and wished him good-night. I drifted off to sleep, only to be awakened hours later by someone in a nearby bunk having a nightmare, reliving the horror of being shot down. Another prisoner woke him up, and his frightened voice and shouted commands stopped abruptly when he realized it was only a dream—only an echo of the original horror.

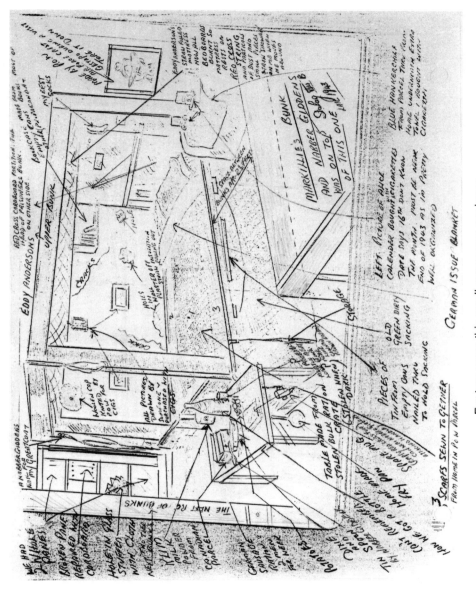

For two years this small space was my home.

Imperial War Museum Photo Hu 47157

Above and below: Prisoners work together to sort food from Red Cross Parcels and to plan menus.

Imperial War Museum Photo HU 47158

RED CROSS PAY DAY

"Toad" Hughes's take on one aspect of the relationship between muckers.

COOKING AT
STALAG VIIIB

CHAPTER 7

Settling In—Day 2

I was awake next morning before the cry of *"Raus! Raus!"* and a deluge of legs from a host of top bunks. It was almost time for my first morning roll call. Markellie was out of his blanket, lying on his bunk and doing his "ride the bicycle exercise." He had two blankets and so had Nabber. I asked them about this and was informed that today I'd probably be issued my second "tablecloth."

I pulled on my boots, laced them tight, and donned my wrinkled jacket and buttoned it to the top. It was dark outside and the snow had turned to rain. The cry, "Outside on Parade!" echoed through the barrack, followed by a louder shout of "Sinclair, have you got Montrose out of his sack? It's a rotten goddamn morning, so move it!"

We stood in a steady downpour of rain as *Unteroffizier* Joe Kussel did his five count. The white snow had turned to a sea of slushy mud under a thousand pairs of feet jostling for position. No one wanted a recount on this miserable morning, and soon we were back in the barrack.

"Let's open all the windows for five," suggested Barrack Commander MacKinlay, and a loud cry of agreement drowned out any dissent. So, for almost ten minutes, the cold Silesian wind was welcomed as it wafted out the foul, smoky air. Someone had hung a clean, dry shirt on a nail below a window, and whoever opened the window had not moved it to a safer place. The rain blew in and soaked the shirt. The owner of the shirt held it up and said, "How would you like to dry a shirt in this lousy place and then have some unthinking ass leave it to get wet?"

The person he vented his anger on, instead of returning with a similar outburst of emotion, put his arm around the shoulder of the unhappy man and said, "Into every life a little rain must fall. Hang it up somewhere near the stove tonight and it will dry. If you've got a date before it's dry, I'll loan you mine." Looking a little sheepish, and probably a bit disgusted at his own outburst, the first man went off without another word, his wrinkled wet shirt over his arm.

Today was special. Instead of mint tea we were getting a ration of Red Cross tea. Apparently there was bulk tea in the Red Cross Store, so this morning some of it would be used.

I made my way to table eleven and sat down with my mug of tea. There was only one other person at the table, the quiet person I'd seen yesterday absorbed in reading a book on banking. He turned a page, then looked up. Quickly I said, "In the banking business before you joined up?"

"Yes, I was," he replied, and right away I noticed the Irish brogue.

"What part are you from?"

"From County Longford," he replied, "I worked in a Drogeda bank."

Now that the ice was broken I discovered he'd been a prisoner since early 1942. He introduced himself as Jimmy Grier.

He seemed a lonely sort of person, and I asked was he in a group or did he have a mucker.

"No, I'm on my own—don't have a mucker." This surprised me; he seemed a reasonable type of person, a year in prison camp, and on his own regarding food parcels.

"How do you divide things?" I asked.

"I don't," was the surprising reply.

"What do you mean?"

"Easy. Joe Blair at table nine looks after himself. We have an agreement. I get a parcel one week and he gets the next issue. We take our chances on English or Canadian parcels."

"I suppose if you like it that way it will work," I said, and added, "How does that end up? A full parcel for each of you every two weeks? Do you have to pull a lot on willpower to prevent eating all the rations in maybe a week?"

With a smile he said, "I did that about a year ago and tried to sleep away my hunger the second week. I guess you get used to looking after yourself."

Was he trying to convince himself it was okay? I had the feeling he was lonely and would like to be included in some sort of group. Perhaps he was too proud or too Irish-stubborn to break down and ask to be accepted again into one of the organized groups.

The Senior Man interrupted with, "All new men to be at the compound gate opposite barrack 18A in five minutes for a clothing parade." A young German guard was detailed to escort us.

At the "stores," a British army Sergeant Major waited, all spit and polished, as though he were back home on Aldershot parade square. With him was an army corporal equally shined up. Wearing his white aircrew sweater and battledress jacket was an Air Force pilot from our compound. He stood by unconcernedly as the major commenced to give us his words of wisdom.

"I am Sergeant Major Lewis." He said this with an air of importance.

"Bet he's a real prick," said someone, loud enough for all to hear.

At this remark the Sergeant Major hesitated for just a couple of seconds and then continued, "The German *Kommandant* has put me in charge of stores. My job is to ensure that all, and I mean *all* supplies that get through to this camp, are equally divided. This assignment of mine covers all Red Cross food parcels and Red Cross bulk rations, and clothing. You men are in luck. We have sufficient Air Force clothing to kit out each of you. I must warn you, be careful of it. Treat it with great respect, for these bits and pieces of clothing could some day save your lives. Don't be tempted to sell your greatcoat on a hot day in summer because your belly says you're hungry and you don't need that damned heavy coat; you need an extra couple of loaves of bread, and anyway the war might end before winter comes around again."

One of our group laughed and Lewis retorted, "Go on, laugh, young fellow. Laugh if you like, but I've seen the likes of you many times. I've seen imbeciles barter their warm clothes in summer, and I've watched them shiver their way through frigid days and nights long after the taste of that extra bread has been forgotten. And the odd one didn't make it to see another summer's warmth. Remember, some day this war will catch up to us and we don't know what time of year it will be, and I don't think any of you have the slightest idea of the chaos that occurs when there is a breakdown of discipline. All of us may have to make our own way back west if the Russians overrun this camp, and that is very likely. So for Christ's sake, but mostly for your own sake, remember my words, because this will probably be the one and only clothing issue you'll get, even if this bloody war lasts ten more years. Once again I say to you, don't sell any part of what you get here today. If you do, you could be driving a nail in your own coffin. On second thought, I don't think you'd get a coffin." He stopped for a moment. "Before I proceed with this issue, you take it from an old foot-slogging soldier, be good to your boots. Treat them with loving care. Make love to them by breaking them in gently. Polish them frequently, even with Jerry polish, and they will someday return that love by saving your life. That great French soldier Napoleon said, 'An army marches on its stomach,' and he meant that without food an army couldn't march for a long time. But you remember that Sergeant Major Lewis said, 'If an army has no *feet* it won't march anywhere,' so I say again, don't try to make love to your mucker or anyone else's mucker. Just love your boots and they will love you and take care of you. Don't sell your greatcoat, don't sell any part of your clothing. With good clothing and enough food, you might survive the war."

He turned and strutted into the clothing shed, saying, "Now let's see what we can do for you flyboys."

We were issued a regular RAF uniform, plus shirt, tie, socks, underclothes, and so on. In fact, it was less hassle than on some of the clothing parades back on the Squadron.

I was able to get a new pair of Air Force regular service boots and also kept my German issue. With the boots slung around our necks by the laces, and our other prizes in our hands, protected as best we could manage from the rain, we fell in line. The guard marched us back to our barracks. On the way, we passed our old naval *Kommandant*, who was accompanied by the Swiss Red Cross Inspectors. I don't think it was by chance they happened to witness the new prisoners with bundles of freshly issued clothing. We certainly made a good propaganda picture. This was a bonanza I never expected, but a very welcome surprise, even if there was German propaganda mixed up in it. New uniform, underclothes and boots—it was really a "red letter day." Tomorrow would be my birthday; these were like early presents!

When I returned, I found an army issue towel, a piece of German soap, and another blanket on my bed.

"The Senior Man left them," volunteered Markellie. "He asked me to warn you to be good to all the new gear. We've been lucky with this good old *Kommandant*, but the situation could change any time. Remember, you won't likely get another clothing issue, even if we are here for years." I realized that he, too, must at one time have listened to R.S.M. Lewis' oratory.

I thanked Markellie and hurriedly picked up the soap and towel. I couldn't wait any longer to have a good wash and change into fresh clothing. Cold or not, I didn't care.

Luckily there was water pressure when I got to the washroom. I turned on the rusty old faucet, found good pressure, put the plug in the outlet of the concrete trough, and filled it sufficiently. I stripped and managed a cold wash-down. I was using my hands instead of a cloth, and the gritty, sandy soap was difficult to work into a decent lather, but I managed to do a fair job. Washing off the soap by splashing myself with cupped handfuls of cold water was a shivery experience, but I felt fresh as I toweled myself dry. I dressed in the new clothes and returned to my bedspace feeling that things were not too bad at all.

During the clothing parade, our daily ration had been issued. My mucker had already picked up both our rations. I wanted to track him down, for my day's bread and spud ration were in his care. Jimmy Grier and I were in the soup line-up. The soup looked thick and tasted not bad. Jimmy supped his, using an old tin spoon that looked very rusted.

I said, "You won't be around much longer if you don't get a new spoon. You'll die from rust poisoning!" He looked at me, then looked at his spoon as if he'd never before noticed the rust. I told him I'd ask Nabber Giddens if he had a cheap new or second-hand spoon with little or no rust and promised I'd visit with him later. Then I was off to find my big Scottish friend.

I found Big Jock stretched out on his bunk. His six-foot frame took up the full length of it. I had, with all the morning's events, forgotten that after twelve we were permitted to relax on our bunks. Jock was lying, eyes wide open, staring up at Peter's bedboards and palliasse. I stood beside his bunk for about half a minute before he realized someone was there. "Well, if it isn't Paddy Mac," he said.

I didn't beat about the bush. "Jock, I need a shave, and someone congenial like you to talk to."

"You need a shave. Any dumb bastard can see that, but we don't need the Irish bullshit about congenial company." He swung his legs off the bunk. Then he grabbed me unceremoniously by the arm and marched me towards the door.

"Where are we going?" I asked. "To the Old Forty Holer, and you want company? Are you going to give me my second lesson?"

"Don't be smart, squirt," he chuckled as we came to the bunks nearest the door and stopped at the last bed but one. Without hesitation, he shook the occupant, who appeared to be sleeping.

"For Pete's sake!" said the curly-headed occupant, sitting up quickly and hitting his head on the bedboards of the upper bunk. He rubbed his head. "That was your fault, Jock. Can't a guy get a little rest around here? I thought it was Ukraine Joe."

"Quit your greetin'," Jock retorted. "Have you got the shaving gear I ordered yesterday for this here Irishman?"

"Did you ever give me an order I didn't fill?"

Ignoring the remark, Jock said, "By the way, I forgot to introduce you two. This Irish friend of mine is Paddy McMahon. Paddy Mac, meet Jack Steves, Canada's last hope in this here war."

Greeting Jock's friend, I found a good strong handshake and the crusty remark, "How the hell can you be unlucky enough to be a friend of this big ass? I thought St. Patrick protected you from haggis-bashers like this?"

"Come on, Steves, cut out the crap," interjected Jock. "You said you were able to fill my order?"

"Sure, sure, Jock." Steves jumped off his bunk. He fumbled inside his mattress for a minute, looking at Jock as he did so. "It was here this morning. I wonder who the hell stole it."

"What do you mean it's not there? You got my cigarettes..." At that, Jock stopped short and looked a little embarrassed. He had never intended me to find out he was paying for the favour.

Realizing his joke had backfired, Steves said, "I'll try the other side of my mattress." With a wry smile, he explained, "When you're in this place for any length of time it affects your memory." He pulled a package from inside his palliasse and handed it to Jock, who in turn gave it to me.

Jock and I thanked Steves for his services and made our way towards his bedspace. "Jock," I said, "tell me how much you paid for this, and I'll repay you when my cigarettes come from home or with Red Cross issue—whatever I get first."

Looking down at me, he said, "When you have those extra cigarettes we'll talk about it. Maybe by then there'll be some other poor bastard who will need your help. Now go grab a towel and take your short ass out of here to the washroom and see if you can shave off that fuzz in cold water. And don't cut yourself opening the package."

Inside the package was a razor, half a dozen three-holed blades, German shaving soap, a brush, and a small piece of broken mirror.

Later, clean-shaven, I returned to my bunk to find Nabber standing at the window, using the window ledge as a bench to work on a new mug. "Where have you been?" he asked.

"Haven't you noticed I've become a new man?" I said. "Can't you smell the fresh aroma of German soap and new clothes?"

"Yeah, I noticed," said Nabber, nodding towards my bed, where my greatcoat was folded up neat and tidy.

He pointed to my bunk. One of my new boots was sticking out from beneath the folded coat. "Just a bit of advice, Paddy. Don't leave boots out in view, especially new ones. Do you realize that those new boots would fetch 500 cigarettes? And cigarettes buy food."

"Thanks, Nabber," I said. "I should have known better."

Picking up my boots, I decided the best way to protect them from thieves would be to put them on my feet. I put on the new uniform.

Nabber looked up from his work, grinned and said, "Got a date tonight? Has she got a sister?" We both laughed.

"See Toad about getting your name put on all your new stuff," Nabber advised.

"What with?" I asked, "and who is Toad?"

"Toad," Nabber hesitated for a moment. "Toad is the little chubby guy three top bunks over from where we are. Hughes is his name. He's a great cartoonist. You'll see a lot of his work around the barrack. He makes quite a bundle of cigarettes from selling cartoons. I think he got the nickname back on his squadron. On finished work he puts his initials below a drawing of a little toad. He has the proper ink (black market of course) for putting names on clothing and he won't charge you too much. He never does for essential things like that, and especially not for new prisoners. I'll introduce you to him later."

I thanked Nabber for the information and made my way back to Hobbs' bedspace to check on our dinner ration. I tried to sound enthusiastic when Arnold suggested that for dinner we mash our potato ration in with the canned bacon.

My new uniform felt a bit uncomfortable. I returned to my own place and took it off to a jibe from Nabber, "She let you down? Stood up, eh? Sure can't trust these German sheelaghs!"

"I wasn't too fussy about her anyway," I shot back. "It was the sister I was after."

I made another super effort to be congenial and stayed with Arnold while we ate our mashed potatoes and bacon, but it was difficult trying to converse. Then Archie Vickers came bouncing along with his usual jubilant outlook and constant prattle.

I left Archie to bend Hobbs' ear. Once again I had missed the mile walk around the compound with Peter and Jock.

After five o'clock parade, I snoozed on my bunk until I heard Markellie say, "Hi! Paddy, there's someone here to see you." A stranger stood by my bedspace, a tall soldier with rank of sergeant and the Royal Irish Rifle insignia on his uniform. He introduced himself as Mike McQuaid, from the town of Lisburn in Northern Ireland, just a few miles from Belfast. After the usual enquiries as to why, where, and how I got here, he invited me to walk a few circuits of the compound. On the second circuit he volunteered the reason for his visit. Our conversation had been mostly about home and how things were when I was last in Belfast. "How are you making out on Stalag rations?" he asked.

"Pretty tough right now," I answered, and followed with, "Hope my stomach will shrink ."

"How would you like a few extra cooked potatoes, maybe every day?" I acted very surprised. I was not going to say that Archie Vickers from Hut 15A had already told me about the Irish Spud Racket. My new friend went on to outline the procedures of how the potatoes would be obtained. I listened intently, as if all of this was new to me, and when questioned as to whether I could take the chances involved to get the potatoes, I replied that I certainly would be interested in taking part. After another circuit, Mike said, "Someone will contact you regarding the extra potatoes." He wished me luck and returned to his own compound.

The barrack was a smoky, crowded place after the fresh air of outside, but at least it was warm.

"That sergeant works in the cookhouse, and we know there is an Irish Spud Racket," Markellie said.

"Trust a hungry farmer to know that," I jibed, and related the conversation with Mike.

With my bread ration and tin mug, I dashed off to collect my ration of hot water.

Returning via Hobbs' bedspace, I opened our Red Cross parcel with its meagre remains. The three-ounce tin of processed cheese I divided into two equal pieces before Arnold arrived with his hot water. "Tomorrow there's another parcel issue," I reminded him, "so I'm getting rid of what's left in this here parcel."

I made a mug of cocoa and spread the cheese on my bread. Arnold didn't like it, but I was making sure he recognized that the food in this Red Cross package was not all under his jurisdiction.

What should I do with the potatoes if I pass the test and bring them back? Why should I give this guy half of the extras? I'd prefer to give some to Nabber or Markellie, or better still, to Peter and Jock Martin. Picking up my mug, I bid him adieu and made my way to the centre of the barrack, where a number of men stood with their backs to the tiled surface of the heater, soaking up its warmth.

At the firing end it was the same as the previous evening: a number of gallant cooks stoked their own little home-made stoves with the usual assortment of fuel. One partnership was smashing a bedboard to pieces. I'd no idea which one of the muckers was going to be short a bedboard until I heard big Jock's voice, his Scottish accent filling the airwaves and directed at the one who was now using his boot-clad foot on the board. As it splintered into pieces, Jock said, "Hi! MacDonald, how many boards have you left now?" "Four good wide ones," came the reply, "but they wouldn't hold up your big ass!"

"He'll be falling through on McIsaac one of these nights," volunteered MacDonald's mucker. "He burnt his clogs last week and tried to get mine for tonight. I've told him he'll be in deep trouble when Ukraine Joe finds out. Says immediate needs get first preference. So here we are boiling up these oats, with part of his bed in the fire."

"I hear there's going to be a clog parade and bedboard inspection this week," Jock said, looking seriously at MacDonald.

"I don't give a damn," was Mac's reply, "as long as this bloody porridge boils."

After sitting with Jock for a while I told him my story regarding the Irish Potato Racket. With a knowing look he said, "Just be careful, don't take a chance for a few spuds. And if there are any of those ex-Hitler Youth bastards on guard, forget it. Always wait until the older guys are on duty." I thanked him for the advice, then returned to my bedspace.

Markellie and Anderson both seemed to be asleep, and Nabber, reading by his illegal light, gave me his good-night salute as I clambered into my bunk.

I was tired and fell asleep quickly. It must have been hours later I was awakened by Eddy Anderson clambering down. The usual bits and pieces of straw and dust that accompanied this movement settled on my blanket, face, and hair. I could feel but not see the shower of unwanted residue. In the morning I would talk to Eddy Anderson to see if there was some way we could prevent this disturbing occurrence.

A little light filtered in from outside, but during a period of intermittent brightness, as a searchlight's beam crawled by, I turned to find a face so close to mine that I could feel the owner's hot foul breath. A pair of black eyes stared at me from above two rows of small, clenched yellow teeth circled by curled-up lips. It took me a few seconds to understand what was happening. Eddy Anderson was on his way to the big wooden urinal, which was often placed in the square vestibule area at Barrack lockup time. He was trying to get his feet into wooden clogs without using his hands. Leaning forward to do so, his elbows rested on the side of my bunk, resulting in the closeness of his face to mine.

I didn't move or say a word, just stared back into that scary countenance for a number of seconds. Then it was gone with a clippety-clop, clippety-clop sound as his clogs played their tune on the concrete floor. Eventually he reached and opened the big door leading out to the vestibule and let it close with a bang as he passed through.

I lay and waited, in my mind giving him enough time to do what he had to. Soon there came the bang of the door's closing and the faint clippety-clop getting closer and louder, but now overlapping with another pair of clogs as someone else made the trek to the same place, wearing his own wooden masterpieces.

Anderson returned with maximum wooden music and got a blast from Markellie: "Can't you go to the can in your goddamned boots? They make a hell of a lot less noise!"

"Don't get so excited, Marc," came back Anderson's reply. He had a habit of shortening Markellie's name that way.

With my eyes closed, I waited as Anderson jumped up to his bunk, and when the bits and pieces of straw and dust had settled, I opened my eyes again. In the shadows I could see two dangling legs. Instead of getting into bed Anderson was sitting on the edge of his bunk and doing something with water, or a cold brew—perhaps tea, cocoa or coffee he had left over from the 8:00 p.m. call. I listened and realized that he had two receptacles and was transferring the liquid from one to the other. He then reversed the transfer, apparently holding one mug high above the other to make a noisy trickle as he poured. He kept on with this, chuckling all the while. I couldn't see in the dark, but I could visualize Anderson's odd grin.

Suddenly Markellie jumped from his bunk. "You rotten bastard,

Anderson! I'm going to get you for this some day!" And with a swipe of his hand he knocked a mug out of Anderson's hand. The tin mug bounced and rattled around the concrete floor. I felt nothing wet, and guessed it was the empty one that Markellie had hit.

Markellie put on his boots, then went to relieve himself, leaving Eddy Anderson laughing happily at the achievement of making Markellie go to the can.

There was a rustle of straw as Nabber turned around in his top bunk, and in a very quiet but forceful voice laced with a much stronger New Zealand accent than usual, he said, "Eddy me friend, if you don't get into bed and go to sleep like a good little boy and stop all this water running crap, I'll have your balls for lunch tomorrow!" From nearby came other exclamations endorsing Nabber's intention.

Eddy said very solemnly, "Okay, Nabber, I'm sorry," and then snuggled into his bunk like a child who had been chastised by a parent. When Markellie returned, he pretended to be asleep.

I didn't partake in this controversy at all, so with Markellie back in his sack, Anderson quiet, and Nabber snoring a little, I too chose the serenity of sound sleep.

Imperial War Museum Photo HU 47134

Above and right: Two views of *Unteroffizier* Josef Kussel, better known to us as "Ukraine Joe."

CHAPTER 8

Settling In—Day 3

The banging of a rifle butt along the wooden bunksides brought me back to reality. One of the guards was doing his thing through the barracks, calling the usual *"Raus, raus, raus! Antreten! Es ist sieben uhr."* ("Up, up! On parade! It's seven o'clock!")

It was my birthday: February 23—I was twenty-two years old. What a place to spend a birthday! I didn't expect any gifts from my hosts— well, maybe that was wrong. It was Red Cross food parcel day, and that was a gift from the Germans, since they had control. And I'd had clothing parade the day before.

We streamed through the stench of the vestibule to the cleaner air outside, again through a check parade, then returned to the barrack to tidy our bunks. We kept our bedspaces clean and ready for inspection at any time. This same procedure was to become so familiar I could do it blind.

The morning brew was again a welcome mug of real tea, and with a full mug plus the small piece of bread I'd saved from yesterday's ration, I sat down next to Jimmy Grier at Section 11's table.

It was Jimmy's turn today. He would get a full parcel for himself, to last for two weeks instead of one. He had been unlucky enough to get English issue a number of times, but this issue was going to be Canadian.

It wasn't much of a breakfast. I knew Hobbs and I had an empty food box except for a small three-ounce tin of powdered eggs.

I asked Jimmy Grier had he been approached regarding the Irish Potato Racket. He said yes, but seemed unwilling to talk further.

It was only eight o'clock. I put on my greatcoat and ventured outside to fresh air. I'd washed and shaved, and I felt clean. Now I was about to clean the stale barrack air out of my lungs. I wandered round the compound perimeter by myself—but not alone, because there were a few hundred other men doing the same thing. Looking closely, I could see pilot's wings, navigator's half-wings, air gunner's insignias, and so on—survivors of crews that had flown together and bailed out together still held a bond as they "walked the wire."

For me, it was a little different feeling. There were no survivors of my crew to share the discomforts and the fears of this new existence or to help boost my morale if I needed it. I shivered, yet I was not cold. My heavy coat kept me warm; but there was still a loneliness.

I could see the tall figure of Big Jock Martin across the compound, with Peter Chadwick bobbing along beside him. Quickening my step, I wended my way through four groups of walkers to catch up with my friends.

"Well, if it isn't 'Bump' himself," cracked Jock, putting a friendly hand on my shoulder.

"Good morning. How's my haggis-bashing friend today?" I asked.

"Just as rotten as ever," said Peter.

"What are you two getting me for my birthday?" I asked.

"Let's wait till then," replied Jock. "I'll send home for a haggis."

"Are you going to request the *Luftwaffe* to fly it out from Scotland? Because today is the day."

"I don't believe you," said Peter. "Why would anyone want to come here to spend a birthday?"

"I came to celebrate it with you guys. I had to get special leave," I replied, and the three of us chuckled.

I didn't count how many circuits we did, but my lungs were cleared and filled with fresh winter air, and the brisk pace had got my heart pumping quickly.

Unteroffizier Kussel was standing at the main compound gate when we completed another circuit. As we passed, Jock said, "Tell him it's your birthday. I'll bet he'll bring you a present!"

"One more circuit and then we go in," said Peter.

"Still thinks he's the pilot, giving orders," jibed Jock.

"If you're too tired I'll excuse you," Peter told him.

"I'll struggle around once more," Jock replied, quickening his pace. His long legs took him so fast we almost had to run after him. That last circuit we did in record time.

On entering our barrack, we discovered that the bread ration had already been issued, along with a ration of German sausage.

My mucker exclaimed, "Oh, there you are!" Arnold seemed to be in a friendly mood as he slid his hands behind his back, first with the sausage and then with the bread. I noticed that once again we'd been unlucky enough to get a heel. "Which hand?" Arnold asked.

"Left," I said, Arnold hesitated for a moment before stretching out his left hand with my heel of black bread.

"Guess I'm unlucky again," I said, looking at the ugly heel covered in sawdust and the usual touch of mould.

I was about to take the spoils to my bedspace when Nabber, who had been watching Hobbs, suddenly got up from the #10 table and very quietly and deliberately took the ration of bread out of the hand Arnold held behind his back. Then he picked up Arnold's sausage ration.

"These are yours, Paddy," he said. "I've been watching this jerk of a mucker you have. He changed rations from one hand to the other after you picked the bread that wasn't the heel. If he hadn't first changed the sausage I might not have noticed."

He took the heel of bread and the piece of sausage from me and offered them to Hobbs. "Here you go. Have a good day," he said. "And my advice to Paddy is to find a new mucker. And my advice to you, Hobbs, is to go have a look at the big cesspool behind the Forty Holer. It's smelly and it's deep, and people like you sometimes find themselves up to their necks in that stuff. Do you get the picture, Mr. Hobbs? Because if you don't, I'd love to arrange a demonstration, with you as the central figure."

Hobbs looked pale and his lips trembled. He made no effort to accept the exchanged rations but stood staring into space as if he were some sort of statue. Nabber grabbed one of his hands and thrust the bread into it. Then he flipped up the lapel on the top pocket of Hobbs' battledress and he pushed in the sausage ration. Finally, he turned him by the shoulders, pointed him towards his bedspace, and gently pushed him in that direction. It was a defeated-looking figure that slunk slowly away from the table.

I looked at Jimmy Grier, who sat at the end of the table. I caught his eye and thought there was a message there. Would he appreciate someone to share rations? I hadn't seen Jimmy cook anything since I arrived. He ate all rations as they came, cold or hot.

I shrugged my shoulders at Nabber. "How can I change muckers?"

"Go and talk to MacKinlay before we get our Red Cross issue. Tell him you want to change."

"Okay, Nabber, thanks. I think I do know someone who might want to change his status."

I walked over to Jimmy Grier and told him I'd be willing to muck in with him if he would like a change. I was surprised at his immediate acceptance.

"Then let's go to the Senior Man," I said.

We had our little session with MacKinlay, who had no objections. When I put the proposal to Hobbs, he seemed pleased. So, after two and a half days, I split partnership with my first mucker.

Partnership with Grier would mean an association, here in Germany, of the North of Ireland and the South joining forces so that each of us would have a better chance of surviving the war.

With a happier outlook on things in general, I returned to my bedspace area. It was close to 9:30 a.m. when a continuous stream of men poured in from outside, cutting short their usual morning walk. I looked out the window and saw a couple of guards putting their rifle butts to a few stragglers.

A little scared, I rushed towards Peter and Jock's table to ask what was going on. In the aisle I ran smack into Nabber and Markellie, and before I could ask any questions, they said, "Chains." The Red Cross Swiss Inspectors had left camp, so now we were to be chained again.

"Keep on your battledress," Nabber volunteered, "It's easier that way. Means you don't have to pick the locks of the handcuffs to put on outside clothing."

"Okay," I said, not quite sure what to expect. MacKinlay was shouting for quiet as he stood atop his favourite perch, Section 1's table. He waited until there was a lull in the hubbub to say, "Line up in sections as you are called. Our friends would like to present each of you with a bracelet."

I stood and watched with great interest as the first prisoners of #1 Section returned with their wrists encased in steel handcuffs joined by a chain about eighteen inches long.

The line moved forward and my turn came quickly. I stretched my arms forward and felt cold steel snap around each wrist.

Jock sat at Section 10's table, a big grin on his face. He held up his chained wrists and shouted, "Happy Birthday, Paddy! I told you the Germans wouldn't forget your birthday!"

"Thanks a lot, pal!" was the only answer I could think of. Stopping for a moment I saw that of the seven or eight people at the table, four of them had only one handcuffed wrist.

I looked questioningly at Jock. He produced from his pocket a small key of the kind usually attached to tins of meat—the ones you use to roll back a strip of metal from the cans. He started to work on the spring lock of the cuffs, and within half a minute he had one released.

"Here," he said, handing me the key. "See how good you are at picking locks."

I worked at that spring-loaded handcuff for five minutes without success.

I laboured on and eventually became aware that someone was watching me. It was the curly-headed pilot, Mark Watson. He leaned over, casually took the key from me, and with a professional air said, "Watch carefully."

It took Watson no more than twenty seconds. He worked his mouth and twisted the key, and presto! My left handcuff came undone. Before it completely released my wrist, Watson quickly snapped it closed again.

"Now," he said, "watch again. This time pay close attention." Then for the second time he repeated his performance, and to my consternation he again snapped the irons closed on my wrists. "Two free lessons, Paddy," he said. "Now if you can't follow through with your next try, it'll be two cigarettes for each future lesson."

I picked up the key and was about to try again when my teacher clamped his hand over my wrist and laughingly said, "Let's see who is the strongest this time." And with that he had his elbows on the table and my hand in an arm wrestling grip.

Grimacing in the mock battle of strength, he whispered, "It's the chain *Feldwebel* (Sergeant Major)." I had realized that something was amiss. Already I was becoming accustomed to things people did upon seeing a guard, like using their bodies to conceal from view forbidden items that someone had carelessly forgotten to hide. It didn't matter who it was they were covering up for. It was a matter of principle to outthink the guards at all costs.

I looked up. Behind Mark Watson stood the sharp-featured *Feldwebel* in charge of the chaining process. He had a bad habit of making quick checks at odd times to ensure that everyone was handcuffed. Mark had only one handcuff fastened when he started my lesson. I was surprised when, with a sinister smile, the *Feldwebel* stretched forward and with his long thin fingers tested both of us for securely handcuffed wrists. We hadn't moved from our arm wrestling position, and as he pulled at our cuffs to see if they were locked properly, I was certain Mark's would fall off one wrist, but he must have made a lightning move to lock them and so prevent instant trouble.

The German looked puzzled for a moment. Knowing he had been outfoxed, he looked with half-closed eyes at Mark and wagged his finger close to Mark's face. In perfect English, he said, "Next time, mister, next time." Then he marched quickly towards the washroom on his way to the adjoining barrack.

"He knows it's too late to catch anyone now," Mark said with a grin. "Sure thought he had me. Lucky that Sam gave me the high sign. I'd sure hate being chained up to that compound wire for a couple of hours in this weather!" For a moment he looked surprised that we were still in the arm-wrestling position. "And what the hell am I holding your hand for?" He grinned and asked if he could borrow the key for a moment. In seconds one wrist was again free. I asked him what high sign Sam had given.

"Oh, he just held both chained hands above his head and I got the message. Otherwise probably you and I would now be chained to the wire with our hands behind our backs. It's a horrible feeling. You can't even scratch if you itch. When I was caught two months ago I got twenty minutes chained to the wire, and I itched all over. Could send a guy crazy!"

I was about to go off to find my newly acquired mucker when Watson said, "Don't you want one hand free?" He held Jock's little key between his finger and thumb. I extended my wrists and watched for the third time as he swiftly released the lock.

He handed me the key, saying, "Maybe I'll go into the housebreaking business when I get home. Go ask your big friend if you can keep the key for a while so you can practice."

I thanked him for his help and for his quick cover-up. Then I looked for Jimmy Grier.

I felt very comfortable with this man. I had no fears of him cheating me or being miserable. Maybe he wouldn't be the bubbly type or chatter away with a continuous line of stories, but he appeared to be a good, solid person—in plain words, someone I could trust.

"Seeing that you are going to be in charge of our food from this day forth," he said, "I think you should go and get our Canadian parcel." I had not said anything about taking over control of the food.

"But what about dividing..." I was unable to finish my sentence. Jimmy said, "I haven't cooked a hot meal for over a year. I eat whatever hot rations come up from the German kitchen, and the Red Cross I just eat as it is. Saves time," he said with a wry smile. I felt he was more than just happy that someone had asked him to muck in. He seemed a lonely person who hid in his books.

"Do you really think that's what you want?" I asked him.

"Yes," he said. "I think it's best that one person look after the menu. When I came here, I mucked in with three others and it was a constant squabble and distrust of each other. I bailed out because of the hassle. I've been on my own for all these months. I learned a lesson from that group. I'd like to try my remedy on you."

"Okay, what's your remedy?" I asked.

"I've already told you. You are in charge of rations—all rations—and I'll go along with any decisions you make regarding menus."

"Well," I replied, "I'm wondering, Jimmy Grier, if I'm not being sucked in by you putting all this great faith in me. Is it not that you will then have a free ride, lie there and read your books, or just stand around and wait for me to call you when your meals are ready?"

"Would you prefer that I take over all the rations, go for the parcels, cook the suppers, divide the rations, and have you wait till I call you?" He looked solemn and sounded like a judge handing down a sentence. I thought, no, I wouldn't want that, and inwardly I knew that really I'd prefer to take charge of everything. It would help keep me busy, and if Jimmy turned out to be the sort of person I had tagged him to be, he would be easy to get along with.

"I don't think you could handle it," I retorted, "you'd only mess things up, burn the spuds, and probably forget to go for our Red Cross parcels. You'd still be reading your books and miss the call when our turn came for seconds on soup. No, I think it would be best if I accepted your challenge and took charge of keeping you from starving to death."

"You see, you know me already. So let's call it a deal. I'll study banking and you study Stalag cooking."

"Fall in for Canuck parcels," came a shout.

"Do you think you'll be okay until I get back?" I asked sarcastically.

"I'm not sure," said my new mucker, "but I'll promise to stay in bed."

It was an odd time, I thought, to go for parcels, right in the midst of the noon to 2:00 p.m. rest period. But I guessed this was a different day all around.

Nabber passed by and I asked, "Don't they take our chains off until after we get our parcels?"

"Are you kidding? Why don't you ask the chain *Feldwebel*?" Then he turned and asked, "How's your new mucker?"

"Just another good Irishman," I said.

"Your tough luck!" he retorted.

Jock and Peter were sitting at their table. With my free hand I dug into my pants pocket for the key. Sitting beside Jock, I plunked it down beside the deck of cards he had carefully stuffed back into their dirty cardboard sleeve. Picking the key up he said, "You've learned to pick locks, I see."

I could have said yes, but he would have found out that I still couldn't get that little "bully beef" key to work the magic of releasing the handcuffs.

"Sorry, Jock," I volunteered, "but this here Irishman isn't much good at picking German locks."

"How did you get them off?" he asked. I told him the story about Mark Watson and the *Feldwebel*. "So what do I do now?"

Peter got up, clipped his loosened handcuffs together, put his arm around my shoulder, and said, "Come on, you smartass Irishman, let's get those Canadian parcels." He looked at my loose handcuff and told me to clip it on, which I did.

At the issue window, I watched the German soldier use his triangle-faced hammer to punch a three-cornered hole in each of the tins.

It was a jovial, chattering majority that marched back to the compound hugging their precious boxes of food. It was this very happy group that made me think of a few lines of poetry I'd seen that morning stuck on the end bunk in our aisle. Actually, it was an old nursery rhyme with a few alterations:

> Little Jack Horner sat in a corner
> Eating a dish of 'Burgoo.'
> He was tight 'round the tum
> For the parcels had come,
> And they lobbed them out
> One between two.

'Burgoo' in Stalag was porridge. I believe it might be a Scottish term for the good old hot oatmeal breakfast. The Canadian parcels always contained a small package of coffee, and in keeping with this, the unknown poet had written five more lines:

> Coffee up
> Through the teeth
> And over the gums,
> Look out, stomach,
> Here it comes!

I found Jimmy Grier still on his bed, reading a new book on 'Modern Banking,' oblivious to the possibility that his mucker was about to concoct a feast beyond his wildest dreams.

"Raus, raus, mein Lieber. Offen das Bet; es ist zwei uhr!" I tried to imitate Ukraine Joe's wakey-wakey cry. Jimmy Grier looked up quizzically from his book as I plunked our Canadian parcel down beside him.

"Look at this!" I said with delight. "Salmon, cheese, jam, corned beef, meat loaf, Klim milk, sardines—and just look at the size of those biscuits. They must each be a quarter of an inch thick. And we have raisins, sugar and coffee—and prunes if you need them—and our Canadian chocolate bar! Bonanza!"

Jimmy casually put his finger on the word or line where he had stopped reading, then looked up from his book and asked, without much interest, "Are we eating now?"

"You don't deserve to eat! You southerners are all alike—lying back and allowing us to look after you. Do you have anything left from your German bread and sausage ration?"

"Can I have my share of the chocolate?" he asked, without telling me what had happened to his bread and sausage ration.

"You put me in charge of food, James," I replied, "and chocolate is not on the menu. Could be for dessert tonight—I'll think about it."

"I'll bet you're an Orangeman too," was Jimmy's only comment, as he turned the page and nestled himself further into his straw mattress.

"Better than being a lazy southerner," I said, "and I don't care if Ukraine Joe catches you in bed. It's after two o'clock now. I won't warn you if I see him coming, because I think you ate your bread and sausage while I was getting our food parcel. I'll get mine to eat in front of you."

I pushed the food parcel into the storage space under his bed and warned, "Don't you touch that chocolate bar!"

It is interesting that one can find in another person of completely different characteristics an instant bond of companionship. Jimmy Grier was a quiet, serious, studious loner. I think his loneliness at having no mucker had begun to take its toll when I came along. Some people might say he was lazy, but as things turned out I didn't mind looking after the catering end of this combine. I had a lot of energy to expend and the running around, the scrounging I was to do, the bartering, the cooking, the stretching out to seven days the food we could easily eat in two or three—this would all help to keep me alert and in good shape, both physically and mentally.

When I returned to my bedspace, Nabber was making a new mug. I touched his arm, and said, "Thanks again, Nabber, for what you did this morning. It has changed a lot of things for me. I feel happier with my new mucker."

"Good," he said, "now is that all you want from me? Can I finish making this mug?" He didn't like praise or anyone making a fuss about the many things he did for people, and I'd noticed this sort of brush-off was typical of him when people thanked him.

"Okay, Nabber, I said, "sorry for disturbing you, but I was going to ask you a question about something that's been worrying me."

"Sure, go ahead, Paddy. Ask me," he replied. "Ask me anything you like."

I looked very serious before replying. "Nabber, have you ever heard of anyone in prison camp dying from rust poisoning by using old mugs and old rusty plates long after they should be thrown away? You know, there are rich people and poor people here, some with hundreds of cigarettes, others with no cigarettes."

"Okay, Paddy," and he looked at me with his brow down. "Just what do you want?"

"Well," I said, "I don't want anything, but I know a poor guy who is eating off an old rusted plate with a rusty tin spoon. I think he bought them from you about a year ago. I'm concerned about rust poisoning." I looked at Nabber and in a sad voice, shaking my head, I said, "Wouldn't it be terrible, Nabber, if somebody died because of a rusty plate or spoon. Worse still, think how you would feel knowing that you made them!"

Looking at me with as much fake disgust as he could muster, and putting on an Irish accent, he said, "Now sure and begorra, Paddy, would this young lad who is about to give us the excuse for a Stalag wake, would he be by any chance your new mucker?"

I faked surprise when I replied, "Now isn't it strange you should say that, Nabber, for indeed my mucker's plate and spoon are the very ones I was talking about, and for a Kiwi you're smart to pick that up! And do you know something else? I think if you were to put your hand into that English Red Cross box under your bed and through the kindness of your heart bring out one of those new tin spoons you made yesterday, then you'd come to me and say, 'Here you are, Paddy Mac, will you please take this new spoon to your mucker with my compliments?'"

"Now what would happen if I did a stupid thing like that?" came the reply.

"Stupid?" I said, consternation written all over my face. "Nabber, my boy, if you were to do that right now you would be forever blessed. Just think! In all probability you could be saving an Irishman from a horrible death—rust poisoning. And do you realize what wonderful things will then happen if you open up your heart and donate a new spoon?" I looked very serious and said, "As soon as the Little People back in old Ireland find out you did this, they will all come out tonight, dancing in those fairy rings, and the news will spread all over Ireland, and everywhere they'll be chanting your name: 'Nabber Giddens, Nabber Giddens!' And I'm sure if you were to really open up your heart and give my mucker one of those special new plates to go with the new spoon, you'd get a double Irish blessing. That would bring in the Little People all around the lakes of Killarney and they would dance across the lakes. Just think, Nabber, you could lie in your sack tonight and know that your name, at that very moment, would be echoing across Killarney's lakes, for you know that in the Little People's world, news travels instantaneously and probably at this very moment they are all waiting with bated breath, fingers and toes crossed, hoping that you will make the right decision and ensure yourself of some Irish Luck in your pocket for the rest of a long life."

Before Nabber could strum up to a rebuff, I said, "Now if you didn't do it ..." and I looked dolefully down at the ground before continuing, "I just wouldn't want to think about it, for sometimes the consequences are tragic."

Nabber put down his work, looked at me for a long moment, and then burst into laughter. "I've heard BS from New Zealand to here, but never in my life have I listened to so much Irish blarney as in the last three days. I don't know how you do it, Mac, but goddammit, you've a way of getting what you want and making other people feel they've just got to do it for their own good."

"Come on, Nabber," I said, "that's just your conscience telling you you're overstocked with unsaleable tin plates and spoons, and as you said the other day, there is a depression here, so maybe a bit of advertising would help, like a free spoon and plate."

Three minutes later I interrupted Jimmy Grier's reading by placing a brand spanking new tin plate and spoon on his chest.

"Sure and bejabbers! Where did you get these?" he asked, putting down his book and taking off his glasses. I noticed he had closed the bound volume on banking, so I reckoned Jimmy was greatly enthused and surprised that I was not yet three days in this camp and already producing these special utensils.

"You've just got to know the right people," I said. "It appears you haven't been travelling in the proper circles. Now why don't you take that rusty plate and spoon and dump them?" Then I thought, where would he dump them? No garbage truck called here! So I asked, "How do you get rid of the garbage around here?"

"The permanent staff clean-up crew," Jimmy volunteered. "Art Scott is on the crew and he does a good job."

"Yes," I replied, "I've noticed him. Looks like a nice guy."

Changing the subject back to food again, I asked, "Where is today's spud ration? With all that's been happening, I forgot to pick ours up."

"Look under the bunk," he said. I pulled up the old ragged cloth curtain and there were six small cooked potatoes cuddled together in my mucker's dixie. It looked like they were in fairly good shape.

"Picked them up when you were down getting our parcels."

It was almost four o'clock and we were being asked to line up again by sections for de-chaining. The same guards who had arrived that morning with the chains were now setting up, ready to retrieve the handcuffs. I had forgotten to ask Nabber, Big Jock, or Mark Watson to release one wrist. I'd been so enthused with the parcel issue and with Nabber and my spoon/plate sales pitch, that both wrists being shackled had not bothered me, and now I was about to be freed of them for the evening. I lined up with the others and waited my turn to be released.

My evening meal was a great success. It was Parcel Festivity!

We sat at our Section 11 table to eat. For dessert I broke the chocolate bar into equal pieces. It was not a bad birthday meal for my twenty-second year. I was finishing when Peter Chadwick appeared with a birthday cake of his own making. It was a sandwich made of two Canadian biscuits that had been soaked in a liquid of water and sugar. They had swollen to three or four times their usual thickness and were then cooked for a while in the old oven to dry out a little. The two swollen biscuits had then been sandwiched together with canned strawberry jam, the top smeared with a mixture of Klim powdered milk and canned condensed milk—a good substitute for icing. There was no writing, but the figure "22" had been imprinted on the mixture with either a piece of wood or someone's finger. "Happy birthday, Paddy me boy, and I hope you'll be spending your twenty-third back in old Ireland!"

I thanked Peter and Jock for once again going overboard to do something nice for a friend. I looked around the table and picked up a piece of thin contraband metal that had been sharpened to serve as a knife. Cutting the birthday cake into six equal pieces, I invited those who were around me to help themselves. It was a pleasant moment of friendship.

"Did you send that message to the Little People that I was a good Joe?" Nabber inquired.

"Didn't have to," I replied. "Remember what I told you about news travelling instantaneously? If you close your eyes and concentrate hard enough, I bet you'll hear the echo of those Little People singing your praises, and my mucker thanks you from the bottom of his heart for saving him from a rusty death."

"I believe! I believe!" Nabber made mock salutations as he sat up in his bunk.

I folded my pants to make a pillow. Leaving on my choker sweater and shorts, I climbed beneath the two blankets. The straw mattress felt comfortable.

It was a cold, clear night with a million stars—a sudden change from what we'd been having. As I looked out one of the whole window panes, the twinkling stars within the sphere of my vision seemed to be sending Morse code messages to Nabber. At least that's what I thought of saying to him. But when I looked up at the top bunk, I saw that the forbidden light was out and both he and Markellie were asleep or quietly meditating. Markellie, as usual, was curled up like a plump little bear.

I lay quietly for some time. Looking through the rows of bunks, I saw a few glowing cigarettes. Then someone a number of bunks away softly recited:

> There is a girl who lives over the hill
> And if she doesn't, her sister will.

Then in chorus a few nearby voices sang,

> That was a funny old rhyme.
> Tell us another one, do!

Then came a series of ditties from different bunks in the area, recited with as many accents as there were ditties.

The impromptu programme went for twenty minutes, then during a minute or two of silence, as people ran out of new material or lay thinking of new lines, a voice from across the aisle requested, "Hi! Kiwi, will you sing us little children the Lord's Prayer?"

I thought for a moment that he was referring to Nabber, but then I heard the request being passed along to somewhere close to the washroom end of the barrack.

"Come on, Kiwi, you're not asleep," said a Cockney voice.

There was a hushed silence for a minute as everyone seemed to be waiting, waiting for something they'd heard before and wanted to hear again. Then, in a beautiful tenor voice that echoed through the barrack, out through the broken windows and through the cardboard repairs, and out and across the compound and the barbed wire to the guards in their stilted machine gun posts, the Lord's Prayer was sung in a way that I will never forget.

When the singer finished there was no applause, no remarks—just a hushed silence. A few people within my vision were still holding glowing cigarettes, each one alone with his thoughts, as we all were. I was to hear this performance repeated a few times, usually when morale was low or at Easter and Christmas.

The searchlights' beams were still crawling relentlessly along the wire when I fell asleep. My twenty-second birthday and my third full day in Stalag were now about to be history.

Above: Prior to the introduction of chains, string was used to tie prisoners' wrists. **Below**: A prisoner holds a 12" Red Cross parcel to show how the chains restricted movement.

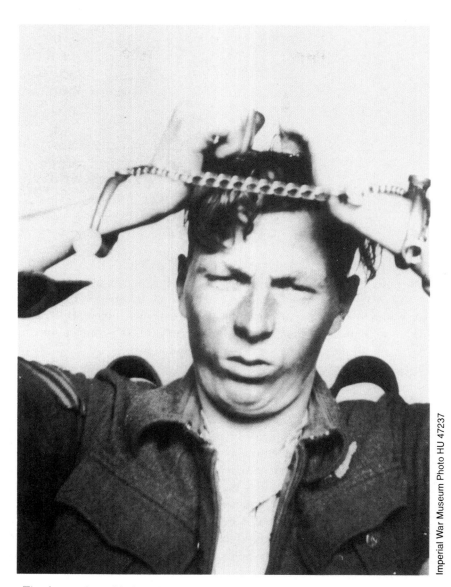

The frustration of being chained is clear on Sergeant Jack Diamond's face.

CHAPTER 9

Spring of 1943

February passed and March was in the autumn of its life. The daily routine bored me, and it took a steady effort to steel myself against my new reality. To dwell on the degrading and humiliating aspects of this existence could only end in disaster. One had to lift oneself mentally to a sort of higher plane and proceed to live there but still keep contact with and carry out all the undesirable rules and regulations.

Each day the German rations arrived at approximately the designated times, then came the weekly issue of Red Cross parcels, daily check parades, handcuffing, walks around the wire, rumours, propaganda carried on the loudspeakers, the continuous fight to ensure as high a standard of cleanliness as conditions permitted, the battle against fleas and lice, the effort to control emotions, the effect of watching another prisoner "flip out" and be shepherded away to the segregated area set aside for such cases. There was also the frustration of being locked at night in a smoky, smelly barrack atmosphere with a hundred men and watching the dim 25-watt light bulbs struggle (like oneself) to clear a circle, no matter how small, wherein there was light and hope of life. There was also the fear that you would come down with some disease, die and be buried somewhere out there beyond the wire. There were rumours that they would never let us go free—that we would never get home—because they were killing Jewish people by the thousands (this information filtered into camp from prisoners who had been sent out on working parties in Poland).

Many discouraging and frightening rumours invaded the barracks, and often, when my morale had sunk to a low level, I had to start climbing the "ladder," rung by rung, to a higher plane of thought, and stay there for as long as possible.

I woke one late March morning to the usual waky call. Out on parade we could feel the season changing. It was too early yet for official spring in Obersilesia, but there was a breath of it this morning, as if someone were saying, "Hang in there! I'm coming with warm sunshine!"

The last few mornings there'd been lots of activity away out on the flat land beyond the camp. Often we would wake before our own parade time to the singing of marching German soldiers in training as they passed by the outside perimeter wire.

I spent a lot of time scrounging for small fragments of wood, even little chips, pieces of paper, cigarette packages and tiny remains of old German newspapers that had found their way into camp. I tried menus that would stretch the meagre supplies—and that was no mean task. But Jimmy Grier never grumbled if food was scarce for a day or two. We ate something each day, and by the end of March I was looking back and thinking, I've managed to get the first two months almost "buried" and I have adjusted well. Of course, that's my diagnosis of my own mental state!

Nabber Giddens built up a nice little business for himself selling tin mugs, plates and spoons and with the remuneration he received (cigarettes, of course) was able to do quite well trading with the few guards willing to take the risk of discovery. Markellie the farmer was looking forward to the possibility of getting tomato and other vegetable seeds in exchange for cigarettes. He had his eye on a little patch of ground in the corner of the compound that he was sure would grow something.

"Are you going to sleep out there, too?" asked Nabber. "You'll have to. If anything grows it'll be gone and eaten before it's ready."

By late March I had survived two trips to the cookhouse to obtain those "Irish Racket Spuds." The first scary journey took place one day when a strange soldier came to the barrack and asked for me.

"You're from Belfast, I hear." His statement was abrupt and he didn't introduce himself, but produced from under his greatcoat a British issue carry-all bag that looked the worse for wear. "Put this under your bunk for now," the stranger ordered. Then he said, "Let's go outside for a minute or two."

I followed the intruder, who had made no attempt to wait for me. Outside, he turned to face me and said, "Take the bag at 1020 hours to the third window at the back of the cookhouse. It will be open at the bottom.

"When you see Mike McQuaid standing inside and facing you, throw the bag to him and wait two minutes. If Mike does not throw out the bag to you filled with potatoes within that two minute period, you will make yourself scarce. You got it?"

"Yes, I understand."

Anyone who obtained extra rations, other than Black Market bartering with guards was known to be "in the rackets," or a "racketeer."

My watch read 9:30 a.m. I had less than an hour to accomplish this expedition.

"By the way," my instructor continued, "when you finish with the bag, take it to a George McNeill in the barrack next to yours. With that he walked away, turning once to say, "Remember, George McNeill."

Quickly I made my way back to the barrack. Jimmy had seen me leave with the stranger. He asked, "The Irish Spud Racket Man?" I answered with a nod of my head. Then he asked, "Are you going?"

"Guess so," I replied.

With no other comment, he continued thoughtfully to sup his tea.

With only fifteen minutes to make my final decision, I thought of the seven other participants who would have to be told, "No extra Irish spuds—the new man chickened out." I imagined them pointing fingers at me as I walked the wire with Peter and Jock, whispering to each other, "That's him, that's the guy who turned yellow and screwed us out of our extra spuds."

I looked around the table. Mark Watson was chewing on a crust of bread. Sam Warnock, the section leader, was printing names on new cards. A German magazine called *Signal* was folded neatly in the centre of the table.

My heart was racing at top speed and I was more than a little scared.

Quickly I returned to my bedspace. Markellie was the only one around and he seemed to be completely occupied with writing a letter card. I tucked the haversack inside my battle dress jacket and buttoned up my greatcoat. I turned to leave.

"Good luck," said Markellie. The gates are open, so you don't have to go through the wire." He did not look up from his card.

"How do you know where I'm going?" I asked.

"Saw the canvas bag and the guy who came to talk with you. Old farmers are not stupid, you know. Hope you think it's all worthwhile."

"Should be back in ten or fifteen minutes," I undid my right handcuff (I had learned to be quite good at this art), walked outside, and joined a group of "wire walkers." At the big open gates I casually walked through, first removing my handcuffs and quickly putting the two cuffs and chain in my greatcoat pocket. Turning down the lane towards the cookhouse, I saw that all of the prisoners using the lane at this time of day were duty crew people going about their jobs without handcuffs (with permission from the German officer in charge, of course).

As I headed toward the BEF compound, I passed duty crews carrying loads of bread rations to designated barracks. Some distance in front of me walked two Canadians from the Dieppe compound. Suddenly they looked to the right and saluted smartly. I made out the naval uniform of our Camp *Kommandant* and quickly understood the smart salutes.

The distance diminished quickly and with the best salute I could muster, I passed the *Kommandant* and a strange high-ranking German army officer with a red stripe down his dark pants. I was only a short distance from the guard who stood outside his sentry box. I knew this was the perimeter of the inner camp. Once past the sentry, I'd be out of bounds. To the right was the cookhouse, standing by itself in a wide open space. Anyone loitering would be clearly visible.

I knew that on an operation like this, you should never hesitate when passing a guard; appear confident that you have a definite place to go. Convince yourself you have a legitimate duty to complete.

I approached the sentry, I looked him in the eye and said, "*Guten morgen, mein Lieber*," and as I marched past him he returned the greeting: "*Guten morgen*."

The two Dieppe soldiers had also gone through the checkpoint and were over to the left in forbidden territory, nearing the Camp *Lazarette* (hospital).

I turned to the right along the isolated path that would take me to the cookhouse. I approached the building and made my way quickly to the rear. It was exactly 10:30 a.m. by my watch. I hesitated for a moment as I passed the third window, which was open at the bottom. A quick look inside revealed the friendly Mike McQuaid standing behind the opening. I made a quick about-turn, took out the canvas haversack, approached the window from the opposite direction, and threw the empty haversack to McQuaid. He disappeared and I stood alone, scared to death that I'd be hailed by one of the patrol guards and led off to the cooler.

The seconds ticked by like hours. I'd forgotten to start the two-minute countdown. I looked at my watch and counted another 30 seconds, and no sign of that bag filled with potatoes or McQuaid. Suddenly there came an explosion of rifle shots. My mouth went dry and sweat soaked my shirt, but as the rifle shots continued, I realized that they were from the German practice range outside camp.

My impulse was to leave without the goods, but Mike appeared and dropped the haversack full of hot potatoes to me. He didn't speak, smile, or give any gesture of recognition. He disappeared quickly.

The haversack was heavier than I'd anticipated. I couldn't sling it over my shoulder and chance that the guard would let me through without checking the contents; that would be tempting fate. I looked down the path, and my heart missed a couple of beats when I saw two armed guards coming my way. I flattened myself against the wall beneath the open window and waited, praying desperately that they'd pass along the front of the cookhouse. I heard them laugh and listened to the crunch of their boots on the gravel when they reached the corner of the lane. Would they follow the lane along the front, or would they come this way and find me? I almost panicked and threw the haversack back through the open window, but I realized that in doing so I would blow the whistle on Mike and the spud racket. Quickly I unbuttoned my battle dress jacket by a few more buttons, enough to lodge the bulky haversack inside, and held my breath as the loud voices of the two guards faded away on the opposite side of the cookhouse.

Tightening the buckle of the jacket around my middle so the potatoes wouldn't fall through, I buttoned my greatcoat and prepared to leave with quite a bulge showing. With the potatoes hot against my chest, steam seeping out and up around my neck. I reached the sentry box, raised my hand to the guard in a gesture of friendship and called out, "*Kalt Tag*! (cold day)." I passed through. He nodded in reply, which suited me just fine. At that particular moment I didn't need him to hail me for a stop and search!

I was three-quarters of the way to home ground when I saw the two German officers on the same side of the lane as me.

I gradually veered to the left, so that when I passed by I would be as far from them as the path's width would permit. A little before they came level with me, I started my eyes right and made a long salute, praying all the while that the buckle on my jacket would hold the weight of those potatoes. My salute was returned by the most senior officer, who was not our *Kommandant*.

As I entered the compound gates I quickly manacled both wrists and joined the stream of wire walkers for a short distance. It would be a sad fate indeed to be caught without handcuffs after almost completing the mission.

Then with a happy feeling of accomplishment, I entered our barrack and signalled Jimmy Grier to follow me to my bedspace.

There were twenty-seven cooked potatoes almost all equal in size. I had seven names plus myself. Jimmy was not on my list. I asked no questions. He didn't volunteer any answers as to why he was not, so I assumed that my previous idea was true—he had in the past refused to participate.

Now, eight times three made twenty-four, and eight times four equalled thirty-two, but nine times three was twenty-seven, so I took it upon myself to include Jimmy in the distribution, for hadn't I risked the possibility of being caught and charged with all sorts of things? Many trumped up charges could be laid at my feet and then I could languish in solitary for months. Thinking about all these possibilities, I decided no matter what the others felt, I was in charge of these twenty-seven spuds. I took out six potatoes, and left Jimmy to take care of them.

With my list of barrack numbers and names, I proceeded like a mailman to tour the barracks, eventually found all seven, and delivered three potatoes to each—almost a whole day's extra ration. I talked to each one and found that only two were truly from the Old Sod. The others were "second-hand Irish" and had never set foot on the Emerald Isle; they could only claim parents, grandparents and great-grandparents who had seen the sun shine on those lush green pastures.

I had deliberately made George McNeill's barrack my last stop. He was from a little town in County Wicklow and taken prisoner while on ground staff duties in France during the spring of 1940. I left George his extra rations plus the haversack, as he was next on the roster to run the gauntlet.

I continued to make cookhouse trips unscathed.

✈

It's amazing how one adjusts to a drastic change in life and learns to admit, this is my life unless I can escape. As the sun rose higher in the sky each day and April was sliding by, the daily happenings around me became so familiar I could tell almost everything that would happen in any given day. This way of life would continue until it was changed by some edict from higher authority or the forces of Soviet Russia, who would definitely be the army of liberation if we stayed in this camp.

And so my mind, body, and soul capitulated to the daily routine. Eventually the aggression and anger at being a prisoner was to a great degree quelled; I was in control of all those destructive emotions that could deprive me of the chance to survive and return home in a rational state of mind.

Time passed slowly. Jimmy Grier and I had few hassles. He was my mucker, yes, but actually my comradeship lay in the direction of my bunk, where Markellie, Nabber, Eddy Anderson, and I resided. The four of us shared the very narrow floorspace between our bunks. Peter and Big Jock were a number of bunks away.

We were like family—the exception was Eddy Anderson. Strange as he was, all three of us made an effort to bring him into a closer bond of friendship, but he always skirted that circle and remained outside. Near the end of April, Alec MacKinlay shouted, "Mail's up!" There was the usual enthusiastic rush. He had quite a bunch of letters. As each lucky man's name was called he'd shout, "Over here!" or "Here, Jock," or just "Yes" or "That's me!" Some would choke up, saying nothing, but push through the crowd, grab the letter, look at the writing, then rush off to their bedspaces to read it. If by the writing they knew it wasn't the mail they were expecting, they would continue to stand, hopeful that their name would be called once again.

I waited and jealously watched each man move away to his bedspace with words from home in his hand, and not until the last letter was handed to George Montrose did I turn away, wondering how many weeks it would be until another mail delivery would arrive.

One morning around six o'clock, Jock was standing on his perch shouting for everyone to wake up because he had a very important announcement to make.

Nabber was first to jump down from his top bunk, almost on top of Markellie, who had at the same instant decided to disembark. He quickly recoiled as the 200-pound piece of Kiwi brawn and muscle descended to the concrete.

Accompanied by Markellie and a few other stumbling, half-awake prisoners, we followed Nabber to hear Jock's 6:00 a.m. information.

"Okay, guys, Joe is digging a hole in the ground near the Aussie barrack and burying items in his possession that have the smell of bartering with the enemy. You know what that means. The Gestapo are coming and must be at Annahof Station, or between here and there, so prepare for searches. Your guess is as good as mine as to what they'll be after."

Many people immediately scurried off to their bedspaces to either dispose of their black market goods or move them to a better hiding place. Nabber quickly returned to his bedspace and snuggled his contraband pieces of metal further into the mattress, along with pieces of tin cans. Others were busy with similar chores, hiding articles they knew would be immediately confiscated if discovered. Activity became feverish as more and more prisoners became aware that a search was imminent.

One prisoner was tearing up an obscene drawing of Hitler.

Jock was shouting for everyone to get outside immediately. Anybody who hadn't hidden his barter goods would be on his own if what he had was discovered. There was also the possibility we could be outside for a long time, Jock said, "So, like good little Boy Scouts, 'Be prepared!'" With that, he made his own way towards the door, his khaki woollen cap looking out of place against the blue of his Air Force greatcoat.

Outside, we lined up in our usual columns of five, and Ukraine Joe solemnly started his count. There were a few brave souls who dared to shout questions: "What did you bury, Joe? Hope it wasn't a *Fraulein*; she'll suffocate!" "Hi, Joe! Can I borrow your shovel? I forgot to bury my radio. I don't want to miss the BBC news."

This morning Joe was oblivious to smart remarks. He was concerned only with a correct count, and hoping the Gestapo would look around, search if they intended to, and leave quickly. It was a scary time for the guards. Every one of them was on his toes: these Gestapo searches were very infrequent, and everyone in camp, from the *Kommandant* down to the newest Kriegy, wanted to keep it that way.

When the Gestapo came to visit it was always for a reason. Could it be they were looking for someone who had escaped their net? It was possible, in a working camp like ours, that desperate people were somehow smuggled into camp to escape the dragnet that was closing around them outside.

It was an hour after check parade and we were still standing, but not in a very military fashion.

Soon, word passed from column to column of impatient men: "They're here!" Now that these notorious people were in our compound, I was interested in seeing what they looked like.

Another hour passed and I realized that behind us, men were moving around in our barrack.

Then a hubbub of conversation broke the last half hour of almost complete silence. There were a great number of people who had things hidden and were concerned that on some very slight excuse, if something were found in their bedspace that upset these notorious people, the result might be injurious to the prisoners involved.

There's no place on earth like a prison camp and a situation like this to trigger one's mind and send it soaring off to all sorts of terrible happenings.

The uniformed figures of soldiers, accompanied by civilians, could be seen pulling beds apart. Then there was the clatter of tin stoves being dumped outside our building. It was another hour before we were given the dismiss order.

At the entrance to our barrack was a pile of masterpieces: single-pot, double-pot, even some four-pot-holder tin stoves. Hundreds of hours of work, all in one large pile. A majority of the stoves had been flattened or broken by soldiers stomping on them. There was an assortment of papers, pieces of cloth, a coil of wire and a large, well-done drawing, crumpled and torn in two pieces. It was wedged between two flattened stoves, but I could see that it was a coloured drawing of the German flag with a Lancaster coming through the centre, ripping it apart. I'd seen it on the wall beside the bunk of a New Zealander. I was sure he would have tried to hide it, but maybe with a touch of bravado he'd left it for them to find.

Beside the pile of broken tin cook stoves stood three of our guards, and a few feet away stood two middle-aged men in black leather coats. At the entrance to the doorway, wearing a shiny black raincoat, stood a younger member of this notorious group. The two middle-aged men could have belonged to any family. They looked like trustworthy breadwinners and could have passed for loving fathers in any circumstance— except the black coats and pants and the black leggings seemed to exude something that wasn't natural. The word would be sinister, like the sallow-faced young man who eyed each one of us as we passed back into the barrack. He seemed to be checking faces, looking for someone. We could see that at the entrance to each of the barracks were three or four civilians, most in dark clothing, watching as the inmates passed through to their bedspaces. They, too, were apparently looking for someone.

When the first members of our group got inside our barrack there was an uproar of swearing and loud protests. Blankets were strewn everywhere. Palliasses pulled off the beds were either lying on the floor or hanging precariously from top bunks. Greatcoats, uniforms, and clothing of all sorts were strewn everywhere. They sure didn't tidy up after their search!

Nabber was ahead of me, helping to push the mass of bodies and feet that were tripping over each other in their haste to see what tragedy had befallen their precious belongings. The mob broke off in pieces, some rushing down aisle one, some down aisle two. As Nabber and I turned down our aisle, Markellie and Anderson caught up, and we reached the wreckage of our "homes" and belongings at the same time. It looked a real disaster, with everyone's belongings mixed up. My palliasse had been opened and some of the straw taken out, but I had nothing to hide. Eddy Anderson's also had been opened and Markellie's pulled from his bunk. Nabber's, for some strange reason, had not been touched. He jumped up, immediately searched the interior, and was delighted to find his makeshift hammers were untouched and the straw filling in his mattress unruffled. He gave a whoop of joy when he discovered that for some strange reason his tin plates and spoons had not been disturbed.

Nabber sat for a moment or two surveying the wreckage of our three bunks. He stared in disbelief and then, shaking his head, he said, "Can't be true, can't be true. They left me alone; didn't touch a thing. I wonder why?"

I pushed straw back into my palliasse while Anderson and Markellie sorted out our mixed up clothing, Nabber sat up like a king on a throne, repeating his disbelief until Markellie looked up and said, "So you're the untouchable one. Even Jerry searchers leave you alone. Bet they've gone for reinforcements and will return *en masse* to search your bedspace."

Pushing the last bunch of straw back into my palliasse, I tied the string and looked up at Nabber. "Don't you know why you were saved from the search and all your precious material and work tools left intact?"

"Because they saw the New Zealand shoulder badge on my tunic."

"Not so, Nabber, not so," I said. "Don't you know the real reason your bedspace was passed by?"

He looked questioningly at me as I continued.

"Your materials and equipment for making the mugs and plates were kept safe from the searching hands by an invisible wall put up by the Little People. Aren't you glad you made that tin mug and plate for my mucker? I told you then that your name would be heralded all over Ireland. Now you can see I was telling the truth."

Nabber was looking at me with a quizzical expression. He had listened intently to what I'd said, and even Markellie and Anderson had stopped their tidying up to listen, and as Nabber went into his "I believe" routine, I was certain that although he didn't want to think my story had any truth to it, he was well on the way to believing in Little People.

Just then a voice from the barrack vestibule rang loud and clear: "They're taking all our cook stoves away!" Immediately a percentage of Barrack 15A's quota of Kriegies, mostly those who were lucky enough to escape a thorough search, trooped outside. The pile of tin cook stoves was gone.

At the open double gates a horse and four-wheeled, high-sided old wagon with its load of precious cooking equipment trundled out of our compound to rousing sarcastic cheers of hundreds of prisoners—that is if one could say cheers were sarcastic—but our message to the Gestapo was, "If this is all you could bag, and what you were looking for got away, tough on you. We'll survive!"

Two muckers were already diligently working on the basic requirements for construction of a new tin cook stove, and soon we were to see a beehive of industry and many busy prisoners. That night everyone was in bed early. I think all of us had lost a lot of nervous energy as those notorious visitors moved among us. It was rumoured the Dieppe compound inmates hid two Russians in a garden patch, covered them with earth and equipped them with breathing tubes. We knew the Gestapo were not here just to upset our personal gear and take away tin cook stoves. Days later the Russians were said to have been smuggled out of camp in a work party.

"The third post and exit to the cookhouse."
The Irish Potato Racket was a scary pastime.

CHAPTER 10

Summer 1943

There would be trading with the enemy if parcels containing cigarettes from home continued to arrive at the camps.

One day Peter, Jock and I walked alongside the wire at the northwest corner of the camp, adjoining the soccer pitch. It was Peter who spied the prisoner throwing to a Stalag guard on the outside what we assumed was cigarettes. We saw a large loaf of bread soaring over the entanglement of barbed wire. It cleared the wire and fell quite a few yards from the prisoner. By this time we were close to where the transaction was taking place and could see he had a small stack of cigarettes on the ground. He was a Canadian.

The guard looked fidgety, but stood his ground while he examined the cigarettes. The Canadian opened conversation again in German and we could understand he wanted the same deal once again. By this time there must have been forty or fifty prisoners converging on the scene. Anything out of the ordinary in Stalag always drew a crowd. These two would have to finish their business quickly—make the deal or terminate discussions before it became too conspicuously "spotlighted" by the spectators.

The bartering Canadian was shouting something about "*Brot, Brot, schnell, schnell*" and cigarettes, and we knew by his actions that this time he wanted the guard to throw the bread over first and then he would throw the cigarettes. They talked back and forth until the Canuck threw over half of the cigarettes. We saw him look in our direction, and then at the guard outside the wire, who had his cigarettes and the second loaf of bread. Two joggers passed by, then three more, and all of them seemed to know this bartering prisoner. They made a wide circle close to him and started running on the spot. Again the bartering prisoner shouted to the guard, "*Schnell, schnell!*"

Looking around, the guard threw over the bread. It landed just a few feet from the receiver, who immediately picked it up. The guard then motioned to the prisoner to throw over the other cigarettes to close the deal. The prisoner pulled a piece of string from his pocket, making it obvious that he was tying together the last packs of cigarettes. This he did, and with great showmanship managed to throw them over the wire to land a long way from the guard. As he did so, he shouted his apologies. At that moment the five on-the-spot runners wheeled around the prisoner who had the two loaves, then six joggers moved swiftly and diagonally across the Kiwi rugger pitch, the shortest route to their barracks, leaving behind on the other side of the wire an exasperated guard who had picked up the packets and untied the string, only to find that they were full of paper and a few pieces of gravel for weight to carry them over the wire.

We moved off, walking quickly, until Peter suggested, "Let's wait for the crowd. We are still within rifle range, and he might think we are part of the suck-in."

Next day, we recognized the same guard snooping around the barracks of the Air Force compound. He came into our barrack at soup up time and watched the crowded tables as everyone supped their soup. I'm sure he knew who he was looking for, because we recognized him, but we didn't hear of anyone being caught for that bit of deceit.

Nabber kept himself busy making and repairing mugs and tin plates, keeping fit with long walks that ended with hundred yard dashes around the perimeter wire.

Water pressure was very poor, as usual, and we'd had no shower parades for three weeks when dark thunderclouds rolled across the sky and then great drops of moisture splattered onto the roofs. Markellie said, "Let's have a shower!" and with that he grabbed his soap, rolled out of his clothing and in half a minute, his round naked buttocks were disappearing out the open window, just as the cloud burst right above our barrack. I hastily followed and made the open space between the barracks seconds after Anderson, who was standing looking upwards, his mouth open to catch the rain.

Markellie had lathered himself with soap he'd got from home and was now standing still while the heavenly shower rinsed him clean. I had more difficulty in getting my German soap to lather, but eventually got well soaped. Then, suddenly, the rain stopped. There were derisive cries from a few dozen prisoners trapped between the two barracks, half-washed, half-soaped, and some with their hair lathered.

Another cry of disappointment echoed down the alley as the bright summer sun peeped out from behind the cloud. The warmth dried the soap on our naked bodies. There was a mad rush back through the windows as we made our different ways to the communal washroom. Markellie had stopped at his bunk and bid us *adieu* as he prepared to dry himself. Being first out, he had been quick enough to get washed off before the downpour stopped. Nabber, who had not participated in the "shower" party, was leaning against Markellie's bunk, a tin mug of coffee in his hand, and eating one of those big round biscuits from a Canadian parcel. He had processed cheese on it and strawberry jam.

"You sure look funny," he smirked as I passed by with my towel wrapped around me.

"Capitalist!" was the only retort I could think of, and I pointed at his biscuit with cheese and jam.

"The chain *Feldwebel* is in the washroom," he grinned in reply.

"You Kiwi liar!" I called back at him as I turned out of the aisle towards the washroom.

There was practically no water pressure and only a trickle of water from three taps at the far end. And there must have been twenty naked bodies caked with dried soap.

"What do we do now?" asked a little English rear gunner who was missing a great chunk of flesh from his right shoulder. It had healed well, but looked horrible.

"Wait till the next thunderstorm on August 18th at three o'clock," came a sarcastic reply.

"Shut up, Albert," replied the little guy. I presumed Albert was a friend, or his mucker.

I returned to my bedspace and dressed over the dried soap, replaced the handcuffs on my wrists, picked up my towel, and headed to the south side of camp to find a washroom with water on. I asked Nabber, if the chain *Feldwebel* should enquire if the Irishman had his handcuffs on, to make sure he told him that I had.

"Be happy to do so," he grinned, and then asked, "Where is Eddy Anderson?"

Markellie wisecracked, "Look out the window, Nabber. He's probably still standing out there in the nude, waiting for the next thunder shower."

Nabber, still with his mug of coffee in hand, took a few paces to the open window, stuck his head out, and loud enough for Markellie to hear, said, "My God! Just look at him!" Then, sure that he had Markellie's attention, he continued, "Come inside, you stupid Aussie. There'll be no more rain for two months. Come on, Eddy boy, I'll help you get back through the window."

Markellie jumped off his bunk. He made one step towards the window, hesitated, then, remembering that Anderson had come back in, pretended to check something underneath in the storage area. "You're talking to a Yorkshire farmer, Nabber. Don't think they fall for your jokes as easily as an Irishman."

I'd no time to banter, so off I went in search of water as Nabber's little joke fizzled out.

Blue sky and rising temperatures chased away memories of dark, miserable winter days. Our spirits rose and an almost cheerful atmosphere prevailed. Markellie had been able to scrounge black market tomato plants and other seeds. He obtained an old spade, worn through in parts, but still usable. We wondered how the Gestapo had missed it.

I watched Markellie swagger across the parade ground, his rolling gait making him look as though he were walking on the deck of a ship heaving in a long, slow swell. He was the happy farmer again—with seeds to plant and with an okay from Ukraine Joe—about to dig the little corner that he had claimed. It would be late planting as June had already lost over a week.

Markellie's seeds were black market but apparently there was a small consignment of vegetable seeds that had come through with Red Cross parcels, so planting was legal, and this opened the door to a new field of bargaining. The old nicotine habit had to be satisfied, whether you were German or otherwise, so springtime meant cigarettes for seeds.

Markellie planted his seeds after turning the ground over. His plot was in the low corner of the compound, close to the cesspool. Smart farmer that he was, he knew that the moisture would stay there much longer than in any other part and the seepage from the cesspool would also be a good fertilizer for whatever he decided to grow. It was a smiling Markellie that returned to his bedspace and hid the old spade under the bunk, and I noticed that about a third of it was eaten away with rust. But this farmer's son could not have been happier if it had been made of gold.

Now, as Nabber put it, the "Great Crop Watch" was about to begin. Nabber had had a bumper few weeks since the Gestapo search. At times he had a line-up of people with orders for new tin cook stoves, plates and mugs. Cigarettes were pouring into his coffers, and we called him the "Kiwi Millionaire."

The sun got hotter, and I spent more time outside. Soon there were lines of prisoners sitting in the dust with their backs to the barrack wall, reading anything printed in English or writing Kriegy letters, while others nodded their heads in the sunlight, dreaming of better times. A few men brought out their blankets to lie on, which was foolhardy because at this warm time of year, the dusty soil was home to thousands of sand fleas.

The flea situation in the barrack was already reaching epidemic proportions, so inviting more by bringing one's issue blankets outside was, to put it mildly, a disaster. Any morning these days would see muckers with blankets placed against the wire and a flea hunt in progress. It wasn't unusual for people to take bets on the number of fleas that would be found in a given person's blanket. I forget the highest total, but a normal count on any morning's forage would be between twenty and thirty fleas. They were exasperating bed partners.

During one of the infrequent mail parades, my name was finally called. I went forward eagerly to claim the letter because it was the first link with home. I recognized that the writing was that of my father—a letter with a simple message and little news. I'd have preferred Dad to have taken the risk of censorship and written about my friends and their well-being.

My first letter from Alice arrived, but not before I had begun to wonder if it ever would. It came in the second batch of June mail.

The letter was full of information about young people we both knew, and it helped so very much to bring the ties of love and friendship closer to prison camp.

✈

Those lazy days of summer were a real tonic, and although each one of us went along with the idea that this time next year we'd all be home and free, deep down we realized that unless something extraordinary happened, we would remain here, lining up for soup and eating that sour bread and shivering in the cold winds at check parades. It seemed a bleak prospect indeed.

One day the soup *du jour* was meat and vegetable. This was always a plus. We wondered what animal had died to become the meat in the soup, and we wondered what parts of that animal had been used. But to hungry prisoners, the soup tasted good, regardless of its precise origin. It was good and thick and smelled better than it had for many months.

"We're 'seconds' today," said Sam. That was good news: being on seconds meant a double ration for our section.

We supped our soup quickly and waited for the magic call of "Seconds up!" When it came, Jimmy Grier and I were close to first in line. We pushed our dixies out for seconds and the duty crewman swilled his tin can around, trying to mix up the remains with the measuring tin. Scraping the bottom of the *kubel*, he dumped seconds into Jimmy's dixie and then mine. It sure looked thicker and better than the first issue. We went back to the table, and as I was dipping a piece of yesterday's bread ration into my soup, I heard Jimmy gagging. I looked to the end of the bench where he was sitting and saw that he had turned away, his shoulders heaving as though he were choking or vomiting. Suddenly he dashed off, wending his way through other prisoners who were in his path of flight. I caught up to him as he stood throwing up outside the barrack. Without speaking, he motioned me to leave, waving his hands in dismissal.

"What's wrong with you?" I asked.

"The eye! The eye!" was all he could manage between heaves.

"Your eye? Did the soup burn your eye?" I asked.

Without any further explanation, he took off towards the Old Forty Holer, indicating in no uncertain terms that I should leave him alone.

Returning to the barrack and the table, where I'd left my unfinished soup, I found members of our table, a few from Section 10, and others who were passing by had stopped to investigate the huddle. I got there in time to hear Sam say, "Looks like a cow's." Someone else claimed that he knew for sure that it was from a horse.

Nabber was there and he asked the question, "Where is Farmer Markellie? He'd know." But Markellie was nowhere around.

Pushing my way through, I asked, "What's wrong with Grier's soup?" I was prepared to see something that shouldn't have been there, but not for the big eye that Sam was balancing on Jimmy's tin spoon. It lay quietly on the spoon, moving gently on the stringy thread-like muscles or whatever was draped over the sides.

"Eyes melt in boiling soup," George Montrose claimed knowingly,

137

"so somebody must have thrown it in after the soup cooled a bit. Sure looks funny," he finished, screwing up his face in a look of disgust.

Word spread through the barrack that Grier had got a "cow's/horse's eye" in his soup and soon there was a big line-up to see this wonderful happening.

Peter went to the front and started calling out, "Come and look, only two cigarettes to see something you will probably never ever have the opportunity to see again. Only two cigarettes. Pay here as you pass by," and he held out his Air Force cap. "Another wonder of wonders you can see only in this great place." He finished up with twelve cigarettes.

I could see why Jimmy's stomach had refused to accept what had already gone down. It was an ugly sight and seemed to stare up at all of us, almost pleadingly. We agreed it was in such good condition that it had not been part of the original ingredients and that someone had thrown it into the *Kubel* after the soup was made—more than likely as a joke—just before we lined up for seconds.

Markellie finally arrived. He'd been washing up. "Definitely a cow's eye," he told us, and launched into a lengthy explanation of how he knew. The crowd dispersed. No one was very interested in the relative size of a horse's eye compared to a cow's.

Having no affection for the rest of my now cold soup, I washed it down the drain. The eye was deposited on a piece of Red Cross cardboard for the purpose of further discussion and examination.

I found Jimmy walking around the compound wire, filling his lungs with fresh air. He was feeling much better, but still very squeamish.

Many things happened when weather turned warm and the daylight hours lengthened. The trading that went on indoors among the men had now moved outdoors. In almost every compound, some enterprising person could be seen standing beside his swap shop, matching his wits and keen business sense against the smart asses, the slightly crooked, and those who just wanted a fair deal.

The weeks of that summer were filled with good-natured bantering, games, laughter, and late evening walks around the wire. Each night we watched the sun sink into the west, along with our thoughts. I think each one of us tried to take in all this pleasantness and tuck it away in the storage places of our minds, so that when the inevitable miserable cold days and nights came again, we could mentally draw on those warm memories.

Farmer Markellie's little garden patch was becoming the talk of the compound, and his crop of vegetables was doing so well that our Senior Man, when reading out daily orders, would often slip in the odd warning: "Please, you guys, leave the vegetable gardens alone. The people who have worked hard to make something grow deserve to have the pleasure of eating the results of their labours. None of us is starving right now. Don't press your luck by stealing a tomato—before or after it is ripe."

The other little patches of garden withered and died for lack of water, but Markellie's vegetables seemed to live a charmed life. Each morning after roll call, the first thing he did was check his garden, and every morning those veggies stood up straight and healthy, as though they were on parade for *Unteroffizier* Joe Kussel. Of course it was where he planted that made the difference: the seepage from the old cesspool kept those veggies alive. Four tomato plants were coming along well, with green tomatoes growing bigger and changing colour every sunny day. Half a dozen lettuce heads, some onions, and a few beets looked almost ready for salad.

The Irish Potato Racket was still alive and well, too, and I continued to share what extras were available. By the end of July, Nabber, Anderson and myself had a couple of times feasted on fresh tomato sandwiches, thanks to the generosity of our farmer friend.

Markellie checked his charges each evening before turning in, and again after morning parade. A couple of mornings after we had those fresh tomato sandwiches, we were standing together at 7:00 a.m. parade. With half-closed eyes, Markellie squinted in the early sunlight trying to see through the ranks of Barrack 19A to his garden.

"Someone's stolen my vegetables," he said.

"Are you sure?" I replied. "You can't see from here."

"I can. I know. It doesn't look right. My tomatoes are gone."

"Too far away to be certain," I said, hoping he was wrong.

Seconds after parade was dismissed we ran over and looked with dismay. Everything edible was gone—even the green tomatoes, lettuce, green onions, beets. Everything. The little garden was trampled down. Farmer Markellie was furious. He stood for a while looking at the mess, then kneeled down and checked the footprints. "They're not Jerry boot prints, they're ours," he said vehemently. Standing up, he looked at the few people who had gathered to view the destruction. "I'll get the bastards if it's the last thing I do," and he marched off to the barrack, his head bowed in dismay. I followed him and sympathized. He kept repeating, "I'll get the bastards. I will, you know."

The word had already reached the barrack, and as we entered there were many sympathetic words, but Markellie wasn't to be consoled. Jock jumped up on his usual podium, Section 1 table, and informed everyone of the tragic event in Farmer Markellie's life. He finished with the hope that it was not anyone in our barrack. As Jock said, "If it was someone from here I think he'd better join the German army, because if he's found out, his chances of survival would be better on the Russian Front." There was a round of applause as Jock stepped down.

It was a foregone conclusion that unless one could stay up all night and watch, some thief would steal at least a tomato or two, but it wasn't expected that some person or persons would clean out the whole works. For a number of days we made a point of snooping around all the barracks in our compound, especially at evening meal time, to see if we could catch anyone eating fresh tomatoes or making a salad, but it was to no avail, although somewhere, someone knew and was covering up.

We never did find out who stole the produce but I'm sure the guilty person or persons spent some disquieting days thinking about their deed, especially when a very official-looking bulletin appeared in a prominent place in the Old Forty Holer.

I had watched Nabber and Markellie write the notice, composing on scraps of paper and occasionally exchanging notes for approval. They would say, "That's great," or "No, that wouldn't do," or laugh together over their notes. Eventually I asked what was going on and was invited to participate and use my Irish brain power to assist in finishing what they had started. With a number of revisions and much laughter, we finished the project and printed it on a large white piece of cardboard, then displayed it in the most prominent position in the best advertising area of Stalag.

> *The camp medical officer has issued a warning to all prisoners who have vegetable gardens close to cesspools to refrain from eating the produce grown in this area.*
>
> *It has been learned that cesspool liquids seeping through the type of soil we have in camp do, in conjunction with the soil, breed microbes known as terminoxites. These microbes accumulate and cling to the roots of vegetables and eat their way into the plant, but outwardly the vegetables show no signs of this infestation. The microbes are so minute that to the naked eye they are impossible to see. Tomatoes seem to be their first target. They lodge themselves between the skin and the tomatoes' pulpy mass, and if eaten*

they can cause disease that in humans is sometimes incurable. The incubation period is about two weeks.

Anyone who has eaten produce that is known to have come from a garden situated close to a cesspool should watch for the symptoms of:

1. *Unusual sweating with no strenuous activity involved;*
2. *A feverish feeling;*
3. *Eyelids feel heavy and sleep-like when you are not tired;*
4. *Shaking uncontrollably after drinking hot liquids;*
5. *Diarrhea;*
6. *Toenails and fingernails will stop growing.*

These are a few of the many symptoms of this disease, which is incurable if not attended to immediately. If you think you have any of the symptoms mentioned above, or anything else you feel is not normal, talk immediately to your Barrack Commander. He will report to the proper authorities and immediate arrangements will be made for a medical examination.

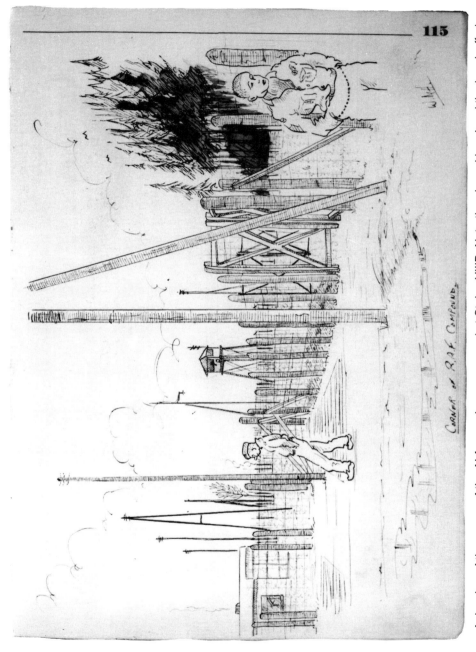

Corner of R.A.F. Compound

A drawing of the corner of the Airforce prison compound at Stalag VIIIB. Note the shaved head and the handcuffed and chained hands.

Prisoners seize the opportunity of a sudden rain storm to take a quick shower. Not quick enough, as it turned out: the "tap" went dry before the prisoners could get the soap washed off.

CHAPTER 11

Food for Thought

I lay on my bunk thinking of the many conflicting news reports and rumours that prevailed in camp this July of 1943. Rumours were rampant about all battle fronts. The German radio broadcasts early in July heralded the great summer offensive against the Russians in the Kursh area. Soon after this our underground BBC news flashes indicated otherwise.

Russia claimed to have destroyed many hundreds of German tanks and the *Luftwaffe* had lost its air superiority on the Eastern Front. Conflicting reports trickled into camp regarding this battle zone. Apparently the Russians had halted the German offensive and counter-attacked around mid-July, causing the Germans to retreat, or in some places, dig in. This was all good news to us as every mile the Russian Armies gained westward was a mile nearer to our prison camp. We looked eastward, hoping the Red Army would sweep back over Poland and so be our liberators.

Word that the German summer offensive had been crushed was encouraging. The camp was alive with news that a Second Front had been started by the Allies' landing in Sicily. American and British armour was now on European oil, so once again the Stalag morale had shot to its highest levels in many months.

From our secret radio came the information that Allied troops were well established in Sicily, and the names of Britain's General Montgomery and America's General Patton came to signify, to us, leaders who might break out from the south and so release us before the Russians could. This, of course, was a prisoner's fantasy. The high mountains and narrow passes of Northern Italy would be well defended. Looking at it logically, "Uncle Joe" was our only hope.

"I wonder how many dried raisins they're fermenting?" It was Nabber's voice that broke into my thoughts. Then, from beside me, Markellie said, "It's Old Nabber, talking in his sleep."

"I don't do stupid things like that, Farmer Markellie." Then Nabber continued, "For three months now we've donated the dried fruit from every parcel issue. When it's ready, if it's good stuff, my share should be enough at least to get a buzz on."

"I think he's having a nightmare," said Farmer Markellie again.

Nabber peered down at Markellie and me. "You guys must be still in the dark ages. Don't you know there's been a voluntary collection of dried fruit—no questions asked. It's being put down in a secret place to ferment, and when some very special occasion comes along, like Christmas, New Year's, or Liberation, there'll be a good strong brew to celebrate with. The guys who donate get a receipt and those receipts are your tickets when the time comes to consume the liquid. Hi! Paddy Mac, they're making potato champagne too. Why don't you get the Irish Spud Racketeers to donate?"

Nabber speech on the underground brew was suddenly interrupted by the voice from Anderson's bunk. "I'M GOING TO ESCAPE, YOU KNOW."

There was expectant silence as we waited for him to continue.

"I'M GOING TO ESCAPE, YOU KNOW," he repeated loud and clear.

"We heard you the first time Eddy," said Markellie.

"When is this great attempt going to take place?" questioned Nabber.

"You said 'attempt.' I don't ATTEMPT anything. I DO things. I'm getting myself a swap-over. I'll go out on a working party and steal a German pick or shovel, find the railway tracks going west and walk along those tracks to freedom. With a shovel on your shoulder, no one will ask any questions because they'll think you're a railroad worker." There was a moment of silence, then, "I was told that, you know."

"Sure, sure, Eddy boy," said Nabber. "A great idea, but what about the swap-over bit? You'd have to find someone with a shaved head, a stick-out beard, and a fondness for those knitted running shorts of yours. Might be hard to find."

"You're making fun of me, Giddens, and I don't like it," said Eddy.

"No! No! Eddy, I wouldn't make fun of you. I was just thinking of how I could help. What about the new guard on duty yesterday? Remember he took off his helmet to hide the cigarettes he'd bartered for the onions he brought? Did you notice his head was shaved? I forgot to tell you, everyone said he could pass for Eddy Anderson's brother." Nabber was really warming up to his leg pulling.

"Maybe, Eddy, you could convince that guard to grow a stick-out beard and change places with you. It would be easier for you to walk out of camp in a German uniform. Bet you could trade in his rifle for a really good shovel. I'm sure he'd enjoy being a swap-over for a while."

"Why don't you guys shut up? You're like a bunch of old ladies." It was Charlie Simpson, one of Markellie's muckers from four bunks away.

"We are planning Eddy Anderson's escape, Charlie. Have you got a spare shovel or pick? Maybe a crowbar would do. Would a crowbar do, Eddy boy?" Nabber was in a mood to tease, so we took Anderson's side to prevent things from escalating.

"Escape is not in your plan, Nabber. Your tinsmithing business is going too well, so why don't you leave Eddy alone? I'm sure his ideas are good." It was Markellie, pouring oil on troubled waters.

Nabber got the message and ceased antagonizing Anderson.

When morning came, Eddy had forgotten all about his escape plans and Nabber refrained from opening conversation on that touchy subject.

August slid lazily by. Prison life was bearable these beautiful summer days. Often we watched trainee fighter pilots from a nearby *Luftwaffe* station play tag with each other as they gunned their aircraft across the blue expanse above. Because they knew that Allied Air Force personnel were being held prisoner in the camp, there were several occasions when *Luftwaffe* pilots made low passes over our compound. One quiet afternoon as we sat in the dust, soaking up the sunshine, two of these aircraft thundered their way across the camp in close formation, almost at roof level, then soared away to chase around in the sky. The aerobatics show was good for a while. Many people shaded their eyes from the sun's glare to get a better view of this display.

Then one of those two pilots made an error in judgment. We watched in silence as the enemy training planes locked together. For a split second it seemed as though they were almost stationary. Then they plunged earthward. Thousands of prisoners stared skywards in disbelief. The silence was broken when someone shouted, "Get out, you silly bastards!"

In an almost-pleading tone, someone else said, "Come on, you guys. Bail out, you stupid jerks."

As the aircraft spiraled earthwards like metal lovers entwined in each others arms, time seemed to stand still. Although those pleading voices still called in a hushed whisper—"Come on, come on, come *on!*"— there was tension among those of us who had gone through a similar ordeal and survived. We knew from our own experiences and memories what would be going through the minds of these doomed *Luftwaffe* pilots.

No parachutes appeared in the sky—just two flying machines, and probably two very young pilots, almost at their destination. They disappeared behind a clump of trees. For seconds there was nothing. It seemed that a magical force had opened up the earth and swallowed them. Then from the crash site behind those trees a great black cloud of smoke rose up to meet the blue sky. A cheer from thousands of throats echoed throughout the compounds, with one exception—our Air Force compound.

At first, a number of Air Force personnel out on the parade square joined in the cheer . . . then realized that most of their aircrew comrades were not taking part in this celebration of joy over the death of two trainee *Luftwaffe* pilots.

Curious how there'd be exclamations of joy if an excited voice crackled over the intercom from the rear gun turret, "I got him! I got him! He's going down!" or how during a dog fight over England we'd cheer loudly when watching a Messerschmidt screaming to earth as a Spitfire did a victory roll. Somehow this was different. To cheer the crash we just witnessed didn't seem to fit any code of ethics. Somewhere there must be a special code for those who fly and often die in air battles, and yet another code applies to those who die in training.

The Burial of Enemies

When I was talking to a friend who had been a member of the Royal Air Force Women's Auxiliary in World War II, our conversation touched on the respect that sometimes shone like a bright star through the atrocities that were being enacted against civilians and uniformed combatants alike.

She told me of a German aircraft shot down near Portobello, Scotland, close to her station. Two crew did not survive the crash. My friend was witness to the burial of the dead enemy airmen. Many residents of this small village gathered in silence as two young men, the pride of absent German families, were lowered into graves. The burial service of these enemy flyers was interrupted by an aircraft of the German *Luftwaffe*. My friend and the villagers were astonished and frightened as the enemy aircraft flew in almost at roof-top level to the graveyard. Instead of gunfire or bombs, two wreaths were dropped. A salute to their dead comrades.

I was informed that this incident was reported on the German nightly propaganda news by the Englishman James Joyce, a.k.a. "Lord Haw Haw," who was tried as a traitor, after the war, and hanged.

But how did the German *Luftwaffe* know where and when their dead comrades would be buried? Even in wartime, channels of information somehow remain open and transmit secretly the information required to carry out such a mission.

"The Portobello incident was not an isolated occurence," I told my friend, remembering a funeral that took place in Stalag VIIIB.

Sergeant Pollard, a member of the Royal Air Force, died on January 20th, 1944 in the Stalag hospital. His burial was next day. Eighty-five Air Force prisoners attended. Considering conditions and, in some cases, the long years in captivity, the turnout was a credit to the high morale.

Sergeant Currie was in charge of the parade. Allotted ground adjoining the prison camp was used as the Stalag cemetery. There a solemn burial service took place.

The coffin was carried by six of Pollard's comrades and draped with the British flag. Preceding the pallbearers was the camp padre. When they passed, the eighty-five Air Force personnel followed and slow-marched to the burial place.

A short service took place, and as the coffin was lowered into German soil, the detail of prison camp guards fired a three-volley salute. Two wreaths were placed on the grave, one by a German soldier and the other by one of the dead man's friends. As we filed past and gave young Pollard our farewell salute, an aircraft from the German *Luftwaffe* base close to our prison camp circled overhead. The pilot of this aircraft then paid tribute to the dead airman by making a low pass over the burial scene.

Under guard we were marched back to our prison compound, and that evening I tried to rationalize the day's happenings at our Stalag graveyard and the rumours filtering in from Poland that special assignment troops of the German army were exterminating thousands of people—most of them Jewish—and burning the bodies. This afternoon, German authorities had shown great respect and helped bury Sergeant Pollard.

CHAPTER 12

Christmas, 1943 and a New Year

The thirty-day month of September passed quickly. Daylight hours diminished and the dark evenings of late fall and early winter crept closer, waiting for their cue. At each day's performance they stole another few precious minutes of light, until once again the world around us was enveloped in early darkness. In exchange for the blue sky and sunshine there was the piercing glare of searchlights and their endless trek across the compounds.

By our secret radio news bulletins we knew the Allies had landed on the Italian mainland at Salerno. With October knocking on those broken and cracked barrack windows, things were not all bad—the war was at least coming nearer to us.

The weeks in October were cool. Days of bright sunshine helped keep our spirits buoyant. This was the month for battening down the hatches—old man winter was not far away. We repaired broken windows with cardboard or any adaptable material.

The dark days ate their way through November. Outdoor activities were restricted by weather conditions, but Markellie, Nabber and myself continued our walking exercise.

November dragged itself to December's doorstep and the weather turned cold. Those dark, weary days slipped by. I'd had no mail from home since a windfall day in September when I'd received two letters from my parents and one (the third, in total) from Alice.

It was my first December as a prisoner of war, and because Christmas above all other holidays is a time of family togetherness, we needed to draw on any morale-boosting activity we could find. As the cruel cold days and nights crawled by, the 25th of December loomed close and morale rose, thanks to the attitudes of fellow prisoners who diligently made Christmas decorations from scraps of almost any material available. People delved into their rations, as I did, for something that could, by a little culinary ingenuity, be turned into a holiday special.

Christmas Day came and no shackles arrived. It was nice to be free officially, so already it looked like this was to be a happier day; at least our hands were free. The soup ration contained more vegetables than usual and numerous small pieces of meat floated here and there (no cows' eyes or dead rats). The bread ration was free of mould, the potatoes were all good, and there was an extra ration of liverwurst on the menu.

Zellbad did his magical bartering with those Germans in charge of heating supplies and came up with extra black market briquettes, and so on Christmas evening the air in our barrack room was like a London pea-soup fog. The old heater's oven was working overtime, tin stoves were stoked to capacity with all sorts of combustible materials, and because our broken windows had been repaired with cardboard and other materials, there were no outlets for the smoke. Rumours were rife that the secret "still" would give up some Christmas cheer, but that thought was squashed when Alec MacKinlay, Barrack Commander, announced that all those who held receipts from summer donations, were to hold them until New Year's Eve, as the "good brew" would definitely be available for that most important and happy time of year, when all good Scots and others would toast in the year that would see us set free—1944!

That day I bought a present for myself: I paid three hundred cigarettes to an army racketeer for a pair of almost-new boots, size 8, that I'd decided was a good investment.

Our German Kommandant also succumbed to the Christmas spirit. We had lights until midnight. The hundred-plus inmates of the 15A side of the barrack took to their bunks, many with transported thoughts of Christmas at home with their families. Our New Zealand tenor, Eric Johnson, sang a number of Christmas carols, finishing his renditions with the Lord's Prayer.

Next day, the chains and handcuffs returned, along with mouldy bread and rotten potatoes, plus "bird seed" soup, but good spirits prevailed.

The New Year of hope was about to be born. We prayed that Alec MacKinlay was correct in saying we would be toasting the Year of Freedom, 1944. New Year's Eve was like Christmas, with relaxed guards and extra rations and the majority of prisoners happy, or pretending to be.

The brew that had been fermenting in some secret place was just as secretly brought out for distribution to those who held receipts. Prison camp life and food had lowered resistance to many things, and alcohol was certainly one of them. There were dozens of inebriated prisoners in the area of 15A and 15B barracks, and many hangovers thereafter. A few minutes after midnight prisoners were exuberantly shaking hands, slapping backs and wishing each other "Happy New Year."

With its tragic memories, 1943 was now history, and back came my own thoughts of lost freedom. We knew what lay ahead if the war dragged on for another year. There would be those crawling days and weeks of 1944. There would be ice and snow, cold winds, rain, dark winter days, mud, spring and summer clouds, blue sky, heat, dust, fleas, lice, hunger, thirst, stench, fear, imagination, sleepless nights, mental illness—and always barbed wire, searchlights, guards, guard dogs, check parades, rumours, tunnels, escapes, Gestapo searches, death, Stalag funerals, hope, comradeship, learning, and the barrack we called Church. What we valued, of course, whether we openly acknowledged them or even understood them, were hope, comradeship, the barrack Church, and the learning experience.

Days passed slowly and changes began to show up in the attitudes of those in charge. The war in the east and in other areas was turning against the German forces. Prison camp guards were gradually being changed. The familiar faces were disappearing—transferred, we were told, to augment forces at the Russian Front. Our new contingent of guards were much older in years. The exception was that *Unteroffiziers* in charge of compounds remained in their positions, so we kept Ukraine Joe, and as my grandmother used to say, "The devil you know is better than the one you don't." So it was in this case.

We struggled through this time of bitter coldness without any tragedies. But in the third week of January, the door into our future opened just a chink: there was no Red Cross food parcel issue. Something had happened to the shipment; we received emergency bulk rations, a blow to hungry prisoners.

Jimmy Grier supped his emergency soup ration with no comment. Probably thought it was a new dish I had cooked. I believe he had lost track of what comprised a food parcel. The Irish Spud Racket had recently become a more nerve-wracking journey because of the new guards. Now, with the possibility of a trigger-happy soldier among those new guards, I breathed easier when my turn to make the Irish Potato Trail was over, but hunger made frightened men brave and the weak-spirited strong.

The days were miserable, with short food supplies making for short tempers and numerous arguments over rations. Muckers, who were always so congenial, now watched each other with suspicion. When Red Cross supplies arrived regularly, the German rations were an extra supplement, but now everyone was clamouring for whatever was edible.

"Wish we had some heat around here," Markellie said one day, as he returned from a walk. His morale was low and he kicked at the small pieces of ice and the tiny mound of snow that had fallen from his greatcoat and balaclava. We had no briquettes for the heater and no warmth, and ice had formed on the inside of the surviving windows. There was little activity this day.

On February second, the first anniversary of my near-miss with death, I spent a number of hungry hours lying on my bunk, staring above me at the criss-cross string pattern holding Eddy Anderson's straw mattress. Nabber, Farmer Markellie, Peter, and Big Jock all took turns at different times of the day to sit and chat with me. They were hungry and cold too, but the warmth of comradeship was always appreciated.

Then Toad Hughes came to see me.

"Hi, Paddy Mac," he began, "feel sick or something? I was here an hour ago and you were asleep." I didn't tell him that I'd been thinking back one year, not sleeping.

"Sorry, Toad, didn't realize you were here."

Looking a little mysterious he said, "I brought you something." He handed me two handkerchiefs, folded neatly to make a square. As I unfolded the material, I could see one was a plain white handkerchief placed over another that had a coloured picture drawn on it.

Toad spoke softly, "Thought you might like a souvenir. I know this night is a rotten anniversary for you to think about, but a few months ago you asked if I'd do one of my aircraft bombing scenes for you, something you might like to keep. I remembered the date you gave me was February 2, 1943, so I did this. Actually, I finished it a week ago but kept it until tonight. For you, Paddy."

I unfolded the two handkerchiefs and peeled back the plain one to reveal a coloured replica of our Lancaster going down in flames. Around the edges of the handkerchief were six crosses, each with the job insignia and name of the crew member. Above my own, the seventh name, a parachute and handcuffs replaced the cross. With considerable emotion, I thanked Toad for his thoughtful gift and beautiful workmanship.

"It was a pleasure to do it, Paddy." With that remark he was gone. I watched him go down the aisle and knew by the manner of his walk that he was proud of what he had done.

✈

April spelled spring and spring spelled summer, and summer was warmth and hope, but this spring was different from other years. Rumours were flying; everyone was certain 1944 must be the year of a great offensive in the West, the Second Front the world was waiting for.

Morale rose as summer took its rightful place in the seasons, and warmth saved many from the depths of despair. Those silver specks glinting in the sunlight at 30,000 feet became more frequent as American bombers increased their raids on Obersilesian industrial targets, and when we heard that Rome had been occupied by Allied Forces on June 4th, our morale was at an all-time high. We had to pay the price for those silver specks. Our Red Cross parcels did not get through because rail transportation was disrupted by the bombings, so the Irish Spud Racket became more important than ever. Those extra potatoes were worth the risk.

It was June 6th, just after midday 'soup up' when we received an important announcement. Barrack Commander MacKinlay looked excited when he called for quiet. He studied the text of a bulletin for a few seconds. Then, in his loud Scottish brogue, he read the news. "Allied Naval Forces, under the command of General Eisenhower, supported by strong air forces, began landing Allied armies this morning on the coast of France."

After the reading there erupted a celebration. A guard passing through looked startled at the sight of so many happy prisoners. I don't think he had heard the news, but soon those who could speak a little German were only too willing to tell him. He looked shaken and went away, wondering I'm sure, how these prisoners would know about such a thing, and I'm certain he must have been completely mesmerized when he found out it was true. Allied armies were back once again on French soil.

Soon a map of Western Europe appeared on the wall in our barrack. Nobody asked any questions about where it came from; it was just there. Little flags were next and were placed on the map at Normandy. As the secret radio blurted out the latest news of advances, the flags and pins were moved accordingly. After the first great furore, things became more normal and there was concern when two weeks passed and the Allied armies were not rushing across France. The little flags did not move far, and we received conflicting reports. German information told us the invasion forces had been halted and the Allies would soon be forced back into the sea.

After the first elated thoughts of quick freedom, reality took its place. Now it was a time of change, a time of fear. If the invasion of France failed, what would happen to us? Would we be doomed to a lifetime as prisoners working in Germany or the occupied countries? For the month of June the main topic was invasion, and in the dust, soaking up summer sun, we played at being generals. We drew battle lines in the dust and wondered why those generals did not think as we did.

Then came July. In the third week there was an unsuccessful attempt to kill Hitler; our invasion armies started to make progress; the Russians continued their advance on the Eastern Front; and we were issued Canadian Red Cross food parcels again. Each new day was a day of expectation, a day to say a prayer, a day to laugh at someone's joke, a day to go hungry, a day to look one of our guards in the eye and feel we knew him in another lifetime, when he was your friend. And oh, yes, a day to cry and a day to regain hope. A day to help a friend out of his despair, and a day when you wondered if there would ever be a time of freedom when you would look back and remember all of these days.

The atmosphere in prison camp changed moods many times. Our *Kommandant* was transferred to the Eastern Front and replaced by a strict disciplinarian. Gone were most of the familiar faces who had escaped the last big transfer, though *Unteroffizier* Joe Kussel and a couple of others were again lucky to keep their jobs.

There came a new challenge for us long-time resident prisoners of this camp. Early one morning, immediately after 7:00 a.m. roll call, there was a sudden influx of hundreds and eventually thousands of Allied prisoners newly captured, plus those from evacuated Italian prison camps. As the Allies fought their way up the boot of Italy, the Germans filled rail cattle cars with prisoners and shipped them north to German prison camps. With practically no food or water or sanitary facilities, they were taken like animals through the cold mountain passes.

When this mass of weary, dishevelled, unshaven, almost starving humanity was dumped on our doorstep, we set about to do what we could to help them. Our own rations were in short supply and we were hungry, but looking at this pitiful group of men, there was only one thing to do—share with them what we had.

Out came the tin mugs and plates, then the last few spoonfuls of coffee or packages of tea. From somewhere, wood appeared and numerous tin stoves came to life. Soon there was hot tea and coffee, slices of sour rye bread with jam, and the odd thin slice of bully beef. Jimmy Grier and I opened a reserve six-ounce can of rolled oats and made a dixie of porridge. I scraped out the last of a tin of Nestle's condensed milk and dropped the sweet, thick substance in the centre of the porridge. Jimmy had taken two of the thin slices of bread we were keeping for breakfast, spread with that questionable Prima margarine. Armed with a mug of hot tea, plus porridge and bread, we looked around the crowd of skinny, tired mankind and picked out a young, fair-haired soldier. His right shirt sleeve was gone, his arm encased in a dirty, bloody bandage. He was sitting at a table with head bowed and one hand covering his eyes. I carried the dixie with its steaming contents, followed by Jimmy Grier with the tea and bread. We approached the young man, then for a moment or two we stood beside him. He did not move. Oblivious to his surroundings, he was sobbing out his pent-up emotions of relief that at last he was now in some sort of an organized prison camp group and was still alive.

I touched him gently on the shoulder. Turning his head slowly he looked up at me as I held out the dixie of hot porridge and the tin spoon. Like an abused and frightened child, he said, "For me?" "Certainly," I said, "looks like you need nourishment."

With disbelief in his eyes, he accepted the porridge, tea, bread, and margarine. Within a couple of minutes he had downed it and was clasping the hot tin mug of tea as if his life depended on it. At that point he probably thought it did. Not until then did we introduce ourselves.

I looked around. It appeared all the 'old hands' were trying to help ease the memory of that dreadful journey. At each table sat new men with strained faces, while others relaxed, and I listened to unfamiliar voices. Curious how voices, like laughter, can be so different. We had got so used to the voices of those hundred plus men in our barrack that it was strange to hear voices with a new pitch.

Peter Chadwick and Big Jock Martin had made coffee and sandwiches from a can of Canadian salmon, and two British Army paratroopers were devouring the feast. One of them, smiling, said to Peter and Jock as he held up the half-full tin mug of coffee, "I think it's better than tea." I knew the salmon and bread was Peter and Big Jock's supper. They had nothing else and food parcel issue was three days away. I guessed we four were in the same boat. The porridge was supper for Jimmy and myself and the larder was empty, so now we would have to depend on German rations for three days. We also knew that everyone in the barrack was depleted to the bare necessities of life in regard to food, yet looking around, one would have thought there was a banquet in progress.

The next project was housing. A number of bottom storage areas were cleared and equipped with German-issue bedboards and straw palliasses. This change meant all new arrivals would sleep on the bottom.

A week passed and the new men quickly became part of the barrack community. Nabber Giddens was lucky, as his storage area was not disturbed, so all his pieces of tin and his unsold wares were left intact. In fact, our spaces were not involved at all in this new change. The floor bunks in our area were very dark and dusty. It was the same all down that wall side of the barrack.

The prisoners from Italian prison camps became a stream that eventually swelled the camp population to three times the builder's plans. Some estimates were as high as 30,000 men in the prison camp. Considering the camp was built to house 10,000 men, one can guess the crowded conditions. But as the old saying goes, "It's an ill wind that blows no one good." What a windfall those extra bodies were for the thousands of Stalag VIIIB fleas!

A drawing by Toad Hughes of his own escape from a Sterling aircraft.

BRITISH RED CROSS SOCIETY AND ORDER OF ST. JOHN

PERSONAL PARCELS CENTRE.

Sent to :

Service No. *1006039*   Rank *SERGEANT* .

Name   *McMAHON. JOHN. R.*

Prisoner of War No. *24468*   Red Cross Ref. No. *RAF/M/344.*

Camp Address   *, STALAG   VIII   B.*

CONTENTS   ¼ lb. Gift Chocolate added

No.	Item	No.	Item
1	BLANKET.	11	RAZER BLADES.
1 Suit	PYJAMAS.	1	SHAVING STICK.
2 Pair	SOCKS.	1	CARD OF WOOL.
1 Pair.	GLOVES.	1 LB	CHOCOLATE.
1 Pair.	GYM SHOES		
1	FACE CLOTH		
3	HANKERCHIEFS.		
1	NAIL BRUSH.		
1 Tin	BOOT POLISH.		
1 Tin	TOOTH PASTE		

11

[P.T.O.

An inventory of items I received from home.

CHAPTER 13

Countdown to Another Year

The camp was alive with rumours that German "plants" had come in with the prisoners from Italy. "Plants" were German intelligence personnel or Allied collaborators masquerading as new prisoners and usually associated themselves with those who had been captured a very short time before. Their job was to pump these prisoners for information. During that summer a dead body was found floating in the static water pool. The German guards came and took it away. There was no special roll call, no fuss, just the quiet disappearance of the body. No questions asked. The rumour mill said that the dead man was a "plant" whose cover had been blown.

Another strange story had it that some dismembered fingers had been found. But no prisoner had reported an accident or requested medical attention, so we assumed that the amputated fingers were the price paid for the life of another plant.

Around that time, as well, we lost Ukraine Joe, who was replaced by a miserable old *Unteroffizier* who took out his frustration on us kriegies. It was said that Joe went to the Russian front, where battle wounds cost him both his legs.

✈

September was almost over, and no more were personal parcels or letters arriving from home. The Germans fought on many fronts—east, west and south—and we felt certain that their defeat would come soon.

Then, in September, Hitler launched his new secret, the V2 rocket—a much faster and more accurate version of the V1, with a range of over 200 miles. With great gusto the propaganda loudspeakers in prison camp told us about this new unmanned secret weapon that would destroy city after city in England. The news dampened our hopes for a quick end to the war, but then our hidden radio came to the rescue. On September 15th we learned that the Allied armies had entered Germany. This information was confirmed and flags on our map were moved over southwestern borders and into Germany near the town of Aachen.

Each day the Russian armies marched closer, but they were still a long way off—and meeting stiff resistance. A consignment of Red Cross food parcels arrived in camp, and this joyful news spread quickly, but then an unheard-of thing happened. On September 16th, the German with authority over food distribution received an order: "All Red Cross food parcels in the stores must be distributed to the prisoners."

Mystified, we took our turn and lined up at the distribution window and received a whole month's rations of Red Cross food, every can with a hole in it. The rationale for this curious phenomenon was that if the Russian armies overran the prison camps, there would be no stock of food for them. But the Russians were probably 100 miles away. We guessed that order had been dictated at some headquarters and our panicky new jailers had taken it to mean immediate action. So here we were, with four weeks' Red Cross food that had to be eaten within a short time. We gorged ourselves for a week and passed up German rations. What a dilemma for hungry prisoners. Eat as much as you can now because there are hungry winter days coming. We had been lucky enough to have a Red Cross rail car get through with food parcels, now because of some stupidity at the administrative level, here was the whole consignment with a hole in each can.

The third week of September we ate and ate. We threw cans over to the Russian prisoners as they were marched along the path that skirted our outside perimeter wire on their way to work. They were a bedraggled, poorly-fed group of men, a pitiful sight. Some picked up a can or two, although other poor fellows who stooped to pick them up were beaten with rifle butts. Russia was not a member of the Geneva Convention, so there were no Red Cross food parcels for them. Starvation, work and death was the lot of these wretched prisoners. We heard stories that the prisoners killed and ate guard dogs that got too close.

Many of us got sick from overeating. Our stomachs had shrunk and it was difficult to refrain from gorging. The food was there. It was ours to eat. One prisoner drew a cartoon to depict the situation: a nude prisoner with a protruding stomach, scratching his head while he surveyed a stack of empty cans and three empty Red Cross food boxes. The caption read, "What a week."

Soon the big feast was over and so was September. Our stock of Red Cross food parcels gone, the outlook was bleak. Great expectations of a pre-Christmas liberation were beginning to fade.

As this new winter approached, our feelings had ingredients of fear and mixed emotions. Certainly there was elation at the thought of Allied armies approaching from both east and west, but depression and fear showed on many faces. The crunch was coming, along with the uncertainty of what would happen when the Russian armies overran this area. (We were certain that it would be the Russians, as they were the closest Allied forces.) Rumours had surfaced that the Germans were killing prisoners before liberation troops arrived, and we heard about the Russian scorched-earth policy—the practice ascribed to the Russian troops of destroying everything and everybody in their path and asking questions later.

Many prisoners prepared for a trek, convinced we would soon be forced to march somewhere, and this started questions in everyone's minds. "What sort of footwear have I got? Will it stand up to a long walk in winter?"

My good pair of boots were in a safe place under my bunk, wrapped in an old piece of green cloth. Thinking of the possibility of a long march, I fished them out, cleaned them once more, and wore them for a few hours.

Hunger was the main problem. As colder days came, the hunger pains grew more intense. We ate every scrap of German rations, even the smelly "fish cheese," a horrible fishy tasting substance the exact nature of which we never determined. There was ersatz jam and something called honey—an extract from coal. Anything that was available, we ate, but each night we went to bed hungry.

Friends who had laughed and joked, told wild stories, tried magic tricks or acrobatics, wrote wonderful poetry, sketched beautiful pictures or lewd drawings, were all very quiet now, with little or no ambition. Nabber and Markellie tried hard to be cheerful, and I did my best to make the meagre German rations last as long as possible. Jimmy Grier did not complain—he knew that the extra potato he got now and then came from the Irish Spud Racket.

October dragged by, and as we moved into November, hunger made the days seem darker and longer. No more did numerous tin cook stoves fill the barrack with smoke and strange aromas. No more did Nabber hammer out his tin plates or make those top-grade tin mugs he was so good at. No more did a jostling, bustling crowd of prisoners walk the circuit. But there were those who defied the general trend. Markellie, Nabber, and I continued our walks, and Peter Chadwick, Big Jock Martin and Bill "Taffy" McLean usually strode ahead or behind us. Our energies were depleted, and as those November days edged towards December, our pace grew slower. We didn't laugh much; we didn't jostle other walkers. We began to look tired. Our youthful faces lost their boyish brightness and showed the stress and fear we had covered up so well. Hunger, I think, more than anything else, can destroy, but hunger and fear together became formidable opponents. It was a very uncertain future, and even the buoyant and mischievous among us could not maintain morale. The bottom line flashed the same message: your future looks dark and foreboding.

One day guards appeared in each compound with picks and shovels. Investigating, we found them digging slit trenches. Russian planes had flown over the area a few nights earlier. The camp lights had been turned off and the searchlights stopped their continuous scanning. It seemed strange when this happened. We had become so used to being watched day and night that we felt almost uncomfortable to find ourselves with only the light from the moon and stars.

The slit trenches were dug, but we doubted there would be sufficient space for all of us if the necessity arose. We inspected the one allocated to our barrack and made dummy runs to it. Nabber, Markellie, and I could reach the slit trench and be down inside within one minute if we had a clear passage to the barrack exit. We agreed that if there was an air raid on the camp, then as soon as the sirens sounded we would dive out the window close to the bottom of my bed, because to make a speedy exit via the barrack doorway amid a hundred men would be foolhardy. We inspected the shutters and the windows to make sure they could be opened speedily. Other prisoners in close proximity had the same idea, but our bunks were nearest to the window, so we had an edge on all comers.

There were no joking remarks about this slit trench order. We believed it highly probable that Russian planes would attack the surrounding area. A mistake on their part could wipe out a considerable number of prisoners.

A week after completion of the slit trench, the camp air raid sirens sounded around 2:00 a.m. Eddy Anderson was first on the floor. He did not jump from his top bunk; he fell off in his haste to be first. His body crashed onto the small night table Markellie and I had made out of Red Cross cardboard and an oblong piece of black market wood that stretched the alley space to join his bunk with mine. We had pictures of our girlfriends, a few little Stalag-made trinkets, and a German desk calendar. Underneath, we kept our tin plates, mugs, spoons and a few other odds and ends. Now, in the dark of the barrack, almost immediately after the air raid sirens, came the unearthly crashing of Eddy Anderson's body landing on our treasured possessions. The wood splintered and the cardboard sides buckled so our tin plates and mugs scattered noisily. The night table collapsed and the splintered wood broke in such a way that it slid Anderson with great momentum as if coming off a slide, whooshing him under Markellie's bunk and in among Nabber's full stock of new tin plates, mugs and spare cans, tearing away, as he went, the only thing he could grab hold of—the green sackcloth curtain that surrounded Nabber's prized possessions and hid them from prying eyes. Now Anderson lay on his back among Nabber's scattered stock, still clutching part of the green sackcloth and yelling, "I think I'm badly hurt."

"Hope you die, you crazy goddamned Aussie," said Nabber.

I don't know which was loudest—the crashing of Nabber's scattered stock of tin utensils or the howls of Anderson that his bare ass was cut to shreds and must have 1,000 slivers. It was like a fox in a hen roost—no one knew exactly what had happened in the dark, and with the noise, the howling of Anderson, the swearing of Nabber and a few others, it seemed like the Russians had already dropped their bombs.

We were the last of that corner community to get out the window, dragging Anderson with us, wrapped in only a blanket and trying to put on the Stalag-made woollen shorts that held nothing in. Then we were outside, everyone else ahead of us or down in the slit trench, the sky above alight with flares dropped from Russian planes, Anderson yowling all the way to the slit trench that he was bleeding to death, and Nabber telling him, "Well, hurry up and die. Then I won't have to murder you."

There was no anti-aircraft fire and no bombs dropped. It was apparent that the Russians knew there were prison camps below. Huddled together in the cold trench, we waited half an hour until the all-clear sounded and we could return to our barracks. Being prepared for sudden events, Nabber, Markellie, and I each night placed our clothing ready for easy access in the dark. It was a cold night, so we had gone to bed wearing pants, shirts and socks. Anderson was in the nude and had no idea where his clothes were when he rolled off and out of his top bunk.

"Could have broken his bloody neck," remarked Markellie.

"Wish to hell he had," replied Nabber, "because one of these days I'm going to do it for him."

In the morning we surveyed the mess Anderson had caused. He made no comment as he picked slivers from his rear end. After check parade we cleaned up and saved the wood and cardboard, thinking that if we got a Red Cross issue soon, we could use it to brew up something, maybe a can of meat and vegetable soup.

With Russian reconnaissance planes overhead, and the Red Army still pushing westward, it appeared to us that the Russians were certain to be our liberators—and we were more than a little scared. Our secret radio was still receiving war news: On the western war zone, at the end of November, Hitler used his secret weapons, the V1 and V2 rockets, against the port city of Antwerp, which was occupied by Allied forces. The British 2nd Army was fighting on the west bank of the Maas River, near Blerick.

December arrived with cold winds and snow. I lay on my bunk thinking, another year almost gone, and in approximately eight weeks I'll have been a prisoner for two years, And here I am, lying on the same straw palliasse, looking up at the same dirty criss-cross string that holds up Eddy Anderson and his smelly straw palliasse.

I was depressed, hungry, and afraid; my morale was at low ebb. Rumours persisted that in concentration camps people were being exterminated, especially those of Jewish origin, and these rumours escalated into the fear that we were all to be executed before the Russians came. When I thought too much about this I felt an inward panic, so I went outside and joined Peter and Jock Martin 'walking the wire.' Their greeting was friendly but subdued in comparison to old times. We walked in silence for a few minutes, then discussed ways of surviving until and after the Russian army arrived. We tried to visualize the German armies falling back and retreating through our prison camp area. If we were not exterminated by them, we would for a time be in some sort of no man's land between those retreating forces and the advancing Red Army. We decided that the slit trenches would be the best place for protection. Big Jock got tired after four laps, so Peter and I continued for another two.

Peter was really concerned about his friend. "I hope we get Red Cross parcels soon, or we will all be in trouble. It's this damned cold weather that eats into your bones." Peter's voice was shaky and he shivered as a cold blast of Obersilesian winter wind caused us both to walk into it backwards for a few paces.

"Let's go inside," I suggested.

"Might be a good idea," he agreed.

From under my bottom bunk I took out the food box and found only three thin slices of sour rye bread, a small ration of ersatz jam, and two small cooked potatoes. I was surprised to feel a lump in my throat, and admonished myself, "You don't have to cry, Mac. There might be Red Cross food arriving tomorrow or the next day." As I looked dejectedly into the food box, my miserable thoughts were interrupted by a voice from above.

"We need Jesus Christ here. Maybe he could make those slices of bread and the two little potatoes feed the whole barrack. Didn't He feed a multitude with a few sardines and something else? I guess you could count all of us a multitude." I didn't look up.

"Sure, sure, Nabber," I said, "but Jesus Christ hasn't been shot down yet. And by the way, I don't think it was sardines. I believe it was five loaves and three small fish. Sardines are small, so if you didn't hit the correct answer, at least you staggered at it. Maybe they were sardines."

"Do you think we are going to make it, or will we starve to death before they shoot us?" I looked up at Nabber. His blue eyes had lost their spark. With an almost confidential tone in his voice, he said, "Paddy, I'm damned hungry all the time."

At our Section 11 table I waited for my mucker. I had the three slices of bread and broke one in two equal parts. The potatoes were almost of equal size, so on the bread I put one potato and equal portions of jam. My mucker returned from a walk and sat down at the table without taking off his wet army greatcoat. The white, clinging, ice-like pellets of frozen rain clung to the lapels and shoulders, but fell off as he ate. When he was finished, Jimmy licked his fingers and without a word left the table and moved quickly to his bunk.

Looking at the ceiling, it occurred to me that the air was clear—no smelly smoke swirling around up there, no cooking odours, and no one around me was jostling for the next turn on a tin stove. It was like an early Sunday morning in a small town, with empty streets and only an occasional human walking in a quiet world. Scanning the rest of the barrack, I saw humps of humanity curled up under thin blankets or lying on top, most of them clothed in outdoor garments.

I noticed Peter carrying two empty mugs on his way to the washroom. A brew of hot water was possible. I had not told Jimmy Grier there was enough loose tea from an English parcel to make a mug each. I divided the tea in equal portions and followed Peter's path to the washroom, where expectant prisoners waited, ready for the call. Five minutes later the shrill cry of "Brew's Up" echoed through the washroom and into the barrack area. It was a very subdued and tired looking bunch of Kriegies who lined up for a ration of almost-boiling water. My two mugs filled, I stirred the tea leaves with the handle of my Giddens' manufactured tin spoon, then made my way to Jimmy Grier's bunk and found him still looking up with wide eyes at the ceiling. It appeared he had not moved and I thought he looked like a corpse.

"Hi, mate," I said, "How would you like a nice cup of tea—real Darjeeling—grown on the bottom lush slopes of the Himalayan Mountains, rich in aroma and flavour, and best of all, picked by the hands of beautiful Indian maidens. It's now being served in the dining room."

Looking at me with quizzical eyes, he said, "Where did you get the tea?"

"Just told you," I jokingly replied, "It was a long trip from India; thought the old Lancaster wasn't going to make it."

"Listen, you crazy Ulster Protestant, I asked you a question. Where the hell did you get the tea?"

I could see that my mucker was almost at breaking point—with all his studying he must have been thinking about the learning he had absorbed over the last years in prison. And wondering if all of it was in vain. Was he going to die in Obersilesia from starvation, pneumonia, or some other disease as his resistance declined? Or was he going to be shot? We were all hungry and had no hope at the moment of being otherwise. We were all afraid. Most of us felt like blowing up at the least provocation. We all knew that after all these many months of survival, death could still be waiting for us around the corner. So I felt a surge of anger at this man I had looked after for nearly two years.

I handed him the mug of tea, saying, "Don't choke on those floating tea leaves. Remember, you and I made a North/South non-aggression pact when we became muckers. Your belligerent outburst just now was out of order. I should tell you to go to hell and get your own tea. By the way, I'm not crazy yet, but looking after you with your present attitude might send me crazy." I stopped for a moment. "And seeing you asked me in such a gentlemanly fashion, I will tell you where I got the tea. I kept those tea leaves for an emergency. I put them away inside my walking boots a long time ago, and the other day when I took my boots out to clean them, I found the tea. Actually, I'd forgotten about it. This was the first hot water brew for many days, so thought I'd take advantage of it. Now does that answer your curiosity? Enjoy it, Jimmy boy, because God knows when we will get another Red Cross parcel."

With that I turned and left my mucker to his own thoughts. As I walked away, he said, "I'm sorry, Mac."

For this propaganda picture, we were spruced up and marched outside Stalag VIIIB to the camp administration buildings. Top row, far right: Barrack Senior Man Alec MacKinlay; Second row, far left: Jimmy Grier; to Jimmy's right, and slightly behind him, Big Jock Martin; I am second from the right in the bottom row.

168

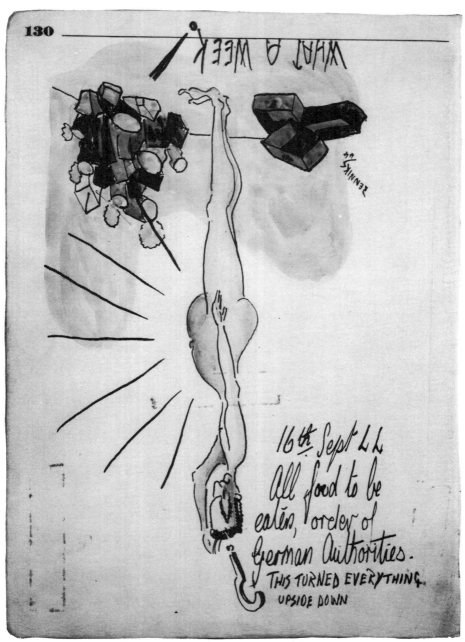

For two years, we were forced to throw a huge amount of energy into making the food last as long as possible. Then, suddenly, we were given a surplus and told to eat it all.

CHAPTER 14

The Year of Hope

I leaned against the wooden upright and looked at Nabber, who was sitting on the edge of his bunk, his long legs moving like he was riding a bicycle.

"What are you doing, Nabber? Your evening exercise to expend surplus energy?"

"I've been sitting for the last half hour trying to write a letter home just in case something happens—you know what I mean. It may never get out of camp in the ordinary Stalag mail system, for as my information goes, that's kaput. If anything bad happens to me, maybe somebody will find it and send it to Mom and Dad."

"You didn't answer my question. And you're still doing it—pedalling an invisible bicycle."

Nabber stopped his exercises. "As I said, I've been sitting here, half an hour on the edge of this bunk, and I must have cut off the blood circulation to my legs and feet. I'm trying to get the numbness out of my legs."

"Don't you think it would be sensible to come down and walk around? You're still sitting on the edge, you big dumb Kiwi!"

At that Nabber slowly and painfully scrambled down and walked to the barrack door and back three or four times until the pins and needles in his legs disappeared and the blood circulation returned to normal.

I finished my tea, and because the usual storage space had been wrecked by Anderson's fall the night the sirens sounded, I peeled back the old sacking surrounding the space under my bunk and set the mug on top of our old tin cook stove, then carefully let down the sacking to hide what possessions we had, which at this moment in time did not include anything to eat. I climbed onto my bunk and lay for a while thinking that perhaps I should also write letters, as Nabber had said, "just in case." Letters had been almost non-existent this last year.

Suddenly I sat up. Something had triggered an appalling thought in my mind. When I'd put my mug on top of the old cook stove, I had not seen my boots—the ones I had bought on the Stalag black market—the boots that could save my life if we had to walk, march, or run out of here in mid-winter! I told myself that they must be there. No one would steal them, only my good buddies knew I had them. For a few more seconds I sat there, the top of my head touching Anderson's sagging, dirty palliasse. It would be a great calamity if my boots were really gone.

I rocketed off the bunk and hastily peeled back the old sacking: there was the old tin stove, my tin mug, the empty food box, the remnants of our smashed night table, a pair of boots belonging to Eddy Anderson— along with a jumble of other belongings— but my new boots were gone! I was dumbfounded, too upset to say anything, until Nabber asked, "What to hell are you looking at, Paddy Mac? I've spoken to you three times and you haven't answered. Are you paralysed as well as deaf?"

"My boots are gone, Nabber!"

"Your bloody boots are on your feet, Paddy. Surely you're not going nuts too."

"No, Nabber, I'm not nuts nor deaf, but the new boots I bought on the market—the ones I paid all those cigarettes for. Remember I found some tea inside one when I pulled them out to clean them a few days ago? The boots, Nabber, the boots I was saving in case we have to get out of here and walk to freedom. You have an emergency pair too, and now I don't."

Nabber looked thoughtful. "Oh, yes, now I remember."

"Well, what will I do now? These ones I'm wearing won't take me very far. They are almost worn through."

Without answering, Nabber pulled back the curtain that he'd repaired after the Anderson episode and produced a pair of good looking boots. They were his own, purchased in the same way as I got mine and kept for the emergency everyone felt was now imminent.

"Mine are okay," Nabber remarked; then raised his voice so it carried a number of bunks. "Some rotten bastard stole Paddy Mac's boots and right now I wish we knew who it was. If I find anyone with his hands in my storage space or close to my possessions, I'll first break his wrists and then listen to him scream as I turn his cowardly body inside out. Someone from this here area did it and probably sold them for food. Only a few people knew there were a couple of pairs of decent boots in the corner. I'm not pointing my finger at any one of you, but Paddy Mac had taken his out the other day to check them, so it would appear to me that some guttersnipe saw those boots and decided to steal them."

Nabber eyed the five army prisoners who had recently come up from Italy. Then he continued. "I hope, I just hope that it was not one of our newest guests. You fellows don't know the penalty for thieving. You were not here when a man was sentenced to the cesspool dunking. That was in good weather. We'd probably have to break a hole in the crap to dunk any new thieves we find, and this time we might let him swim under there and break his own way out.

"If the thief is listening and has sold Paddy's boots, I hope his own boots are rotten and that sometime in the next few winter months they fall to pieces and he has to go barefoot in the snow." Nabber stopped his oratory, and then as if he had remembered something, he picked up his own well-cared-for emergency boots, held them up high and shouted, "These are mine! Doug Giddens is my name. Take a good look at me and my boots! Now any bastard who would like to try his hand at stealing Doug Giddens' boots, come and try it! I wish you would, because I'm mad at the rotten son of a bitch who would steal from another prisoner. I hope he's listening, because we are going to start an investigation. So, Thief, sleep well tonight, it might be your last."

With that parting shot, Nabber put his boots back in his storage area, replaced the old sacking curtain, and turned to me. "Rotten bunch of bastards, Paddy. I know damn fine it must be one of the new bunch. None of our fellows would take the chance, even if they thought about it."

After Nabber's great oration, I said, "Gee, Nabber, you didn't have to go way out like that just for me."

"Now what made you think I was lambasting those guys for you? Did you really think that you and your boots were so very important that I'd waste my precious energy in a long spiel like that for you? I did it for myself, I've been scared stiff for a long time that somebody might steal my getaway boots, so I thought I'd try to shut the gate on would-be thieves by terror tactics. Yes, terror tactics. I like that expression. Do you think, Paddy, I struck terror into the heart of whoever stole your boots?"

"You sure did, Nabber," I said, "you sure did."

Very pleased with himself, Nabber got back up to his top perch and continued with his just-in-case letter. In a few minutes he looked down and with a wan smile said, "I did that big spiel, Paddy, for you and for me."

I felt a kinship with this New Zealander, a bond of comradeship and trust that comes only through living close to someone under distressing circumstances where there is absolutely no privacy and no hope of privacy. Living so close, one gets to know his fellow prisoner almost as one knows himself. You can predict his moods, thoughts, reactions, fears, and a host of other emotions that arise when a number of men are imprisoned together with the knowledge that release may be years away, if ever. Now, with 1944 in its last days, each one of us struggled with the pangs of continuous hunger and strove to hide our fears of what was to come when a new calendar would say 1945 and death for some of us, we felt, was a certainty.

December produced a continuous stream of frightful hungry days, except for one unique happening. For some strange and unbelievable reason, a few personal parcels, along with mail from home, arrived in camp. I got a parcel that contained two hundred Players cigarettes, but no letters. Now I had a decision to make. Was I to buy extra food for Jimmy Grier and myself with my cigarettes? Should I give some of the smokes to my mucker so he could appease his nicotine pangs? I did not wrestle very long with this question. I decided my life was more important. At this moment in time there was something even more important than extra food. Through devious channels, I was able to buy, for my two hundred cigarettes, a pair of second-hand boots in good repair. With the starvation diet we were on, present prices had plummeted for nonedible items. Some prisoners still believed that there would never be a forced exodus from camp and were still gambling with their lives by divesting themselves of warm clothing and footwear in exchange for cigarettes or food.

I wore my new boots every day for a week. About the fourth day they began to feel comfortable. Probably it was closer to the end of the week before I had superimposed my own foot imprints and restructured the shape to suit my feet.

December passed the halfway mark. Our camp loudspeaker system blared out news that the German *Panzer* divisions and artillery units had started a big offensive on the Western Front and were pushing the Allies back in the Ardennes area of France. A great victory was soon to be announced.

Next day we had nothing for breakfast, so the ration of watery "bird seed" soup tasted good. When the bread ration arrived, Jimmy Grier and I decided to save ours for later. Everyone had little or nothing to eat, so no lunch time, supper time or snack time—just the time one could hold out without eating the last of his meagre daily rations. This day our total food supply was one-seventh of a loaf each of mouldy rye bread.

Shortly after one o'clock an army sergeant major, whom we knew worked with food distribution, was seen entering the wigwam to visit our Barrack Commander. Immediately, Alec MacKinlay (a gaunt looking specimen now), called for quiet and stood almost dejectedly for a moment before announcing, "If those people who usually pick up food parcels can find their way outside and walk to the Red Cross parcel distribution area, we will receive one food parcel between two men. Be careful of it. God only knows when you will get another one."

With that almost pathetic announcement, he disappeared into his cardboard-panelled wigwam and in a few minutes was dutifully standing at the doorway, dressed for the cold, wearing his usual little woollen cap. There was no great enthusiasm or pandemonium to line up for the parcels, just a weary bunch of young men who felt that a reprieve from starvation diet was here, but only as a postponement of the severe hunger to come. I tried to make that food parcel last two weeks instead of one, but even with the most stringent rules, it did not work. Two biscuits, the last survivors of that Canadian parcel's contents, were eaten a few days before December 25th, 1944—the hungry Christmas.

There was a cold stillness in the barrack room Christmas morning of 1944—a crispness in the air that probably would have been exhilarating if we'd had food in our stomachs, and of course with no cooking and little or no cigarette smoking, the clear air stayed that way. Morale was at an all-time low, and those damned propaganda messages rang loud and clear their triumphant news that American troops encircled at Bastogne by German armour were expected to surrender very quickly.

It was a shivering check parade by guards with unfamiliar faces. At some point in the past, as the weary months slipped by, we had made an unspoken truce with people like Ukraine Joe and a few other guards. Now the unpredictable mixture of old and very young guardians of our existence could not be trusted. You didn't dare step out of line or you might be disciplined with a rifle butt. Our wavering line of prisoners seemed to sway with each blast of icy wind.

The morning mint tea arrived. No more was it used as shaving water. Soup was dished out in the old rusty 16-ounce tin can used as a ladle. We were happy to get any variety of soup.

Nabber, Markellie, and I, and even Eddy Anderson, had this morning wished each other a Happy Christmas, but not for this year. The wish was for a Happy Christmas, 1945, one year from now.

The daylight hours of Christmas Day faded slowly into darkness. Jimmy Grier and I ate our bread ration together, spreading it with that curious-tasting margarine and washing it down with cold water. It was a sad Christmas, with little joy or hope, and only a smattering of goodwill.

As watches dragged their hands to that hour again, we slipped into our bunks, and Eric Johnston, the Kiwi tenor, sang the Lord's Prayer. I am certain many who never prayed before did so that night.

The days edged slowly towards New Year. It was a week of mixed emotions—so many things we had at one time taken for granted, but never would again, if we survived. We permitted our thoughts to linger around the festive season and what it meant and would mean again some day. We had given up on a few people who went about each day cloistered in their own thoughts, speaking to no one and refusing to answer if spoken to, so eventually and reluctantly they were left alone to wander aimlessly around the barrack or compound.

The morning of New Year's Eve dawned bright and cold with a clear sky of light blue, and as we tumbled out on check parade the crystal sparkles of frozen snow crackled and popped under our feet.

Another whole year had passed, and the silent cold whiteness outside had much in common with the unusual quietness that prevailed in the chilly barrack room. After the five o'clock parade I spent some time with Peter and Jock. Ten minutes before lights out, fully clothed, I wrapped the thin blankets around me and tried to sleep.

CHAPTER 15

A Terrible Venture

Two weeks into this new year of hope, 1945, we existed entirely on the meagre German daily rations. The only bright spot in our daily routine was the radio news. It was the "Ruskies," as we called them, who for better or for worse, would be here soon. News filtered into camp that the Russian armies, if their present impetus continued, would be here in a week. Morale picked up, but rumours persisted that the Germans were killing prisoners before retreating.

A strange thing happened during the second week of January. Bill "Taffy" McLean, Eddy Anderson, and a few others from different barracks were asked to pack their kits and go with the medical people as part of a prisoner exchange. It seemed to us late in the war for exchanges to be made, but apparently arrangements had been in the works for some time. Swiftly they left camp for some rendezvous and then on to Sweden or Switzerland. I asked Peter Chadwick, "Why Taffy Mac? His mental condition is okay."

"We know that, but his name was put on the list and recommended for repatriation by our Medical Officer." So Lucky Taffy Mac was going home the easy way. The rigours of prison camp had taken their toll.

In the third week in January, a large number of men from our Stalag working parties arrived back in camp from Poland. The Russian army was only a few miles from Poznan, and all men from work camps in the area were quickly being returned to Stalag. They told stories of Russian gun barrages that shattered the nerves of German soldiers, who in some places were retreating in complete chaos, and then corroborated stories of atrocities being committed by the retreating German forces. Concentration camp prisoners were being shot—even women and children did not escape. But with nearly 30,000 prisoners in this Stalag, if it happened here, some of us would get away. And if our guards tried to kill us, we could overwhelm them in quick time.

These stories created a hive of industry in the barrack. Now almost everyone was convinced we would have to make a run for it. The message was get out of prison camp if the guards start shooting—get out any way possible and hide until the Russians come.

There was a great deal of activity in the area of our bedspaces. Nabber and Markellie had their belongings strewn on the bunks. Markellie was trying to make an oversize bundle that he hoped to put a stout stick through and carry on his shoulder. Nabber said, "Hi, Markellie! Dick Whittington's carryall was about fifty times smaller than yours. I think you'll have trouble finding a monster cat to go with your big bundle of junk."

Markellie did not respond, but continued to pack odds and sods. I had the haversack we used for the Irish Spud Racket. It had been my turn to go when that channel of supply dried up. I packed a shirt, my extra pair of undershorts, a new pair of woollen socks from home, a razor and my wartime scrapbook, plus a number of pictures taken in prison camp by a Canadian who had a secret camera. I would be wearing my greatcoat, sweater, balaclava, and woollen gloves. Sewn inside the cuff of my greatcoat were the two handkerchiefs that Toad Hughes had presented to me, one of them with the wonderful coloured drawing of our aircraft being shot down.

Barrack Commander Alec MacKinlay interrupted our Stalag exit preparation with a request for everyone to come forward and listen. Alec looked like an old man. These last few distressing months had played havoc with him. He struggled to his table top podium and spoke quietly. "Well, fellows," he began, "the Russian armies are not too far away. We expect they will be in this area within a couple of days. We don't know what is happening; communications are poor. All we have is rumours, some not so good. But unless a battalion of German soldiers retreat this way and through the camp, I don't think we will have trouble from our guards.

"There is the possibility we will have to walk out of here to some place further west, so don't bank on being liberated by the Ruskies. I have information that tomorrow morning we are to take with us on check parade any small kit we wish to have and use on a march. So you are being forewarned. When parade is over tomorrow you will not be permitted to return to your barrack. It's hellish cold weather and I can't understand why they want to take us out on a hiking tour right now. We are 40,000 plus men, and once we move away from here, we'll be camping in sub zero temperatures. Make sure you wear the warmest clothing you have and the best footwear. I'm not giving orders or much advice; you are all free to make choices."

Jock took a deep breath and continued. "If you can find a safe way to stay behind and wait for the Russians, I say good luck to you. The rest of us will have to play it as it takes place. Remember this. Don't forget it. Fellows, all I'm asking is that you be ready tomorrow morning. When you leave your bunk, your bedspace, and this barrack for check parade, in all probability you will never see any of it again. Good luck to all of you. I hope you make it. I hope to Christ I do."

Alec stumbled down from his perch and into his little senior man's special corner. He looked sick, but now it was every man for himself, so I returned to my bedspace and prepared for the unknown.

I closed the Irish Spud Racket haversack and somehow I felt it held luck. Many times I, along with other participants delegated to brave the perils of that Irish Potato Trail returned safely, and so far all survived. It was a good omen, the haversack being in my possession.

Knowing someone was watching me as I pulled the straps tight and pushed the ends through the buckles to the correct holes, I looked up and met Nabber's serious gaze. Before he had time to say anything, I returned his look, and pointing to the haversack, said, "Don't want them to get out. I'll need them with me for luck."

Looking earnestly at Nabber, I said in a low voice, "They are in there you know. The Little People." Then I added, "How's your Killarney Lake ones? Are you taking them with you?"

Nabber looked startled for a moment, and I knew he was about to say something that would throw cold water on the belief in Little People. Then he grew very serious again, probably thinking about the "I believe, I believe" business.

He probably thought this was not the time to stop believing, so he pulled himself up to his full height and replied in an Irish brogue, "Sure and begorra, Paddy, I'm glad you mentioned it. The poor little critters have been sleeping inside my palliasse since the cold weather started, and I wouldna' want to go anywhere without them. I'm keeping this pocket of my greatcoat empty and that's where those Little People from

Killarney's Lakes will sleep tonight, and to be sure I won't forget them in the morning."

"That's good, that's good, Nabber," I said, with a chuckle. Markellie shook his head.

My new boots were on my feet, and tonight that's where they would stay. Our "sack time" attire would include socks, pants, shirt and air-crew sweater, so we'd be ready for any emergency and no one could steal boots or clothing. In some areas of the barrack there was panic regarding footwear. Those cynical souls who said that we would never leave the camp were now very upset because they had sold warm clothing for food, ignoring the warning, "Never sell your winter clothes. In summer you can sweat or take off warm clothing, but in winter you can die in light clothing."

I was ready for whatever tomorrow held in store. In a way, it was exciting. Here we were, Russian artillery fire now within earshot—and by morning it would be closer—and we were going out there into the unknown.

"Well, Nabber," I said, "guess we will see a fair bit of country on this hike."

"All we'll see is snow and ice, Paddy. It's snow and ice from here to the French coast. What we need is a toboggan."

There was no comment from the top bunk any more. It was empty. Eddy Anderson had gone home the easy way—repatriation.

We turned in early and as the three of us lay in our bunks, Markellie spoke his thoughts. "Did you guys hear the rumour that's going around?"

"What's that?" queried Nabber.

"They are going to take us out into the country and shoot us the same way they did with the fifty Air Force guys who escaped from Stalag *Luft* III."

There was no quick denial that this rumour was bunkum; no quick reply saying, "Don't be stupid, Markellie," only silence, because all of us were afraid that something terrible was going to happen. If we were caught on the roads, how could Russian flyers distinguish us from German soldiers? We could be bombed and strafed by their planes. We drifted off into troubled sleep with the dull sound of artillery fire in the distance.

Next morning there was no need for guards to scream *"Raus! Raus!"* Everyone, even Montrose, was up before 6:00 a.m., making last-minute preparations. Peter Chadwick and Big Jock, already dressed for cold weather, sauntered down the aisle to our bunk space.

Peter eyed the three of us grimly, "We came just to say good luck in case we get separated on the way to somewhere."

"Thanks, Peter. Thanks, Jock."

Nabber and Markellie were standing in the aisle, ready to go. Nabber had obtained a small German-type haversack from somewhere, and dressed for winter weather he looked prepared for a long march. Then another terrible thought struck me. Where would all those thousands of men from our prison camp sleep at night, out in the snow-covered countryside with temperatures down below zero?

Markellie was clad in so much warm clothing he could survive an ice age, but the bundle he had slung over his shoulder was so large he looked like Santa Claus prior to delivering his first parcel. It contained everything he had acquired since becoming a prisoner.

"I think you have a little too much," suggested Nabber. "You won't make it to Annahof Station, if that's where we are going, and it's only a few miles. Travel light is my motto, but if you want to carry your 'house' with you, good luck."

Conversation was cut off by the call, "Mint tea up."

Almost simultaneously came the calls, "Bread up" and "Soup up." At least we were going to have something in our stomachs before leaving camp.

Nabber, Markellie, and I were standing beside our bunks when the announcement was made. "All personnel must now leave the barrack and form up as usual in columns of fives for check. You will *not*, remember, you will *not* be returning to your barracks, so bring with you all the small kits you will need for a journey."

I took a last look at the space that had been mine for twenty-three months, with its old straw palliasse, the tin bookshelf Nabber had made for me, the German propaganda books and magazines I'd left. The empty frame that had held Alice's picture looked out of place hanging on the cracked wall (I had the picture in my battledress top left pocket). The little desk calendar I was leaving behind looked so lonely sitting there, with only propaganda books for company. It read January 21st, 1945.

I was looking up at the criss-cross string that once held up Eddy Anderson and his dirty palliasse, when Nabber spoke up. "Come on, Paddy. They are waiting for us. Let's go and find out what our future is."

As we marched out of our Air Force compound, I looked back at Barrack 15A. I had a strange foreboding that all was not well for us in the days ahead. In one way the barrack, with its one hundred plus inmates, was like a big family. It had been our home. And the comradeship, the feeling for each other, the confidences shared, even the odd tear, were somehow good things that were being left behind in there. They overshadowed the pain, the mental suffering, the breakdowns, the sickness and death that were all part of prison camp life. Now we were out here on this bitter cold January day marching with forty thousand other prisoners to some unknown destination. We would probably get mixed up, lose our comrades, our identity, and maybe our lives.

As the *crunch, crunch* of boots on the crisp layer of frozen snow became a steady beat, most men kept in step. With the day's food ration already in their stomachs, they were, for the moment, almost free from the pangs of hunger. Anything that was to happen to us as the day progressed was still too far in the future for us to see. So it was now that we were living. It was now that we were passing the Dieppe Compound. It was now we would pass the BEF Compound and out through the inner camp gates to where the German personnel were housed. It was now we had to help Toad Hughes to his feet after he had slipped on the icy surface. So our life in the foreseeable future would be measured only in what was happening to us now.

I had asked Jimmy Grier to stay close to me, as word had passed down the line at check time that all muckers were to stay together. He was marching in the column of five directly in front of me. As we continued down the hill towards the main gates, I again praised myself for having the foresight to obtain another pair of decent boots when my original spare ones were stolen. That brought another thought to my mind: somewhere in all the marching feet of forty thousand men would be at least one single pair of stolen size eight boots. Watching those five pairs of feet in front of me, I saw that with each step the white frozen snow clung to their boots only for a second or two before flying off amid the next stride.

Checking the condition of the footwear; only two out of the five pairs were in good shape—almost new. My mucker was one of those lucky people. The other three prisoners had footwear that was badly worn down at the heels and that indicated the soles could also be in tough shape. Looking down, I checked the four pairs of marching feet beside me and found them in good condition, with one exception. So out of these ten men, four were stepping out into the unknown Obersilesian winter with poor footwear. If this was an indication of the overall condition of footwear, there were going to be a hell of a lot of frostbitten feet.

At the main gate there was a jam up of prisoners from other compounds, all keeping their ranks but moving very slowly. The guards, who had placed themselves at intervals on each side of our column, now called for a halt. We could not see what the hold-up was, but knew there was much activity as the column ahead passed through the gates. As our contingent of Air Force prisoners neared the activity area, there was much chatter and excitement from those up front. Soon the words "Red Cross food parcels" were passed from man to man. Eventually, we reached the area and each of us was issued an unopened Red Cross food box, so the cans were not punctured. What a bonanza! Mine was English, but who wanted to be choosy at this moment? Here was food enough for a few days. No time was permitted for prisoners to organize this food. In fact we had not halted, but moved slowly as the parcels were handed out. Then it was march again, out through those massive double gates to the frozen road, the same road I had traversed two years ago with eleven other new incoming prisoners.

Thousands of feet had scattered and beaten the snow on this ice-covered road so that it had become a crust of frozen ice, and we stumbled rather than marched out into what once we would have called freedom. It took a careful, well-placed step each time to keep from slipping or falling on the treacherous surface. I tried to manipulate the Red Cross box of food to some comfortable position. Some had it tucked under their arms. Others, like myself, were carrying the box with both hands, holding it in front of them. The food boxes were not large. The exact measurements were 9½ inches by 12 inches and 5 inches deep, so what they held was not a feast, though to us it was life.

As I marched and slipped and slithered, I undid the rope around my middle and tied it around the food box. I shouted to Jimmy Grier in front, "Are you okay, Mucker?"

The wind caught his faint "yes" and whistled it past my ears in a flurry of snow as I watched him change his food box from one arm to the other. I knew that Nabber and Markellie were two ranks behind me, but looking backwards for even a few steps would be disaster. It was necessary to watch the person in front side-step the deepest ruts or see him slide on treacherous ice and then react accordingly. I guessed this method of navigation was being practised from the second column in line right down to the last. It was a stumbling, treacherous journey, and we hoped it would not be for long—perhaps only to Annahof railway station. Then, maybe, we'd get a train west.

The guards were all strange to us, and one of our German-speaking prisoners asked, "Where are we going?"

"To a camp further west and much safer for you."

As we slithered along, the Russian and German artillery slugged it out close enough to send shock waves through the ground. Soon we were flanked by fir trees that muffled the sounds of battle.

There was no turnoff to Annahof Station. There was no train, and if we were thinking rationally, we should have realized it would be so. How could and why would a beleaguered German army allow train transportation westwards for forty thousand prisoners? We were on the road and it appeared the ice-bound country roads would be our home. It began to snow again, not the soft, fluffy stuff, but the hard ice-pellet kind, and wind whipped it into our faces like multitudes of oversized grains of gritty sand. They were so cold that it felt like each one was equipped with a sharp little knife to pierce our skin.

I slung the roped food parcel around my neck, so it hung loosely in front of me. Jimmy Grier was changing his parcel from under one arm to the other every five minutes, but now I had both arms free. My little Irish Spud Racket haversack on my back and my Red Cross food box strung in front along with my dixie and tin mug. Taking off my Air Force cap, I put on the balaclava. It covered my head and face, and I said to the gritty snow, "Okay, do your worst; I've got my Irish protection now."

Undoing the clips on each side of the cap, I let down the side flaps, put it on top of the balaclava, and pulled down the chin strap, fastening it under my chin with one brass button. My feet were in good shape; my greatcoat and other clothing kept me warm; my face and head were enclosed in wool, except for my eyes, nose and mouth; my gloves had only one small hole in the right hand just at my first finger knuckle; and I had a number of days' food bouncing on my chest with every step. I was not in as good physical shape as prior to the starvation diet, but I felt equal in strength and endurance to anyone around me. If our destiny lay westward, we would walk, march, slide, or slither that way.

The afternoon wore on, but there came no respite for weary legs, tired feet, bruised knees, sprains or other hurts caused by falls on the icy road. A number of prisoners seemed to have collected the spare gear others had rejected, and those overloaded people were in trouble. They had been thinking of a train journey west for all of us; now they faced something different. We moved west, yes, but *away* from Annahof Railway Station. The grumble of complaining prisoners was like the low rumbling from the war front. The column of men wound along a narrow secondary road and stretched out in both directions as far as one could see. The sounds of many thousands of marching feet were muffled by the snow. Occasionally someone would take up the cry, "left, right, left, right." It was easier to walk in step if possible.

Daylight began to fade as we came to Neisse, almost twenty miles from Stalag VIIIB. The town was bustling with activity. The inhabitants were preparing to evacuate. Horse-drawn vehicles, including a variety of sleighs, carried household items, and all were heading west.

On the march over that first twenty miles of frozen road, we were given two ten-minute rest stops, and that provided the opportunity to divest of surplus gear. Most overloaded prisoners held tight to their bundles, thinking that perhaps Neisse would be an overnight stop, perhaps even in a German army barrack or camp. They were sadly disappointed. During the first rest stop, Jimmy Grier and I had opened his food parcel and divided the chocolate bar.

Daylight was almost gone when we dragged ourselves out of town and struggled into steeper country, where the temperature dropped considerably as darkness fell. The fine, gritty snow had stopped a long time ago, but the bitter wind whipped it up from the road surface and dashed it everywhere in swirling clouds. Soon the wind had swept clean long stretches of road, leaving only a glassy ice-encrusted surface as treacherous as an undulating skating rink. This was already becoming a hazardous journey, testing the willpower and physical strength of everyone. Cries for a rest period echoed down the line, but our guards said, "No, the Russians are behind us. Keep marching tonight. Tomorrow rest, maybe." Things got worse as darkness engulfed us. The road was like a sheet of glass. Prisoners slid, slipped, and fell, some gently, others with fearsome cracks. It became impossible to maintain a marching step.

As the hours passed the ranks dissembled, and in the cold darkness it was difficult to see where to take the next step. It was up hill and down again in undulating countryside. It was a test to see who—guards included— could stay on their feet the longest. When a prisoner fell, his mucker or friends would immediately jump to his assistance and get him back on his feet.

I called to Farmer Markellie, "How are you making out?"

"Okay, Paddy. Aren't you glad we walked the wire every night?"

"Sure am," I shouted back. "I'll talk to you next rest period."

"Okay, Paddy, if there is one."

We were hungry. We had food, but were not permitted to stop. "Hi! Mucker," I called to Jimmy Grier, "your parcel is not sealed. Can you get out the can of hard tack biscuits and the little can of cheese? I watched him take the box from under his left arm, hold it in front of him, and dig for the biscuits.

Then tragedy struck. Jimmy fell flat on his back, and our box of Red Cross food flew into the air as he fell. The spilling contents made little or no noise as they spread themselves out on the frozen road, to be kicked here and there by marching feet. Almost falling over my mucker as he lay on the icy road, I yelled, "Man down!" The cry was taken up by those immediately around him. The ranks behind divided like the Red Sea and marched around my fallen friend. If the warning cry was not given, the men behind, unaware that someone had fallen, would push onward and cause a pile-up.

I got Jimmy Grier to his feet, a little the worse for his crash landing. The food box was close by, but at least half its contents missing. Someone handed me the tin of jam. Nabber Giddens and Markellie stopped to help search for lost food, but after so many boot-clad feet had already passed, the search was useless. Anything on the road had been accidentally kicked away or picked up. Each minute, we fell further behind our companions. As the surging mass of prisoners passed around us, prisoners offered rebuffs: "Are you guys waiting for a bus?"

"Hey, who said you could have a rest?"

"Give Joe Stalin my regards, eh."

One of the guards quickly ended our search for missing cans. Unslinging his rifle, and with the swiftest action he could muster under the conditions, he hastened us onward. Jimmy Grier quickly pushed the half-empty Red Cross food carton into my hands and made off, pushing his way forward in search of his original position in his rank of five, which was now fifteen or twenty rows ahead. I now had another box to contend with, and my only alternative was to place it on top of the one I already had bouncing on my chest.

There was no way we could force through the ranks to our previous positions, especially with Markellie hauling his monstrous pack; but we did want to get back with our own crowd. I guess we felt more secure with the people we knew and had lived with for years.

More weary, frightening hours passed before a halt was called. During those hours, the call "Man down" rose often. Many men had sprained ankles, bruised knees, and other injuries from their falls. Others had no greatcoats, no gloves or mitts. At this rest period, men flung themselves on the cold, snowy ground and lay there exhausted. Others busied themselves with food parcels, dividing the easiest items to eat, like chocolate bars and hard tack biscuits.

Nabber, Markellie, and I made use of the rest time to catch up to our own ranks, where I found Jimmy Grier sitting beside the road, head down and chin in his hands. I knew we had only a couple of minutes left of the ten-minute rest.

Without a word, he struggled to his feet and held the box while I divided the biscuits and the four ounce can of cheese. Putting his rations in the box, I said, "You are in charge of what's left, so don't drop it again. We will take stock in daylight." I was about to eat my first biscuit when the guards started their *RAUS! RAUS!* and *MARSCH! MARSCH!*

We scrambled and slid into our proper ranks and marched throughout the night.

It was a short time after I'd finished my hard-tack biscuits that I heard Markellie curse. Daring to look back, I saw him dragging the Santa-like bundle along the icy road. Nabber Giddens grabbed one part of the bag and Kiwi Tim the other. Between the three of them, they trudged along until Markellie could unload and leave behind his overstock.

Dawn of the 22nd brought a little light, and just as little hope. Sure, the sound of gunfire had been left behind a long time ago, but the question remained in our minds: "How long can a man walk on starvation rations?—especially in these conditions."

Another winter day shed its miserable light over thousands of weary prisoners. Each man tried to show that he was in control of his emotions and that he was equal to the gruelling trek.

Stumbling and sliding in what seemed an endless upward path, we reached the summit of yet another hill. As usual, the road fell away on the other side in a spiral of treacherous ice and snow. Before commencing the descent I looked down at the twisting snakelike road we had traversed. The columns of prisoners quite literally stretched for miles. As far as the eye could see against the white expanse of winter, the long line of Air Force blue uniforms filled the narrow twisting road like some great blue serpent making its final wriggle.

Men now threw away everything that would not preserve life. The winter daylight showed roadsides strewn with discarded possessions. The night had taken its toll in discarded and lost possessions as prisoners fully realized that this was no boy scout walk to freedom—it was turning into a nightmare march that struck fear into the hearts of everyone. We'd had no hot food or drink since leaving Stalag, and only bits and pieces from the Red Cross food parcels, and a deep hunger now joined forces with the bitter weather. If only we could stop somewhere for an hour or two—some place away from the snapping wind, perhaps with a place to cook up some sort of a meal.

At the next ten-minute break I had to relieve my bowels, which I did along with hundreds of others in the snow by the roadside. A dozen or more German civilians—men and women who passed by in a horse-drawn wagon—jeered and shouted.

Just before noon we reached the outskirts of a town and what looked like a German military camp. The column headed through the main gates to a barrack square.

A cry passed down the line: "They're going to feed us!"

At the far end of the great parade square were five large containers, and beside each one was what we presumed to be German cookhouse staff waiting to serve us hot food. The column of fives marched towards those containers and were halted approximately twenty paces from them. Each man was to have his dixie ready. Five abreast we moved forward, one to each container. After receiving our ration we formed up again in our original ranks and proceeded to a lower parade square. It was good vegetable soup and hot—a life saver—an unexpected gift from our captors. With time only to consume our soup, the order came to march once again to the open road.

Jimmy Grier and I found our old positions with Nabber and Markellie a couple of ranks behind. We had made it clear, just as others had done, "This is our column—we belong here." A bond was perhaps unknowingly forming with our comrades in the two or three columns of five immediately in front of us and behind—a little marching community who depended on each other, at least for the present moment, for moral support, vocal encouragement, and physical help where necessary. In a sense we were oblivious to the multitude of struggling humanity around us. Taking care of ourselves and those in our little group was the ethic emerging this January 22nd afternoon.

The hot soup had lifted our morale. We assisted each other when necessary and shouted encouragement into the wind to those in front and behind. I maintained the outside position in my line of five and Jimmy Grier did likewise immediately in front of me. It became a habit to keep my eyes on the two brass buttons that held closed the slit at the bottom of his army greatcoat. With cold temperatures and the wind chill factor, my woollen balaclava was a Godsend. We struggled through the afternoon hours with the usual slipping, falling, getting up again, swearing at our guards or trudging silently along with our own thoughts. The terrain was the same—slide up, slide down. Now and again a cry for rest rose above the ranks, but our guards were adamant—keep marching. I think they were happy to be marching westward and away from the Russians. The sky had become ominously dark with snow an imminent possibility, and our fear was that we would be forced to continue this struggle for another night, which could be disastrous. We needed sleep.

As time passed, the chatter of voices became subdued; vocal encouragement and morale-boosting one-liners from spirited prisoners died away, and there was only the occasional cry of "man down" as some other poor tired body crashed to the icy road.

We were one little group of marchers, only four ranks of five, twenty men—a small drop in the ocean of 40,000 struggling prisoners, but we were sustained by a single thought, "Each step is a step westward and closer to freedom and home."

Late in the afternoon it began to snow. The darkened sky had held off for some time, almost as if it was waiting for us to take refuge somewhere, but eventually it permitted the first few million snowflakes to fall as a warning of what was to come. They were great large flakes, like so many paratroopers with white chutes. They fell slowly at first, but within a few minutes it was almost a white-out. I bowed my head into the curtain of white and watched Jimmy Grier's two brass buttons at the bottom of his greatcoat dance a jig with each step he took. Soon the icy road surface was covered in new white snow.

The column slowed to a crawl. Something was happening up front. At dusk we were halted and directed off the road and into a large farmyard with numerous buildings. The reason for the column having slowed was clear. The front of the column had been billeted in farm buildings. Now it was our turn. We were left standing for a long time, and gradually ranks began to break up as curious prisoners started to investigate.

I asked Jimmy Grier to open the remainder of his parcel to see what could be done regarding food. A few enterprising prisoners congregated in the centre of the square while others emerged from an open barn door carrying handfuls of straw. Soon a fire was going, fuelled by continuous armfuls of straw. Industriously, muckers filled dixies with snow, melting it over the burning straw. Soon another fire was burning. Unslinging my Red Cross box, I opened the cans of mixed vegetables and meat loaf. They fell out in frozen sixteen-ounce blocks.

Nabber knelt beside a few handfuls of straw he was trying to light with damp matches. He looked at me. "Isn't this one hell of a mess, Paddy?" In his dixie was a frozen replica of my mixed veggies.

"You'll need more straw," I ventured.

"Yea, I know. Markellie has gone to get it. Damn these Kraut matches!"

Suddenly, Nabber shouted with delight—his straw had ignited. Markellie arrived in time to feed the flames with more straw. Plunking two dixies in the middle of those flames, one with the frozen vegetables and the other filled with snow, Nabber exclaimed, "All I want is to melt the ice off those vegetables and brew hot snow for tea."

Those who originated the straw-burning fires had an assortment of canned Red Cross food heating and almost ready for a hot meal when suddenly loud cries came from their direction. A German *Unteroffizier* had suddenly gone on a rampage with his boots and a heavy stick. Wielding his stick and using his boots, he kicked over dixies of food, scattered fires and prisoners alike with his wooden club while he screamed, "No fires! No cooking! No stealing fodder."

Quickly we were housed. About fifty of us were relegated to a large empty stable. We bedded down on the stone floor, making ourselves as comfortable as possible. I broke the frozen vegetables and meat loaf in two and gave Jimmy Grier his share. The only light came from the open double doors where two lanterns were hanging.

Most of us were suffering exhaustion from almost thirty-six hours of treacherous hiking. Because of the winding trail we had followed away from the main roads, we were probably not more than fifty miles from our prison camp. We presumed that all main and secondary roads were being used to rush all possible military personnel to the front line.

After gathering a few bits of straw from the floor, I took off my boots and socks and extracted a pair of warm new socks from inside my shirt. It was a smart move to have saved the socks and stored them next to my body—they were warm and clean. I rubbed my cold feet. They were not wet, just a little damp from the long hours slugging through snow and ice. The boots had served me well. Others were not so lucky, and already there were complaints of foot problems. Pulling on the socks, I felt their magnificent warmth. The doors were closed and the lanterns taken away, so we were engulfed in blackness. I lay down with my greatcoat over me, my boots tied together by the laces, one boot on either side of my head, the laces running under the back of my neck. As a safety measure against theft, I also had one of the laces through the top button hole of my greatcoat.

Jimmy Grier had found a corner spot. A little short Canadian made a bed for himself in the manger close by, and he fitted perfectly. "Hi, shorty!" someone shouted, "Better get up early before they bring in the horses, or you'll be their breakfast."

My battledress jacket, as usual, was my pillow. For a little while I lay trying to pierce the complete blackness. I rubbed my hand across my stubbled face and wondered if there would be a possible chance to shave. Nabber and I had made a pact that we would shave every day. I tried to blank out other fearful thoughts, then I slipped off into sleep.

I awoke to a hubbub of activity. The stable doors were open. It was dark outside and the two lanterns appeared again. Stiff, sore and very cold, I quickly removed my socks and replaced them with what I now called my "day socks." They were no longer damp, having dried in the heat of my body. My boots were a different story, as the temperature in the stable, even with all the body heat, was cold enough to make my wet boots stiffen considerably during the night. I put them on. Getting my feet in was okay, but I had difficulty lacing the half-frozen footwear.

It was 6:30 a.m., and our guards were ready to march. The temperature outside was freezing cold as we struggled to form up in our old ranks. There was no sign of food. Prisoners were opening Red Cross tins and eating cold whatever was left. Nature's call was being attended to anywhere one could find a place. Soon the order came, "March in five minutes!"

As I hustled into line, I asked Nabber, "Where do we shave?"

"Some time today, Paddy, during a ten-minute rest period. Snow, German soap, and a razor. Okay?"

"Okay with me," I replied.

Then we were off again.

It was Archie Vickers, as usual the fountain of information, who told us that he had talked to Zellbad. Zellbad had talked to one of the guards. "Apparently we're going to a prison camp about 150 miles from here, and according to the guard, it's a bad camp. Zellbad and the Aussies are bailing out now. They say that hundreds of prisoners left the column that first night and are hiding in the woods until the Ruskies come."

"What do you mean, 'bad camp'?" I asked.

"Zellbad didn't say. Just that he wasn't taking any chances on how bad it might be. He'd prefer the risk of staying behind and hoping the Russians will recognize the Allied uniforms."

As we trudged along, this conversation did nothing to allay the fear of being taken to some place that would eventually be the death of us. We were more convinced than ever before by rumours that filtered through about extermination camps.

"Should we stay with the crowd?"

"Should we make a break for it and hide in the woods?"

"Should we hide close to the next village? Then we could scrounge or steal food."

"What's the Russian word for friend, or Allied Air Force, or British Army?"

"Better stay with the multitude."

And so it went on as we discussed the pros and cons of breaking away from the column.

This day was similar to the previous one—the same type of road, the same slipping and sliding up hill and down, the same nagging hunger pains, the same cries for rest, and the same fear of the hours and days ahead. The sky was clear and temperatures had plummeted. It was damned cold!

Eventually a halt was called and we rested. I was about to open my Red Cross box to see what food remained when Nabber said from behind me, "Where's your razor, Paddy Mac?"

I found my German safety razor, a stick of shaving soap, and my old beat-up shaving brush. "Have you a mirror?" I asked.

"Scrape the bloody snow off a patch of road and you'll have an ice mirror, you dumb Irishman."

I removed my balaclava, took a handful of snow, and rubbed it through my two-day beard. A few applications and the stubble was wet enough so that I could rub the shaving stick over it. The impossibility was getting a lather. It was a poor attempt at shaving, but eventually, and without a mirror, we were able to scrape away most of the stubble. We cupped snow in our hands and washed our faces.

"Feels good, Paddy," said Nabber, with a question in his eyes.

"Sure! Sure!" I replied with difficulty. "Feels great. Only thing is, my face is frozen."

"Move your mouth, Paddy. Sing an Irish song and everything will

191

work again." With that, Nabber set about finding something to eat, and so did I.

With the few minutes left, there was time to open a small can of oatmeal flakes from my English food parcel. Calling Jimmy Grier, I divided the four ounces of flakes as equally as possible. I took my share in a handkerchief and I gave my mucker his in the can. "Chew on these," I said, "a good Scott/Irish breakfast."

As we wended our way northwest, I chewed on my small portion of oatmeal flakes and thought that if I could get a drink of water, they would swell up in my stomach and kill the hunger pains.

Before we reached the prison camp at a place called Gorlitz, the Obersilesian winter took its toll. Each morning around 7:00 a.m. we marched, walked or stumbled along until approximately 4:00 p.m., when the guards started to count us off in fifties, hundreds or whatever number they thought could fit into designated barns and outbuildings in the immediate area. Sometimes we had to retrace our steps for a mile or two.

We were herded like so many sheep crammed into cold dark barns and farm sheds built for animals only. From late afternoon until 6:30 a.m. we tried, sometimes unsuccessfully, to maintain some sort of sanity and meet the basic survival needs of human beings. As these terrible days dragged by, there was one person who deserved great praise for his tenacity in trying to accomplish and tend to the needs of many. A little Scottish Medical Officer did a valiant job of walking up and down the ranks of weary men, giving verbal encouragement and assisting those who could not go on. Somehow he had acquired a horse-drawn wagon as a medical rest centre. He permitted the sickest and most weary prisoners to ride on it for a time at the back of our column. Half hour or an hour's rest on the wagon helped people to continue the journey and may possibly have saved their lives.

Art Scott had been a prisoner since Crete, and the years in camp had undermined his resistance. Art had a chill and coughed continuously and we were worried about him. During that long trek, a number of people disappeared. One day they were struggling along like the rest of us, and then suddenly their spaces in the ranks of five were vacant.

During those days we received the odd bread ration and dixie of soup, but nothing substantial that would give us strength or help to sustain it. I had to force my legs to take the next step. Uphill grades were becoming a nightmare.

Close to the town of Lauban, approximately twenty miles from Gorlitz, our column of weary prisoners moved at a pace of no more than two miles per hour, and the shout of "man down" became a constant repetitive cry. Those around the unfortunate fallen prisoner were themselves almost too weak to help him to his feet.

Jimmy Grier and I had finished the contents of our Red Cross parcels and all we had left was a couple of two-ounce packages of Maypole Red Label Tea, with a Christmas message on the label that read, GOOD CHEER AND GOOD LUCK FROM ALL IN THE HOMELAND and an additional plug that said OUR FAMOUS RED LABEL BLEND. At this particular moment, all we needed was good luck. We had no hot water to make a brew, and hungry as we were, I don't think we wanted to eat tea leaves--not just yet. We would keep them and hope for better days.

It was seven o'clock before we were bedded down that night, and in utter exhaustion I lay just as I was, somewhere close to the double doors. All night the bitter cold wind whistled through the large gap at the bottom of the doors. I awoke in the dark early hours—my feet felt like blocks of ice. It was the first time I had not taken off my boots, and had not continued with my ritual of changing socks and rubbing my feet with the ointment I had received in a personal parcel from home. My feet felt as though they were both in a concrete cast. I discovered that the low temperature and the bitter cold wind had caused the wet leather almost to solidify. I could not feel my feet! Quickly I set about beating the laces with my fist. When I had both boots and socks off, I went to work on my feet, kneading them until the feeling returned. I rubbed in a little of the green Zam-Buk ointment, put on my warm, dry socks, and decided to wear the good warm socks this once, since we were nearing our new prison camp.

Nabber Giddens, I knew, was close by, but in the pitch blackness I could see nothing. Someone was snoring next to me, so I curled up once again on the concrete floor. The next morning, the open doors would bring a blast of bitter wind into the warehouse. And so February 2, 1945 would begin.

On the evening of February 2, the second anniversary of my capture, we reached Gorlitz Prison Camp, an ominous, forbidding place. As hundreds of us stood in the dusk waiting for admission, I had visions of horror behind that tangle of barbed wire. Archie Vickers echoed my thoughts, "It's a bloody scary-looking place."

"Hope there's bunks in those barracks," said Bob Pierce.

"And bedboards and straw palliasses," added Vickers.

"Don't forget food," I said.

Another shivering hour passed before we received permission to enter those ominous gates. This place had a different atmosphere than our Stalag at Lamsdorf. The guards were different. Their faces and the set of their shoulders spoke of cruelty.

We crowded into a barrack and were at liberty to take whatever bunk we wished—first come, first served. All the lower bunks were already occupied. I chose a top one, but found to my consternation I had great difficulty pulling myself up. There were no straw palliasse—just the bare boards. I lay on my stomach, looking over the foot end of the bunk, and was concerned about my physical weakness. I saw Archie Vickers help Bob Pierce to a top bunk when Nabber's face popped up near me.

"How the hell can a guy get up here? Christ, these bunks must be higher than our old Stalag ones."

Relieved, strangely, that even this tough New Zealander had fallen to the rigours of the march, I said, "Just swing yourself up the way I did."

It took Nabber three attempts to make it, and when he looked at me he said, "I guess, Paddy, Old Giddy here is getting weak." He put out his hand and gripped mine in a handshake that spoke of many things—friendship, comradeship, fear, hope, and a string of unspoken thoughts: Please help; I need you; we need each other; I don't want to die now; I've had enough; I'm tired; will we make it? He was hurting my hand, he gripped so tight. Then he said, "Welcome to Gorlitz Winter Holiday Camp."

"It's a pleasure to be here," I joked, "What time do they serve dinner?"

"They will bring us menus very soon," he replied.

"Where is Farmer Markellie?" I asked.

Nabber grew serious. "Don't know. He couldn't keep up the pace this afternoon. He kept falling back. I tried for an hour to keep him with me, but he kept falling. I hope he made it. The last time I saw him he was six or seven ranks back. He had stopped on the road and was allowing everyone to pass him by."

"Maybe he got on the wagon," I volunteered.

"I hope so," replied Nabber, who was upset because he was unable to keep his friend mobile and was now remorseful that he had allowed him to fall back. But I could see that it wasn't that simple: like me, he had just now realized that his own stock of energy was depleted to a danger point.

Nabber and I talked for some time, and the conversation always reverted to wondering where our friend Markellie was. Later, an army sergeant called for quiet and announced that soup would be served in fifteen minutes.

With dixies ready, Nabber and I descended with great difficulty. I had to hold onto other bunks as we made our way toward the soup ration. How could I have walked all those treacherous miles today, fighting and winning against the elements, only to stumble weakly in the relative warmth of the camp. Perhaps it only was my stubbornness that had carried me through.

I looked Nabber's way and was about to ask him if he saw me having trouble keeping up the pace today, when suddenly he put his hand on my shoulder and leaned heavily as his step faltered. Realizing that he also felt weak, I grinned at him and said, "Steady up, old man. I thought we were both indestructible."

"The way I feel, Paddy, someone might have to pick me up."

We decided that hot soup and a night's rest would help us regain energy. We had reached our destination. Frightening as it was, it was still a sort of oasis in this snow-covered wilderness, and perhaps our bodies were turning off their energy output for a period of renewal. Instead of the buoyant spirits that had kept us going for two hundred miles, lethargy now set in, and our weary bones and starved bodies were taking their revenge.

The soup was watery but hot, and the majority of prisoners moved a little way from the line-up to immediately consume the warm liquid. As Nabber and I stood supping this renewal of hope from starvation, Peter, Big Jock and Archie Vickers joined us. The conversation centred around the prison camp—why were we here and for what? Half of the camp's barracks were empty. What happened to the inmates? Where do we go from here?

They wouldn't march us two hundred miles to get away from the Russians and then leave us here until the Red army advanced this far, so the consensus of opinion was we were going somewhere else--that this was only a brief rest stop and so we had better take advantage of it.

I found my mucker and realized he had survived this crazy march better than I had anticipated. We talked for a while, then he dismissed me with two words—"I'm tired"—and staggered towards his bunk.

I ate a bread ration, a little margarine, and a small portion of sausage, then turned in. There was considerable conversation, and I slept only for very short periods of time. People were huddled together, talking instead of sleeping. They were scared, unsure of what to do, and planning escape from the column, if and when we hit the road again. Quite a number were convinced that the column of marching men was not a safe place to be. When people got tired and stopped talking, silence did not reign, for there was continuous coughing. Many had really bad colds, and young Art Scott was in rough shape. He had trouble breathing and was wracked with coughing bouts.

The next day we had regular Stalag rations: one-seventh of a loaf of bread, three potatoes, soup and hot water. I used some of that Maypole Red Label Tea to make the first cup of tea in many days. I still had to hold on to walls and bunks to get around; I was weak, and I prayed that we would stay here long enough for me to regain strength.

In two days I felt equal to exploring the camp with Nabber. We discovered that it was not half empty, it was almost deserted. There were a few South African army personnel captured during the North Africa Campaign. They had been brought by train from another Stalag, and the camp was vacant of prisoners when they arrived.

It was a strange and eerie situation.

This sketch, made by Lee Kenyon of *Luft* III, captures something of the blinding cold through which a seemingly endless column of men marched day-by-day.

To all Prisoners of War!

The escape from prison camps is no longer a sport!

Germany has always kept to the Hague Convention and only punished recaptured prisoners of war with minor disciplinary punishment.

Germany will still maintain these principles of international law.

But England has besides fighting at the front in an honest manner instituted an illegal warfare in non combat zones in the form of gangster commandos, terror bandits and sabotage troops even up to the frontiers of Germany.

They say in a captured secret and confidential English military pamphlet,

THE HANDBOOK OF MODERN IRREGULAR WARFARE:

". . . the days when we could practise the rules of sportsmanship are over. For the time being, every soldier must be a potential gangster and must be prepared to ad...

"The sphere of operations should always include the enemy's own country, any occupied territory, and in certain circumstances, such neutral countries as he is using as a source of supply."

England has with these instructions opened up a non military form of gangster war!

Germany is determined to safeguard her homeland, and especially her war industry and provisional centres for the fighting fronts. Therefore it has become necessary to create strictly forbidden zones, called death zones, in which all unauthorised trespassers will be immediately shot on sight.

Escaping prisoners of war, entering such death zones, will certainly lose their lives. They are therefore in constant danger of being mistaken for enemy agents or sabotage groups.

Urgent warning is given against making future escapes!

In plain English: Stay in the camp where you will be safe! Breaking out of it is now a damned dangerous act.

The chances of preserving your life are almost nil!

All police and military guards have been given the most strict orders to shoot on sight all suspected persons.

Escaping from prison camps has ceased to be a sport!

Fifty officers had attempted escape from Stalag *Luft* III. After their recapture, they were taken to a wooded area and shot. We believed that the same thing could happen to us.

CHAPTER 16

On the Road Again

We stayed in Gorlitz six days—enough time to gain some strength. War news was now only rumour. There were no secret radio bulletins any more, but the South Africans told us that the German radio broadcasts had said the Russians were across the River Oder at Brieg and only thirty miles from the big city of Breslau.

With two days' ration of bread and cooked potatoes, we left Gorlitz on the fifth morning with new guards, who insisted we march, not straggle along. They were fresh and well armed, with haversacks bulging with their own rations. Behind the wire and machine gun posts of that eerie prison camp, we had to leave a very sick Art Scott, who was taken to the barrack relegated for use as a hospital. We hoped he would pull through.

We knew nothing of Farmer Markellie, and that disturbed Nabber, who was convinced he should have tried harder to help his friend. I reasoned with him that he'd done his best. The future would be survival of the fittest. Others were left behind at Gorlitz. They had various problems—frostbitten feet, broken limbs caused by falls on the ice-covered roads, a few cases of pneumonia, and a half dozen nervous breakdowns.

We marched southwest and listened to the crunch of frozen snow underfoot. We were a refreshed army of still-weary prisoners, but in a way we were happy to put distance between us and Gorlitz. We continued our forced march towards the Western Front, buoyant with hopes that our own Allied armies would liberate us if we continued westward.

As usual, padding along in front, was my mucker, Jimmy Grier, the two brass buttons at the bottom of his greatcoat glinting in the winter sunlight.

Days passed and we covered many weary miles with the same routine and the usual country-barn accommodation. One could not truthfully say we were marching. That was utterly impossible for people in our condition. Some days we covered no more than twelve miles, and it was apparent that the orders were simply to move us west.

We picked up the occasional bread ration but we did not stop to distribute it properly. The man on the outside was issued one loaf of bread to be divided among seven men. We were five to a rank, so two men from another rank had to be included, leaving three to be included in another rank of five, which would pass on only two shares. The odd man out usually suffered hunger.

The bread was usually hard and frozen. I watched people trying to divide the bread as the column passed them by. They sank to their knees and hammered the loaf against frozen ground, and guards used rifle butts to keep them moving. It was a ridiculous way to give out rations and meant that some men took double rations while other men starved. When one who had gone without asked for their ration, asking—sometimes with tears in their eyes—who had their ration, they often heard only the old British rebuff, "Bugger off mate, we don't have it." I was lucky to have four good friends in my line of five and Jimmy Grier in front to make six. We always found some poor soul who was odd man out with no ration. Usually we kept our bread until there was an opportunity to divide it equally.

It was the middle of February in a forested area, where trees laden with snow made a beautiful sight. We stopped for a rest period, and the echo of our voices resounded through the forest. Occasionally there would be a crack like a rifle shot as a branch overloaded with snow broke under its load and crashed to the ground. Our guards said we were about thirty or forty miles south of Dresden. Progress from Gorlitz had been slow.

We lucked out, one day, and billeted in a round stone building, almost like an old castle, which had a winding staircase to a lookout area. The date was February 13th, and Allied Air Forces were busy. The heavens were alive with pulsating aircraft engines, and from the north, towards Dresden, came the sounds of bombing. We were not permitted to watch, but our guards said the sky was red from fires.

Next morning was dull and overcast as we marched towards the town of Freiburg, and still we heard the drone of heavy bombing aircraft. We did not know then that in a way, by hearing those bombers this day and the previous night, we were by sound witnessing the most merciless bombing of an almost defenceless city crowded with refugees fleeing from the Russian armies. The old city of Dresden was destroyed by RAF Lancasters and other heavies, and now in daylight the American Air Force was unloading fire onto the decimated city. (According to some post-war reports casualties, mostly civilians, ran to 130,000, about 20,000 more than the first atomic bomb raid on Hiroshima.) We marched south of the city. We did not know it at the time, but we were lucky to be away from Dresden after the bombings. There may have been no mercy for men in Air Force blue if surviving citizens had known we were there.

This march to the Western Front was becoming one of hope, of fear, frustration, and pain. And it was being accomplished at the worst possible time—January and February. We trudged mostly through snow, ice, and sometimes break-up conditions, always hoping tomorrow would be better. Each day was now a test of physical and mental endurance, as every part of our exhausted systems cried out for rest and release from this awful daily punishment. There were many untold human interest stories—some tragic, others miraculous in their dedication to the spirit of comradeship. I wondered how, after my first two-hundred-mile trek to Gorlitz (where I had been unable to stand up without the support of a wall or bunk), I could be here days later with my comrades on another stage of this frightening and torturous trek across Germany.

Closer to the western fighting there was more air activity, and many times we took cover as British planes appeared overhead on reconnaissance, not bombing missions. Everyone hoped they knew what was going on and who we were. As we passed through one small town, the sirens shrilled an air raid warning. Quickly we took cover in a small shed behind a house. With us were four Australians and three resident plump white rabbits in a cage. The air raid did not materialize and soon we were back on the road in marching columns, all tidy in ranks of five. The Aussies were a number of ranks ahead of us, but their numbers had been augmented by three dead white rabbits. Those rabbits were somehow skinned, gutted and chewed on raw as the march continued. They risked the consequences of getting caught; we did not, so we remained hungry.

We had come to the third week in February, and my twenty-fourth birthday was two days away. For some time now the awful conditions had taken their toll; each day the ranks were depleted. Men just did not appear. They were either too weak or decided to make this place their last stand, for better, for worse, right where they were. Our guards had changed again and they were nervous. We passed through the towns of Jena and Weimer. Morale and hunger were at their worst when we reached a military camp that seemed devoid of personnel—only a few cookhouse staff waited to issue us hot soup, and a can of horse meat plus a loaf of bread between seven men. A real bonus for starving prisoners. We were given time to divide the meat and bread ration. Jimmy Grier and I consumed it right there, as did most of the others. The horse meat was salty and soon we grew thirsty. Often snow had quenched our thirst, but this time we needed water.

We skirted a large mound covered with branches of trees and earth and a number of German army helmets on top.

"A quick mass grave," suggested someone.

"Probably a column of German soldiers strafed by our planes," Nabber said.

"I agree. You're right. And there's about thirty helmets," answered an Australian.

"Nice conversation," interjected someone. "Hope they don't come back and think we're German soldiers."

A few minutes later a ten-minute rest was called, and to quench our awful thirst we requested from the nearest guard his permission to draw water from the stream that was running by the roadside. It looked clean and clear. The temperature was above freezing, so the stream had some momentum and the water looked good. We were permitted to quench our burning salty thirst.

It turned out to be a terrible day of slushy roads, and by afternoon, freezing rain and sleet. My feet were wet, as after all the hundreds of miles my good old boots were also beginning to feel the strain. This day we stopped early, around 2:00 p.m., outside a large warehouse on the outskirts of a small town, and were surprised to find that once again we were to be issued rations—supposedly for the next day. This was a very unusual occurrence and started rumours that Allied armies were very near and our captors were giving us extra rations in the hope that our physical condition would improve before the roles were reversed and they were taken prisoner. It was the usual loaf between seven men, and this time a ration of German sausage.

I had asked Jimmy Grier to get our sausage ration, and I would look after two bread rations.

Jimmy and I had a fallout. To appease his nicotine craving, he had bartered to four Australians almost all of our sausage ration for two cigarettes. Immediately I broke up the 'mucker' relationship. I told him to go join the 'Aussie' group.

I scrambled and slithered my way back to where Nabber was munching on rye bread and Kraut sausage. I said, "Did you forget that's tomorrow's ration you're eating?"

"There might not be a tomorrow, Paddy." That brought us all back to the reality of our situation. Thousands of men in columns and ranks of five marching closer to the war zone.

"I've got a strong hunch," said Nabber, "that tomorrow, or someday soon, there's going to be a dumb 'sprog' fighter pilot out on his first mission, and seeing all us jerks sprawled along a ribbon of road, he's going to strafe hell out of us and fly back to base expecting the Victoria Cross."

I explained to my buddies the situation regarding my mucker and they agreed I had made the right decision.

My thoughts turned to yesterday's march and today's, with so many faltering footsteps around me, and more men with tragic looks in their eyes as they stumbled out of the column. For hours they would try desperately at least to keep within sight of their pals, but would finally fall behind to disappear among the disoriented rabble of struggling humanity back down the line. It was like watching men drown. Our little medical officer, who had so often passed down the ranks with his remark, "Keep it up lads. Each step is a step closer to home," was missing.

We had not seen him for a couple of days, and although we had come hundreds of miles westward with those encouraging words ringing in our ears, there was now an overwhelming feeling of fear creeping into our thoughts. We knew the crunch was coming—the war, the fighting, the dying, were creeping closer to us and we would be enveloped in it before liberation.

The men who were still in fair physical condition were stepping out in the front ranks of their designated column and that's where the majority of my friends had been through this nightmare march. The first five ranks was always our goal. Our daily walks around the Stalag compound, our 100 yard dashes, our games of tag, our soccer and rugby games, our mental battle of wits with each other, had stood us well. But now as the days passed, each of us felt—but dared not say—that the time was coming, and coming fast, when it would be every man for himself. The ones who stayed on their feet the longest would survive.

We had already lost a fair number of friends. And there was still no news of Farmer Markellie.

We stopped early and lucked out with billets in a farm building with an upstairs loft-type room above a cow barn. It had a wooden floor and lots of straw, and it was warm. I slept deeply that night.

Next day, of course, we were on the road again in the cold. It was February twenty-third—my twenty-fourth birthday. I had a touch of diarrhea, which made for a difficult routine of stopping by the roadside and then struggling to catch up with my buddies again.

For two days I tried to satisfy nature's calls in a sanitary fashion, but a number of times I was too late. It was a depressing and disheartening situation. As the afternoon wore on, the temperature dropped and the cold seemed to pierce me through to the bone. That night we slept in a barn, where I managed to maintain my routine of changing socks and rubbing ointment into my feet. For days I carried on, drawing on some inner strength that kept me walking with my friends. After the interruptions that sent me on hasty trips to the roadside, I would always catch up and Big Jock would force a grin to his bearded face and say, "Paddy Mac, I admire your courage, I'm proud of you, my little friend." I would look at him and watch his faltering steps and wonder just how long his own reservoir of strength and courage would last.

The others spoke little now. They just plodded along with grim-looking faces covered with a number of weeks' growth of dirty stubbly beards. I had dysentery and my stamina was fast being depleted. It was probably caused by quenching my salty thirst with water from that stream a number of days back. I heard that some prisoners had seen the floating bodies of dead German soldiers in the water upstream from where we quenched our thirst.

Another evening. Another barn. Another night of fighting to keep our sanity until morning. It was my concern that I wouldn't make another day's march, but there was no alternative. I had to try.

I had no idea where my former mucker was. He did not show up in his rank the morning after the cigarette/sausage deal. Archie Vickers said he had joined the Australian combine.

I started out next day with willpower cranked up, but my energy bank refused to credit the account of motion, so with continuous stops for nature's frustrating disease, I was fast becoming one of those scared people who fell out of the ranks and then tried for many hours to keep my friends in sight, only to fail. I tried desperately to draw on energies that were no longer available. A couple of times I almost made it back to my buddies and Big Jock did his best to encourage me, but that was all he could do, for he was also using his own last dregs of willpower to keep himself mobile.

Dysentery had taken its toll over the last number of days. Now I stumbled along with strangers, jostled on each side by other men who were tripping and sliding, cursing and crying. This stream of prisoners was now nearing the end of another day's march. It was getting dark and I fully realized that for the first time on this nightmare journey, I had faltered all day. Gradually I had lost ground and lost my friends. Now I was with strangers, way back in this column of perhaps a thousand men, and I was scared. I was slipping fast and knew it—disappearing like the others into the rabble of struggling humanity who had lost all sense of discipline, but I said, "Paddy Mac, you're not going to disappear. You're not going to lose your sense of judgment. You're going to beat this thing. You're going home." The day wore on and I struggled to stay upright. I spoke to no one and no one spoke to me.

I spent a horrible night in a farmyard billet with no straw, no warmth, no rations, no sanity, and no discipline of any sort. It was a drafty barn, crammed full of sick and tired men, the majority of whom had lost all hope and will to survive. But even in a weakened state, a few had acquired an aggressiveness that may never have shown up in their normal makeup, but here in this stink hole of a dirty country barn they preyed on weaker fellow prisoners with forced exchanges of footwear, openly stealing meagre remains of bread and sausage, and forcibly moving someone from a space more sheltered from the cold wind that whistled through the cracks. I huddled up in a corner, skipped my nightly ritual of sock changing and foot massage, kept my boots laced tight and on my feet. From that dark corner I listened to the squabbles, the moans, the curses and cries of this small army of helpless men—proud men whose pride had been torn to pieces by circumstances beyond their control.

With fearful thoughts that I wouldn't make it, I struggled through the next two days. That flickering flame of self-preservation had not yet been extinguished, so my legs kept moving, and somehow, by the grace of God, I found myself, at the end of each day's march, someplace out of the elements. At times I would not have cared if it had been the frozen road—just somewhere to lay down my weary body. The days were hell and the nights worse, but I survived, and each morning I joined the ragged ranks of stumbling creatures, a number of us the pitiful remnants of what once were vibrant young Air Force flying crews . . . a thousand years ago, perhaps, on some other planet, for this one bore no relation to the one I had been a part of.

I asked an army corporal who was limping alongside of me, "What happened to the doc?" "Not sure," came a gruff reply. "Heard he stayed at one of the villages way back there. His legs refused to take that 'one more step nearer home.' Anyways, he couldn't do much for this God-damned lot."

CHAPTER 17

My Battle Lost

It was another horrible, slushy, wet day, and at the end of this terrible February afternoon, we were stumbling along as daylight began to fade. I thought it must be the last day of February—maybe the 26th—no, the 28th—or a new month. Someone fell in the dirty slush. The man behind me stumbled over him and they both just lay there while the column moved around them. Gone was the energy and the inclination to help.

The slippery roads had given way during daylight hours to break-up conditions. Rivulets of water made great gouges in the hard-packed snow, resulting in almost unbearable walking conditions. My boots were soaked and leaking, so I just squelched along in the wet mass of slush. Some men had frostbitten toes and many had bleeding feet. Looking around, I saw men with pieces of cloth wrapped around worn-out boots in a vain attempt at protection.

Now, with darkness falling, the temperature had dropped considerably. Wet rivulets no longer made gouges in the road bed; they had slowed down to almost freezing. Road conditions were becoming more horrible all the time, with frozen ruts everywhere. Men fell, slipped, slid, and swore at each other as they went. Close to me a big man hobbled along with no heel on one boot, and the other completely worn through at the toe. What was left of the sole and toe piece flopped open with every step, gobbling up water and pieces of ice to be squelched out again as he stumbled forward. He was crying like a baby: "I'm going to die. I'm going to die. I'll never see my little son." He had no greatcoat, just an Air Force blue sweater under the tunic that bore his faded pilot's wings and the distinguished flying ribbon underneath. Here was a war hero decorated by his country for bravery, broken by years in prison camp and now the hell of this march. The very same thoughts were beginning to hold in my own mind, "Will I die before liberation?"

It was almost dark and the wind chilled us to the bone. The wool balaclava around my face felt colder than usual, and as the temperature dipped, each breath exhaled its own little fog into the evening air.

I now answered nature's call whenever it came. With dysentery, and under these conditions, men just let things happen and walked in their own stench, hoping at least to stay on their feet and keep putting that one foot in front of the other until the nightmare ended. The spirit was willing, but the flesh was very weak. My "tank" of energy and stubbornness of will was running out, and the stark reality was that after hundreds of miles, I was close to the end. With each faltering step in the nightmare of these German country roads, I had to accept the fact that I was weakening fast.

After two years of surviving the rigours and mental strain of prison camp, it was ironic that a ration of salty horse meat became the original cause of my pitiful position. If only I hadn't eaten that ration. If only I hadn't drunk of that polluted brook. If, if, if—I knew I could have walked forever if dysentery had not come into the picture.

It was dark and oh so cold. I could see my own excrement clinging half frozen to the bottom of my greatcoat, and there was no wonderful wakening up to find this just a horrible nightmare.

A big chunk of the column in front of us had now been marched off the road and was being "billeted"—herded like cattle, more like—into two big barns. Three or four old fashioned storm lanterns, probably borrowed from the farmer, helped guide the men down a narrow lane to the barns. One of the guards had sat down in the snow beside our now-stationary column to light one of the lanterns. It seemed strange when he asked a prisoner to hold his rifle while he did so. He must have used five or six matches before several other prisoners gathered around to give protection from the wind. Finally he succeeded. Retrieving his rifle, he gestured his thanks and moved off down the lane to light up the billeting.

We had been standing for almost twenty minutes, shivering in the cold night wind, and hoping that there would be another barn close by for the rest of us, but this was not to be. I stood near the front of this remaining column of stumbling men. Two swinging lanterns appeared to dance towards us in the darkness. As the lights approached, we saw that a little fat corporal carried one of the lanterns and the *Unteroffizier* in charge of the whole column carried the other.

At the "*Marsch!*" command, we valiantly moved our stiff legs forward. It was a painful effort to get started again. We trudged dejectedly along for another couple of kilometres before the "*Halt!*" command stopped us. For another ten minutes we stood in the cold. Then we were segregated, marched through a big gate and along a short lane, and delivered into in a square of farmyard buildings. I found an old can and planned for its use.

There was "hushed" silence and expectation as we stood shivering in the farmyard. My teeth chattered. "Geezus, let's get in some bloody place so I can sleep!" This came from an Australian, a tall kid I'd seen in camp.

The corporal, still swinging his lantern, counted off the ranks. I reckoned there were ten or twelve rows of five men in front of me. I was on the outside, and as the German and his lantern passed by, he touched my arm and exclaimed, "*Zehn*," and on down the ranks—"*elf, zwölf, dreizehn, vierzehn*," each time touching the arm of the man on the outside. "*Fünfzehn, sechzehn, siebzehn*." I listened to his voice as it faded away and I tried to count even after I could no longer hear him.

"Wonder how many tonight," someone said.

"All depends on what size the barn is," replied a little Canadian.

"Oh, you're really smart, Charlie," replied the first speaker.

I didn't know any of these people, but it was good to hear *someone* banter like that.

Back trotted the corporal and his lantern.

"*Komm*," he shouted, and we followed the light across the farmyard, all struggling to stay on our feet. We stopped at the far end of a very large square and entered a barn through double doors that were painted red. It was pitch black inside—the light from the corporal's lantern at the doorway shed its yellow glow only a few feet inside.

Someone said, "Hi, guys, there's straw in here!" The wooden floor had straw, at least covering the entrance where the lantern's light was shining.

If there was straw elsewhere in the barn, it was a sort of bonus night. We had slept on concrete floors, dirt floors, dry wood floors, wet wood floors. We had slept huddled together for warmth, arms around each other like little children. We had snoozed standing up when too many people had been crushed into a small barn. Straw was a bonus.

Before our guards closed the doors and left us to complete darkness, I gathered straw from the floor—in fact, there was enough around to make a sort of mattress. This done, I began my nightly ritual of sock changing. Having made the bed of straw deep enough, I inserted my trusty tin can in a hole I'd made in the "mattress," undid my pants and slid them down to my ankles, then lay backwards in the straw with my rear firmly in the can. With my greatcoat over me, I spent the shivering dark night that way. I'd come to the point of exhaustion. With the knowledge that I'd survived all this way, and was close to the western battle front and liberation by the Allies, I was running out of the necessary energy to make it much farther.

It was a night to forget. In the pitch blackness, other stinking men spewed their urine and excrement around and on me. We were a mass of hopeless humanity, almost all at the end of a nightmare journey. The end might be liberation and a hospital. Or it might be something else: we could be mistaken for the enemy and killed by our own would-be liberators. And any one of us might fall down on the road, unable to get up, and die of exposure and malnutrition.

It was still dark when the barn doors were opened. I pulled on my waning strength to get up and out of the stinking hell hole. I fastened my pants and left the tin in the hay and staggered to my feet. Realizing I was still wearing my dry socks, I slid down the wooden partition that divided this part of the barn. I sat with my back resting against the divider and untied my boots, which were attached to my wrist by the laces—now a must against theft.

My socks were wet and ice-cold, and the boots were not much better, but this morning at least I was able to lace them up. Laces tied, dry socks warming next to my skin for tonight, I staggered out to clean air.

Standing there, we looked like a herd of neglected cattle. All traces of human values were gone. I knew that Peter, Big Jock, Nabber, and the others must be far in front. The guards tried to keep us in some semblance of marching ranks. I didn't know the person stumbling along beside me, nor did I care that he was babbling away, talking to himself, and had only one whole boot—that the other's gaping sides were stuffed with straw from the barn, tied and wrapped with an old cloth. I knew it wouldn't work. The cloth and straw would soak up the water like a sponge when the frozen road surface thawed, but perhaps he had prayed to his god or to whoever or whatever he believed in and asked that the temperature stay low, and for his sake, the roads remain hard frozen. If his prayers were not answered, he would walk in slush and water again, and he would go slopping along until he fell down from sheer exhaustion. If he stayed on his feet, he might suffer frostbite when the temperature dipped once again.

It seemed like days ago that we passed through the town of Weimar. The sky was alive with the drone of aircraft engines. I thought that maybe this was not a good thing, remembering Nabber's words about 'sprog' pilots and first missions. There was a bread ration and more sausage, and I ate all of it at once. Today I knew it would be a miracle if I finished the allotted span of miles. I had already fallen twice and lain in the wet slush, watching for a time all those pitifully clad feet scramble and slide around me. The second time down I wanted to stay down. I had no energy left to drag myself up. Feet splashed ice and slush over me as I lay on my back, and I thought, "Will this ugly parade above me never end?" How many hundred, how many thousand more were behind these stragglers? They could go on forever. I could be buried in sloppy slush if I stayed there. Someone tripped over me and fell, got up and took time to bombard me with every swear word he knew. I struggled to my knees, then two strangers jerked me to my feet as they passed. Once again I laboured along with the mass.

Thawing ice on the roads created more ruts that seemed to me like miniature mountains. I staggered along for a while in the middle of a jumble of men pushing and swearing at each other as we tried to negotiate the rivulets and uneven icy surface. For some time I continued without remembering a thing, then came back to reality to find myself stumbling along with different prisoners. There was no Air Force blue anywhere. They were all wearing army uniforms—a mixture of regiments. How did I get with these people? My heart beat like a runner's, and I was aware of passing out somewhere and then somehow joining up with this column. When and how long ago this had happened was a mystery to me. My watch had been lost a long time ago, but I knew it must be well into afternoon. These people were stragglers from numerous columns, and like myself, unable to make the grade—a collection of those prisoners who were doubtful finishers.

A halt was called—a ten minute rest—but I had no rations to eat, no mucker to look after, no Nabber Giddens or Peter Chadwick or Big Jock to talk to. A ragged-looking army private stood nearby, and I asked, "Do you know what time it is?"

"Who knows?" he answered, "and who cares? It's bloody near time somebody got here before it's too late. Why don't some of your "fly boys" drop a load of paratroopers to liberate us, or better still, a plane-load of food? The time, you ask. It must be after two o'clock. It'll be dark in three hours." The command "March!" cut short any further conversation.

With dysentery continuing to play havoc with my innards, I tried to carry on, but spells of dizziness caused me to move out from the column. I tried walking by myself beside the moving, swaying line of prisoners. I knew if I fell down once more, to get up again by myself would be almost impossible. I also realized that in a few short hours it would be dark. Into my fogged brain the message kept repeating itself, "Stay on your feet. Pass out in the dark and no one will know. You will freeze to death before morning." So at this crucial moment in my walk for life, four words hammered in my brain—KEEP ON YOUR FEET, KEEP ON YOUR FEET.

Another hour passed and I noticed our guards were now sparsely allocated along the road. I could see only two in this area. I slipped and fell to my knees a number of times, but struggled to my feet and carried on. Soon the temperature changed and there was a cold stillness that spelled winter. It felt, and looked, by the darkening sky, like late afternoon was close.

The column of prisoners had thinned out. Looking back, I was shocked to see the end of the column, and behind it an empty rutted frozen road. I thought they must have divided the column and diverted the mass of stragglers in another direction, because all of them could not have passed me by, I thought.

Turning my face into a new chilling wind that had joined the day, I tried desperately to reach the summit of a small hill, and was surprised to see that the column of prisoners were making better progress than me. That shouldn't be, according to my thinking, because they were all stragglers, but they were passing me by, and yet I was moving my legs, putting my feet out in front of me in the proper manner that I knew— or did I only think I was making my other leg pass its mate and carry my foot in a forward step? Those were the instructions my brain was putting out, but somehow I felt my legs were not responding properly, because the crest of the hill seemed to be further away than when I started five minutes ago, or was it ten or fifteen?

Now the column of prisoners seemed to be moving faster than before, and somehow I had got turned around, facing down the hill again.

Something was wrong. Once again I sternly rebuked my rebellious legs and feet. My one and only aim was to get to the top and look down the other side. Resetting my course for up the hill, I said to myself, "Paddy Mac, if you accomplish this, I'm sure you can then catch up with Nabber, Peter and Big Jock, for I bet there's a long downhill for miles on the other side, and you'll be able to run down to meet with your pals." Feeding this message into my foggy brain, I was certain it got through, because I started to sing, I thought, loud and clear, "The top of the hill, the top of the hill."

A guard was telling me, "*Schnell! Schnell! Schnell!*" but my legs wouldn't work. He said something in German about night-time coming. I knew that without him reminding me. It was the reason I wanted to get to the top of the hill. He gave me a gentle enough push to assist me in take off once again, but I walked only half a dozen paces before my legs gave out again—although I kept feeding them that same message, "The top of the hill, the top of the hill." The guard was now in front of me and striding quickly away up the hill. He turned as I looked up, and with his hand he waved a signal of disgust. And then he was gone over the crest of the hill. I looked around to see how the other stragglers were doing. The road was empty. They had all disappeared over the brow of the hill.

In desperation, I tried once again. I must get to the top of that hill. It was my only hope of survival. I tried to will all my remaining strength to move uphill. I kept turning around, facing the wrong way, and as I looked back along the road I had travelled, it turned and twisted away and over a small bridge, then behind snow-laden trees, reappeared for a short distance, then once again disappeared into a clump of pine trees. The road sparkled like a new mirror, and even the ruts seemed to reflect magic light from the new cold of this afternoon.

I could see all this very clearly, so why was it that my eyes played tricks on me and my thinking went foggy? Why could I not keep up with the stragglers? Why did I keep facing down the hill when I wished to continue going up? Why was I making no progress—losing ground, in fact? I must be staggering around in circles. No! Paddy Mac wouldn't do a stupid thing like that! I MUST GET UP THAT HILL!

Pulling on all my remaining resources, as well as the fear of being left to die alone in the freezing cold, I turned once again to the hill. I knew that this might be my last chance to reach the top.

With slow, weak steps, I gradually made progress. I wheeled a few times, then corrected my error, straightened out, and again set course for the top. I felt lonely on the hill, with the dark clouds above, the frozen, rutted road at my feet, and the great silent expanse of freezing enemy country around me. And the great fear in my heart was that it was here everything would end. My two-year battle for sanity and survival, the many hundreds of criss-cross miles trekking across Germany—only to come so close to the Allied armies and liberation and die here on this lonely freezing hillside.

About halfway up, things started to go wrong. I floated off some-where and my thinking began to fog, but I snapped out of it to find myself knee deep in snow by the side of the road, again facing the wrong way—downhill. Great gusts of frigid air whipped loose snow in all directions. The finer snow seemed to scurry along the road's deep ruts, trying to find a place to hide from the chasing wind, and I felt kin-ship with it and hoped it would win the race. I called myself stupid and tried to turn around to attack the hill again, but my legs refused. As I looked to check on the fleeing snow, the road appeared to move, and things around me began to change—the white snow, the dirty snow, the ruts, the ice, the sad trees, and my hill to freedom all merged into one great whirlpool. I fell into it.

I had lost the battle, but that was no shame.

I had fought with the tenacity of a true Irish spirit.

I had asked for strength and willpower when there wasn't any left—and got some.

From my tired, frozen feet and legs I had demanded more miles—and got them.

I had pushed my muscles beyond all normal endurance—and still they had worked.

I gave no quarter and asked for none—they gave me all they had.

I asked my heart to pump more life-giving blood and oxygen throughout my tired body—and it did.

I had suppressed my own fears and flaunted my hopes—it helped many friends.

To the best of my ability I had helped the morale of fellow prisoners when their strength, willpower, and mental capabilities broke down—and I had my rewards.

I had watched stalwarts of physical height and strength cry like ba-bies, falter, and disappear on the march—and I could do nothing.

While still on my feet I would never surrender to the elements or anything else. I WAS GOING HOME. But sometimes fate twists life cruelly. I had travelled my road. I had finished my course, but short of my goal—the top of the hill and beyond. Now I felt no pain and I had for company, the road, the white snow, the dirty snow, the ruts, the ice, the snow-laden trees, and my hill to freedom. Now they were all mine here in this great whirlpool, and I did not have to strain or cry out in pain or stumble or fall. Dying was easy . . . As I lay there in the glittering snow I lost consciousness and found myself a passage to some other galaxy, all within my own great whirlpool.

Later I heard, away in the distance, a human voice. Someone was speaking to me, and somehow I was sitting up in my cold snow bed.

"*Kriegsgefangener, ya? Kriegsgefangener, ya?*"

Yes, I was a prisoner of war, but I could not answer. I knew someone was bending over me, but everything was a blur. My lips would not form the answer, *ya*. The voice seemed so far away that I would have to shout to be heard, and I did not feel like shouting. And anyway, I could not speak. Who was holding me up? Someone who had been close by. It must be the same person, so why did I think that person was so very far away? Again came the question, and it penetrated my fuzzy brain, "*Kriegsgefangener, ya?*" I think I nodded my head—at least that's what I tried to do. Maybe I was dead, and because I died in Germany I was being asked the question in that country's language. I must be dead because my body was leaving the cold bed and I was floating above the ground and moving along without any effort on my part. No! Someone strong was carrying me out of the snow. I could feel arms beneath me, then I drifted off.

It must have been the shaking that brought me back. I was laying crosswise on the hard floor of a horse-drawn wagon. There was some brightness left in the sky, so this winter's day had not lost all of its light. I don't know if the journey was a long one, because I slipped out of consciousness and returned to find it was night and the wagon had stopped.

I heard voices, then a lantern's light illuminated the wagon's interior. Willing hands carried me into a small hut where there were bunks similar to the ones in Stalag. My benefactor did not follow these new people. The horse, wagon, and driver continued their journey, so the opportunity to see who had saved my life was gone.

I felt myself fading again.

When I returned to consciousness, the room was quiet, my only company a small circle of light coming from somewhere behind me, and I was having strange thoughts. Maybe God was driving the wagon. He had denied death its victim when our plane was shot down two years ago and I the only survivor. Death had come back to collect an old debt and because God was driving, it was again denied payment.

If that wagon had not passed by until morning, it would have been too late, and I couldn't figure out what quirk of fate made the driver stop, look in the dimming light, and find me. Then my thoughts came to life. I could visualize Nabber Giddens and hear his New Zealand brogue with a loud and clear answer, "You stupid Irishman, how could you forget it was the Little People from Killarney's lakes, and God too—all together on that wagon. They knew you needed help." I'm certain if Nabber was here in person that's the sort of answer he'd give me, but I wasn't satisfied with those thoughts.

I wanted to see and thank the person who picked me up in my stinking state—if only I had a name—who was this man who saved my life? He must be a civilian. Was he old? Was he young? Probably not young—the young were all at the fighting front. Old? Probably a farmer in his fifties. Fifty was old—I was only twenty-four, and just turned at that. Maybe he had a son or sons who were prisoners of war, but who knew for sure? He could be an old bachelor. Now he was gone, and I would never know.

✈

The willing hands returned. One person could speak a little English. The people were Serbs, themselves prisoners. Their work parties in the area were serviced by this four-hut Red Cross Unit. They gave me hot soup and bread, and my half-frozen body soaked up the warmth of the room. Soon a Russian medical officer visited. He could speak English and was also a prisoner of war. His home town in Russia was Omsk; he wrote his name and address on a scrap of paper. Producing a jar of black powder (charcoal, it turned out), he insisted I swallow three good-sized spoonfuls—sufficient, he said, to bung me up for a short period of time. As soon as possible they would try to transfer me to the British Prisoner of War Hospital at a place called Obermassfeld.

My curiosity about the wagon driver still was not satisfied, and I asked the doctor did he know who was driving the wagon that brought me here. The man had saved my life, I told him, and I wanted to thank him personally.

He knew that the wagon passed once a week about the same time, in the late afternoon, but never stopped. His presumption was that someone drew weekly supplies from the village. Putting his hand on my shoulder, he said, "I can inquire for you. Now rest. You are a very weak and sick man."

I thanked him and my thoughts turned to the British Prisoner of War Hospital they were sending me to. How I was to get to this place, Obermassfeld, my befuddled brain could not fathom. They had told me I would go by train, but how would I be given permission to ride on a train in my stinky condition, unless it was a cattle car? My balaclava, cap and greatcoat were the only clothing my attendants had removed from me, and they were hanging on a nail near the door. I reminded myself that sewn into the sleeve of that greatcoat was my handkerchief with the colourful scene of a Lancaster bomber in distress, from Toad Hughes. How was I to retrieve it before that putrid piece of clothing was destroyed with the rest—probably at this place called Obermassfeld? I MUST TELL SOMEONE.

Before solving this problem, I drifted into a restless sleep. I dreamed that it was snowing heavily and I was standing outside this small Red Cross hut. The same old wind was drifting snow against the building, but I felt no cold. My Air Force uniform was clean, and my boots were new, like my heavy greatcoat. Then, out of the blizzard came a horse and wagon. With unbelieving eyes, I watched the plodding, straining horse as it pulled the wagon closer. Rooted to the spot, I waited. The animal came to a standstill beside me, its straggly knotted mane encrusted with frozen snow that looked like so many tangled icicles. Instinctively, I put out my hand and touched its dripping wet nose. In return there was a friendly nudge, but it was the driver I wished to meet—the man who saved my life.

He sat motionless, the reins wrapped loosely around his wrists. I could not see his face, which was hidden by a familiar-looking, snow-laden coat slung around his shoulders like a cape. The large collar hid the man's features. I couldn't wait for him to descend, so I raced to the side of the wagon. I was shocked to see the man's boots were in terrible condition. Part of his frozen right foot was sticking through the broken toe cap. Swiftly I was beside him. I reached out to pull back the cape and realized that it was a British Air Force greatcoat, stinking and dirty like my old one. Underneath, his battledress jacket and pants were in the same condition. His dirty white aircrew roll neck sweater was like a block of ice.

His face was the face of a young man, his hair laced with white streaks of winter's frost. His face lacked colour—just a bluish grey sculptured frozen look like it was chiselled from an iceberg. The unseeing blue eyes were wide open and the long frost-coated lashes were reflected in a mirror of frozen tears. As the horse waited patiently for the word to continue, I looked in horror at this pitiful frozen figure, and the ghastly truth hit home—IT WAS ME! Then I fled in terror towards my warm room and the people with willing hands, crying NO! NO! NO! I stumbled and fell numerous times before reaching my goal. Blindly, I wrenched open the door to my room and flung myself through—but something was wrong. There was no cozy warm room. There were no willing hands to pick me up. There was nothing on the other side of that door but the empty sparkling road, and around me was a great expanse of white snow. I was on my knees, looking down the road as it twisted and turned away and over a small bridge, then made its way behind snow-laden trees to reappear for a short distance, only to once again disappear for the last time in a clump of trees. I watched fine snow scurry along the road's deep ruts, trying to find a place to hide from the chasing wind. Behind me I heard a swish as one of the lonely tree's branches shed its overload of snow. I turned to watch as it cascaded like a great waterfall of turbulent white that formed a grave-like mound beside me. Then fear and desperation clutched at my heart, for in front of me was THE HILL. At the top, looking down at me, was the guard, along with all the stragglers—a great multitude silhouetted against the skyline. Before they disappeared over the crest, a thousand pairs of hands waved their signal of disgust that I was too weak to make THE HILL. I screamed after them into the wind, "No! Wait for me! No! Wait for me!"

✈

The Serb who spoke a little English was shaking me gently. When I opened my eyes, he said, smiling, "You were dreaming, my friend, but now it is time for us to go."

Still shaken by my nightmare, I permitted those willing hands to help me into my stinking greatcoat and headgear. It was very early—perhaps 3 a.m.

"Where to?" I asked the one who understood English.

"The train station," he answered.

Looking at my right boot, I saw that someone had made an emergency repair by wrapping a piece of canvas, fastened by string, around the toe cap—useless for walking in the slush, but the repair would help keep out the cold, and I believe that was the reason for it, as in my condition I would not be doing any walking.

Another face appeared in the doorway. It was the Russian medical officer. In his hand he held the big jar of charcoal. "Thought I'd make sure you will have an uneventful journey." He smiled as he said "uneventful" and held up the jar. "Another two spoonfuls and you will be okay." I was sitting on my bunk, so he sat silently beside me as I downed that black powder. Then, very softly, he spoke.

"I promised to make inquiries regarding the horse and wagon that brought you here, and of course its driver. Late yesterday evening I was able to carry out that mission."

Immediately he had my full attention. "Yes," I said, "did you find the man who saved my life?"

Ignoring my question, he continued, "You must remember that this civilian wagon driver is German, so at the moment also the enemy of my country and yours. But my request to talk was granted, and I received permission from the German authorities here to make the contact. I also speak some German. My assumption was correct. The wagoner picks up weekly supplies at the village. I was able to make contact and delivered the message that you wished to render your thanks personally. I am sorry, your request was denied, but I did glean some information. The wagoner is a very lonely person, having lost life's marriage partner six months ago in an air raid on Frankfurt. Then tragedy struck again last month when their only son was killed at the Russian Front. Your remarkable discovery was the result of the horse's unusual behaviour. He stopped and refused to move, even under pressure of a few smarts with the whip. Eventually your wagoner descended, knowing that the horse had sensed something was wrong. Nothing could be seen, but further investigation found you lying in snow close to where the horse had stopped. The wagoner is very sad and very bitter at having lost loved ones at the hands of both yours and my comrades in arms, so knowing you would die before morning if left there in the freezing temperature the decision to help you was not an easy one to make.

The doc paused for a moment before continuing.

"Your wagoner at this point broke down and cried, then said quietly but firmly, 'At that moment I felt I was God, for this one time in my life I had the power of life or death in my hands. The decision was mine and mine alone. Let him die in the snow. He is my enemy. It will help to even the score. Pick him up and hope he lives so that some other family might rejoice in his homecoming. There was little time to ponder, so I made my decision.'"

I listened in awed silence as this man related the story, and I thought—IT IS TRUE! IT IS TRUE! I was right, for out there on that bitter cold wasteland, as my life or death decision was being made— GOD WAS THE DRIVER. With great emotion, I asked, "What sort of man was he? Must be a strong character. He had to be to make the decision regarding me, considering his own great loss. But what was he like? Middle-aged, if he also lost a son in the war, and he must be in good physical shape because they were strong arms that held me and carried me out of the snow."

The doc stood up to signify he had ended the conversation. He held out his hand and grasped mine in a firm handshake. "Your wagoner is probably a little over fifty, a strong, wonderful civilian enemy, and accepts your gratitude. So may I wish you a quick return to good health and a safe journey home when all of this over."

Stepping back, he looked at me with a mischievous smile on his lips. He crossed the room to walk out of my life, then paused at the door and turned towards me. His words rang strong and clear, "YOUR WAGONER, MY FRIEND, IS A WOMAN!"

✈

I will never forget the transportation ride over rutted roads and cobbled streets. Transport was a two-wheeled wooden push cart. Those willing hands picked me up gently and laid me on the barrow, but almost shook me to pieces during the journey.

I was bundled onto a train after all passengers were aboard, with permission only to be in the corridor a short distance from the exit. I was of great interest to many who came to look at the enemy airman lying in such a degraded state. The majority of passengers on this crowded train were women and children, most of them carrying bundles of personal belongings. They too were fleeing west. At each of the numerous stops boarding passengers looked incredulously at my dishevelled and dirty condition. Soon there was standing room only on the train, including corridor space. With furtive looks and pointing fingers, these German civilians discussed among themselves the filthy enemy flyer, and kept their distance.

No official had asked me for a ticket or made any attempt to converse with me. I had no idea where or when I was to get off for Obermassfeld, but I trusted that my Serbian hosts had made complete arrangements. The train clattered to a stop at another station, and this time the activity included me.

Two British Army Medical Corps people appeared at the doorway, and within minutes I was being carried out of the station on a stretcher. I must have passed out again, because I could not recall if the stretcher bearers walked all the way or if there was transportation to the gates of Obermassfeld Prison Camp Hospital. One of the Medical Corps people shook me to consciousness and asked if I had anything I wished to get past the German guards at the entrance gate. If so, he would do it for me. I had the pictures taken in Stalag by the Canadian with the secret camera, and I had paid good cigarettes for them. Shakily, I took them from my pocket and handed them over, a dozen in all. That was the last I saw of them. There was no need for alarm—the guard made no effort to search me.

It was early morning, not yet daylight, but the camp was coming to life with numerous Medical Corps people preparing for the day's duties. The overhead lights showed them looking like they were ready for some special parade back in Britain. Their uniforms were spotless, their trousers had knife-edge creases, their spit-polished boots glinted in the light. It was evident these soldiers of the medical corps and this prisoner-of-war hospital had not yet been touched by the advancing battle fronts. They had not endured the horrors and tragedies that were being inflicted on so many thousands of their fellow prisoners, some of whom were still stumbling along German secondary roads in bitter weather, with no sustenance or warmth to ease their aching bodies—only hope in their hearts that somehow they'd make it.

I was in no condition to take notice of anything more. The wonderful knowledge that I was in the care of Allied medical people, at last safe and in good hands, was sufficient for me to capitulate to defeat whatever little embers of stubborn resistance I had left, so once again I retreated softly into oblivion.

When I woke up, I was sitting on a stool in a communal shower room. Behind me stood an orderly clad in swim trunks. His hands were on my shoulders to steady me—I was nude. Quietly he said, "You will now have a shower." Immediately the warm soothing water streamed on my head and body and my medical attendant lathered me with soap. For the first time in over forty days I was having a shower. I was going to be clean. The spray of water bounced strangely against my head. I put up my hand and found that my head was shaved clean.

A quiet voice behind me said, "We did it when you were 'out.'"

CHAPTER 18

My Battle Won

It was a new month—the 3rd or 4th of March—and I felt a wonderful cascade of warm water was cleansing me of all the filth and dirt. I thought of it melting the ice and snow and clearing the road of those sparkling, treacherous ruts so that my wagoner and her horse would have a clear, safe road. It was warming the earth. The green grass would grow again and the sad trees would shake off their heavy blankets and burst into wonderful foliage, with birds building nests and singing their freedom songs and rejoicing in the sunshine, because now I had reached the Top of my Hill. The stool, the medical attendant behind me, the warm water—and those thoughts of warmth, of melting snow and green grass and birds and the Hill to Freedom—were the last things I remembered for many days.

There is a gap in my life when I must have been fighting for life. I recall nothing between the shower and the day I opened my eyes to see a uniformed British medical officer beside my bed. With a strong Scottish accent, he said, "You are with us again." Another face immediately came into my sphere of vision. It was the orderly who had kept me upright on my shower stool.

"We thought you were going to leave us for good; you had a few tough days," continued the Scot. *Leave us for good. You had a few tough days.* I had no intention of going anywhere, especially now that I had reached this oasis, and I'd had more than a few tough days—I'd had more than forty.

He must have realized that I did not understand. "You have been in

222

a different world for a week, and Bill here has done a valiant job bringing you back to us." (Bill, apparently, was the orderly's name). "Maybe soon we can take away this gadget and feed you a little nourishment by spoon. Good to see you in our world." With that he was gone.

Some time later, Bill returned and sat beside me for a few minutes, took my pulse rate, my blood pressure, and informed me that I had been unconscious for the best part of a week—delirious at times—and he had feared that I would not make it. A week—and I thought it was only a day since my shower. Checking my intravenous tubes, he said, "I'll be back to take this away and bring you something else."

Aware that someone was in the other bed beside me (Bill was talking to him), I turned my head but could see only a portion of Bill's back. I tried to turn on my side but the bed felt like a hammock. I wallowed in it, so weak I was unable to push myself over onto my side. I gave up the effort and sank back and tried to listen to the conversation, but nothing registered.

A short time later he returned. My wrist was freed and he assisted me in drinking a sweet liquid from a mug with a spout. Later I was permitted a small cup of warm tea. I graduated to bowls of soup a few days later and was able to sit up and introduce myself to the man in the next bed.

Charlie Mawhinney was from the English Midlands. He was a Royal Air Force corporal and he had been brought here with his buddy a few days before me. They were from a prison camp northwest of Dresden. This was the hospital attached to Stalag IXC and close to the towns of Weimer and Jena.

The bed beside Charlie was empty, but his mate, Phil Wilson, was in the next one. I raised my arm in salute to him and he returned the greeting. It was another week before I was able to get out of bed and walk to the bathroom, although for a number of days I had been able to sit up in bed.

After lunch Bill came to my bedside with a large paper bag and set it on the table beside me. "Your precious worldly possessions, I believe," was his only comment. The bag contained my prison camp scrap book (or wartime log, as it was called), my letters from home, and snapshot of Alice. There was also the coloured drawing of the Lancaster in distress.

Looking up at Bill, I asked, "Did you destroy my clothing?"

"Of course. We couldn't keep that mess."

"I don't recall telling you where this handkerchief was hidden."

"But you did!!" he exclaimed with a knowing look. "You told us when we carried you from the shower room that first day. You were delirious, but you made sense on one point: 'The handkerchief hidden in the sleeve of my greatcoat—please, please, somebody save it.' Lucky I heard you mumbling the request before you passed out on your way to the ward after your shower. By the way, I came by to tell you and Charlie that in a couple of hours you will be transferred to the convalescent barracks. I'll be back in an hour, so get prepared."

As he turned to go, he said to Charlie, "We're keeping your mate a few more days, just to make sure he's okay."

I lost my haversack somewhere during those last desperate days, but I guess those precious Little People were able to get out because they found me, and I am certain they must have known all along that God is a woman.

Around 2:00 p.m. a strange medic came to our ward. Bill had been called to the railroad station on an emergency, and so this man would assist us with our move. That afternoon Charlie and I were transferred to the convalescent barracks. Before leaving the hospital I was given some of my own clothing, plus reconditioned clothing. My own battledress jacket, my shirt and white aircrew sweater had been washed. With them were my "warm" socks, a small can of Zam-Buck ointment, and a strange pair of well-worn size 8 boots.

The convalescent huts were comfortable and warm. Temperatures had risen considerably since I entered hospital. There was green grass all around and the snow lay here and there in small islands, dwindling in size as the hours passed.

The village was small, but had a creamery. It was a collection and distribution centre for the milk, butter, and eggs. Wooded hillsides flanked the village on two sides, and to the west, open flatland spread out in a plateau to far-off hills. There was a question in our minds: "Will we see the army of liberation coming across that open space?" And another frightening one, "Are there German panzer divisions and other armour lurking in the surrounding hills ready to pounce on our would-be liberators?"

Rumours were numerous, and for a number of days German military vehicles passed through the village in ever increasing numbers, all re-treating east. There were no heavy panzer divisions, more like administration personnel accompanied by light armour, and the odd heavy mixed in here and there.

On Good Friday evening a "fireworks display" lit up the western sky behind a range of hills, so we knew the real war was closing in around us. An air raid alarm sounded and we were taken back to the hospital and down into the cellars used as air raid shelters. A number of villagers had gathered there, mostly women, and they were petrified, certain that enemy soldiers would soon be here to destroy their village and rape the females. One of our German-speaking prisoners assured them it was not so—this would not happen here. Strong rumours had filtered through from other fronts that this was happening in the east, so it was hard to convince these hysterical women that no harm would come to them. When the all clear sounded we returned to our huts, leaving behind very frightened people.

The retreat of army and *Luftwaffe* personnel continued all day Saturday. We started the day early and discovered that our guards were gone. There was no guard at the gate and none to be seen anywhere. From the hospital staff of British medical corps prisoners came the order, "Stay put! Don't try to leave. Stay behind the wire. Something is happening out there." We watched throughout the day as German vehicles filled with army personnel retreated. I stayed up all night with Charlie and his friend Phil (who had joined us the day before). We did not wish to miss any of this second show of fireworks.

The next day was Easter Sunday and a day to remember. There were no more German vehicles retreating. The wide flat tract of green plateau in front of us was empty of both friend and foe. We watched for signs of our liberators, but we saw nothing. There was a hushed silence and a sense of expectation, broken only by the occasional battle sounds coming from afar. Something was definitely happening out there.

In the afternoon, we were inside our hut—the end one, closest to the perimeter wire that divided this part of the small enclosure from the tree-covered hillside. Charlie was looking out the window when suddenly his mouth dropped open and he struggled to speak. Finally he pointed to the hillside and shouted, "Out there! Look! A tank with a big star on the side."

We heard the crashing sounds of small trees and brush. Everyone leapt to their feet and headed for the door. "The tanks are here," Charlie exclaimed.

Someone shouted, "The Russians are here!"

"You dumb bastard!" someone else cursed. "It's not a red star—it's white. That's an American tank."

The crashing continued as we tumbled outside. Within minutes, a half dozen Sherman Tanks had positioned themselves around the compound—guns pointing outwards—while others rumbled towards the hospital.

Our liberators were part of General Patton's third armoured division.

For years, to cross the Stalag trip wire was to court death. "Keep this side of the trip wire," was burned into our brains. And so we stood along the wire, making no attempt to cross it, conversing with a tank crew.

"You guys are sure lucky," yelled one of the crew. "You came out of your huts so fast we almost opened fire. Why are you standing in line along that wire?"

"Because we are not permitted to . . ." The man suddenly realized what he was about to say. He did not finish his sentence.

"Stand back, we're coming through!"

To the sound of our cheers, the big Sherman nosed its way through the barbed wire entanglement as if it were a flimsy spider web.

The tank rumbled through the wire, then did an about-turn, the big tracks chewing up the ground until it was again in a position with guns pointing out. I joined a happy crowd, shaking hands with Americans and asking many questions.

The village creamery had received some of its daily milk, butter, and eggs, so already a number of enterprising ex-prisoners went investigating and returned with plentiful supplies of eggs, butter, milk, and bread. Soon the small cook stoves in each hut were turning out fried eggs by the half dozen. A rectangular dixie was ideal for six eggs. With our own appetites satisfied, we supplied fried eggs, fresh bread and butter, and fresh milk to all and sundry. Yanks lined up at the windows as though it were a quick-service joint, ordering eggs over easy or sunny side up, and everyone was going full steam ahead to fill the orders. Fresh eggs and fresh milk were not usual items carried in Patton's tanks.

This impromptu catering had been in progress about an hour when overhead we heard the whistle of a shell, followed by another, and yet another. Rushing to the door, we saw them bursting quite a way out on the flatlands, but as we watched, each salvo was exploding closer. "A creeping barrage," someone exclaimed, and that sent little demons dancing in my stomach. I had heard of creeping barrages in the First World War, and how terrifying they could be. We watched in awe as this line of exploding shells grew closer with each salvo fired. We should have immediately gone to the basement shelters at the hospital, but something kept us watching as the deadly bursts crept towards us.

Suddenly we realized that only three tanks were left. The others were moving quickly down the road in the direction from which the shelling was coming. The tanks that were left had manoeuvred to positions behind walls and buildings that would give them some protection. Above the noise we heard and saw for the first time an American military policeman. He was perturbed and screaming at us to move it, move it, move it, quickly to the hospital shelters. Realizing how vulnerable and how stupid we were, we took very little time to make that short journey to the basement shelter. Charlie exclaimed, "Why the hell did we stay out there so long? That was pretty stupid." I had to agree, but fifteen minutes later we were given the all clear and learned that the tanks had very quickly disposed of the German artillery. Soon we were back to cooking.

Around us, tank crews hustled to carry on their advance—no time to stick around. Patton's armour was spearheading thirty and forty miles per day, and I heard tank crews say, "We are going to the River Oder, and if necessary we'll push the Russians back to the other side." At that time, we did not know that lines had already been drawn, that agreements had been made—that already the seeds of the cold war had been sown.

Next morning the tanks were gone and we were left with a few military police for protection. In the village, white surrender sheets hung from windows but we were a little apprehensive that small groups of trapped German personnel might be waiting in the surrounding hills and decide to recapture the village once the armour had moved on.

It was a big relief when, just before dark, a column of American army trucks rumbled into the village and we got our orders to climb aboard— destination, a safer area behind the lines. With tailgates down, the transportation waited. Our group was assigned a vehicle and we climbed aboard. With a full complement of ex-prisoners, the trucks headed west.

"Where are we going tonight?" someone asked the MP.

"To a village southwest of here. Quite a way yet."

It was in the small hours of a new day when the column slowed. Proceeding down a hill, we heard the chatter of small arms fire. We were ordered to lie on the truck floor, which was impossible for all of us to do. The trucks stopped and we quickly took cover in the ditch. Orders were being shouted, "Douse those lights." The column had been driving with wartime covers on the lights. Now all were switched off. Again fear gripped many of us. We crouched in the ditches on each side of the road, thinking we could still be recaptured. An American voice in the dark shed light on the situation as he called to another buddy, "Don't those silly trigger-happy bastards know we are coming? Bet it's Doherty's crew on guard duty. They couldn't hit a cow on the ass with a baking board."

His friend chuckled and the reply came from somewhere in the ditch. "You may be right, Mike, but just in case, I'm staying down till we get the okay to move out. If it's Doherty's guard crew, we'll razz hell out of him tomorrow."

Back came the quick reply, "Today is tomorrow, Jake, and it's almost 2:00 a.m. I could do with some shut-eye."

"Where are we billeted? Did you find out before we left?"

"No, I guess they'll turf out some Kraut family to make room for us."

"Maybe they'll leave a couple of frauleins—anything over sixteen will do."

"Then I wouldn't get any sleep, Jake."

"Okay, you can sleep. I could handle two."

And so it went—a typical conversation between army buddies close to front-line fighting.

Within ten minutes the okay was given to move out, and all aboard. The convoy moved slowly down the hill and into the narrow village street, the roar of motors echoing around the building and sending frightened residents rushing to don their outdoor clothing.

"What's the German for 'get out and hurry'?" asked another M.P.

"*Raus! Raus!*" came a chorus of voices and "*Schnell! Schnell!* for hurry."

Soon, automatic rifles were hammering on doors, and frightened residents were made to quickly vacate the homes in approximately half the village so that accommodation for all of us was plentiful. We were allocated a comfortable two-storey house that was the *Burgermeister's* residence. What a contrast to our years in prison camp! We languished on beds with clean, white sheets and warm coverlets.

Next morning we received coffee and hard tack front-line rations and discovered that only one truck was in the village. The others were gone and we were informed that very soon foot soldiers were coming. The infantry men would mop up a number of small pockets holding out in the hills. That day a few German prisoners were brought in. One was an officer, and I took a ceremonial dagger from him—a beautiful piece of work, with pearl handle and beautifully carved oak leaves with the swastika embossed on top. It looked like it was done in gold. But I possessed that souvenir for only one day.

We saw the American M.P.s setting up machine gun posts and preparing for defence. Inquiring what was wrong, we learned an elite S.S. fighting unit had encircled the area and we were cut off from the advancing infantry that was coming to protect us. I quickly exchanged my prize with another ex-prisoner for a German luger and ammunition. Others had a variety of weapons, and I waited with them. We would not be taken prisoner again.

There was no need for panic. The S.S. did not appear, but the relief infantry did, and what a welcome sight! Jeeps, small armoured carriers, cookhouse wagons, and trucks full of soldiers rolled toward us.

The Americans set up a front-line kitchen in the street. In a great barrel-like affair were cans, 'dancing' together as they popped up and down in boiling water. The cans contained delicious soups of many varieties, and all we had to do was ask for one or two and the cook would take a large pair of prongs and deposit the request in a dixie.

On the fifth day of liberation, an American military police sergeant told us, "Tomorrow you move out, but this evening at the village school hall there will be a dinner." Our stomachs were not ready for the change to richer food. Evening came and we entered the school hall to find a line of tables covered with white cloths, real plates, and eating utensils. On a makeshift stage a three-piece ensemble played for us. The menu was varied—a variety of soups, meat, vegetables, and fresh white bread out of cans (we thought it was cake), coffee and dessert.

Then we were told that we would fly back to England the next day.

On the way out we were guided past a long table loaded with all sorts of necessities—soap, toothpaste, toothbrushes, boot laces and polish, small mirrors, and so on. "Pick up what you need," we were told. A high-ranking American officer with two guns in his holsters stood at the doorway and shook hands with us as we filed through. We crossed the road towards our billet. I was clutching soap, toothpaste, and other goodies. Charlie and Phil were beside me, "Who was that officer who shook hands with us?" I asked.

Looking surprised, Charlie said, "Didn't you know, Paddy? That was General Patton himself."

I was unable to confirm Charlie's statement, and the American soldiers we asked were noncommittal. Since then the question has often crossed my mind: Was General Patton in the frontline village of Oberwed, Germany, the first week of April, 1945?

| McMAHON | JOHN | RADCLIFF | BRITISH |
| LAST NAME | FIRST NAME | MIDDLE INITIAL | NATIONALITY |

| W O I | 100639 | 27468 | R.A.F. |
| RANK | A.S.N. | P.O.W. NO. | BRANCH OF SERVICE |

| OBERWED | 5 DAYS | OBERMASSFELD | 24 DAYS |
| PRESENT ADDRESS | HOW LONG CAPTURED | PREVIOUS CAMP | HOW LONG |

| 2ND FEB 1943 | HOLLAND | E.T.O. |
| DATE CAPTURED | PLACE CAPTURED | THEATRE OF OPERATION MISS. |

EVAC., BY SHIP, AMB. TRUCK ___ DATE EVAC. ___ DESTINATION ___

DATE OF RETURN TO U.S. CONTROL — 2ND APRIL 1945

R.A.F.
UNIT

G. R. McMahon
SIGNATURE OF P.O.W.

G. Zrelinski
Capt Inf U S
CONTACT OFFICER SIGNATURE

ER FOR BATTLE OR NON-BATTLE

Liberated—and a flimsy piece of paper to say that on the 2nd day of April, 1945, I was under the control of the United States Army. A nice feeling.

CHAPTER 19

Going Home

We were going back to England! Back home! Back to freedom, where we would be able to walk the streets, come and go as we pleased!

The trucks arrived and we piled aboard. We moved southwest again. The trucks were canvas-covered. Destruction and death were stamped heavily on the landscape. By the roadside sat burnt out military and civilian vehicles. Most bodies had been taken away. The majority of villages and small towns in this area were untouched; others had gone through hell.

Finally we heard aircraft overhead and then the familiar sounds of an air base. Soon the trucks wheeled in through a gate, stopping for identification check. British Air Force personnel were everywhere. We were in Germany, but the uniforms were Allied. Quickly we were gathered together at one end of the dispersal area and ordered to stay put—if we wished to see England today. No one strayed.

Suddenly there was a commotion a number of yards away. A small crowd had gathered around someone. Curiosity took Charlie, Phil, and me to see who was commanding the interest. It was a pretty young woman dressed in slacks and a jacket—an American newspaper reporter. With the exception of those frightened women in the cellar at Obermassfeld, this was the first woman I had seen close up for years. She chatted and asked questions, made notes, and joked with those characters who asked her what she was doing for the next hour or two. "You would only miss your plane home, and it wouldn't be worth it," she told one persistent character.

"It sure would," came the instant reply, "Afterwards I'd fly home without an aircraft." He hesitated for a moment, then with a grin he said, "And you'd be on cloud nine."

With laughter in her eyes, the reporter said, "I'll make a note of that." Then away she went, notebook in hand, towards the next group of ex-prisoners. Halfway there she turned and waved her notebook, and the wind carried her tinkling laughter back to us.

Moments later Charlie nudged me and said, "Listen, Paddy, lots of aircraft coming," and sure enough, there was an ever-increasing sound of aircraft engines.

Someone shouted, "There they are!" A squadron of DC3s passed overhead to cheers from hundreds of men. A number of men stood with tears running down their cheeks, both arms held high above their heads in salute to the small armada in the sky above. I too had a great lump in my throat as I watched those work horses of the Air Force settle on the runway and taxi to positions nearby. The runways had been damaged in the fighting for possession of this air base, so great steel mesh carpets had been rolled out to cover the damaged tarmac.

Fifteen minutes later we were segregated into groups for boarding and were directed to line up close to a designated aircraft. The whole area was now crowded with liberated prisoners. An almost continuous stream of trucks was arriving to unload their complement of freed humanity. Some were in a carefree, happy mood, making for an almost carnival atmosphere around their group. Other batches of men were quiet and haggard looking. Many hobbled along, helping each other struggle to their designated positions, where they stood with wistful, trusting looks on their faces, content to know they were being taken care of.

Some crew members stood beside the aircraft—smart-looking, healthy young aircrew. One of them called out, "Five more minutes, no more than ten, and you'll all be aboard." Looking around the group with a smile on his face, he added, "Will that be okay with you fellas?"

I had acquired, at Obermassfeld, an old cowhide German army haversack. In it were my scrapbook, my letters from home, and another dress bayonet (I had given away the luger and ammunition to one of Patton's tank crew). Standing in the sunshine I watched the line-up at the aircraft closest to us and thought I recognized a familiar figure standing there, head and shoulders above the others. It looked like Nabber Giddens. The bright sunlight made it difficult to see. I cupped my hands around my eyes and yelled his name. His head turned immediately. I dropped my haversack and stumbled across the uneven ground towards him, ignoring the shouts of a military police officer whose job was to ensure we stayed in our respective line-ups. When he saw me coming, Nabber left his line to meet me. We were two prison camp buddies glowing with the knowledge that we were both alive. I weighed no more than 112 pounds, and Nabber, as he stumbled toward me, was a skeleton of his brawny former self. With a big hug, he almost lifted me off my feet, saying, "Where the hell have you been, Paddy Mac? I thought for sure you were dead."

"Do I look dead?" I replied, ecstatic at finding my friend, "Well, I was pretty close. I think I've been to hell and back again, but don't you think I look good?"

Nabber looked me up and down, "Not bad for a sick Irishman."

"You look pretty skinny and sick yourself," I replied.

"Wait till I get a few weeks on mutton stew and rack of lamb—I'll put it back on again."

"Where's Peter and Big Jock and the others?" was my next question.

"I don't know, Paddy Mac. Big Jock took dysentry about the same time you fell behind and disappeared. There must have been hundreds with dysentery. Hope Jock made it. I lost contact with Peter and the rest of our gang. We were all in bad shape."

A hand grasped my shoulder and I was gently but firmly turned in the direction of my designated aircraft.

"See you in London, Nabber. We can look for each other when we land."

As another MP guided Nabber toward his flight, Nabber turned and called, and a gust of wind carried his New Zealand accent to me. "We're not going to London. Come to New Zealand, Paddy."

I shouted into the wind, "Some day I'll try, Nabber, I'll try."

I picked up my haversack just as the captain of the aircraft, who looked about nineteen, shouted, "Anyone for the first leg of our trip to England can now climb aboard."

I turned to the MP and said quietly, "See? I wasn't going to miss it."

We flew west over Frankfurt and its ghastly remains of gutted buildings, then turned northwest to land, eventually, at LeHavre on the French coast. "Thought we were going to England direct," we asked the Skipper. He laughed and said, "England is not ready for you yet. They haven't finished the decorations—maybe tomorrow."

We were served tea and buns, and later, dinner. No one was permitted to leave the base. The day had been strenuous enough. I was content to relax and dream of tomorrow.

After a light breakfast of tea, toast, and a boiled egg, we assembled at 10:30 a.m., and by 11:00, we were in the air. The White Cliffs of Dover reflected the sunlight like a welcoming signal as we passed over England's south coast.

A short time later we landed and taxied to prearranged dispersal points. Air Force buses transported us to the reception area. One of the aircraft hangars had been decorated for our return. A giant sign was strung across outside: "WELCOME HOME PRISONERS OF WAR." The girls in Air Force blue were waiting for us as we got off the buses. There appeared to be hundreds of them. Each man received a welcome home kiss and hug and was accompanied into the hangar by at least one of the Royal Air Force's young ladies.

A number of high ranking officers and numerous NCOs were there to greet us, and tables were laid out with tea and coffee, plus a variety of other goodies. We were among the very first prisoners of war to be returned to England. The war still raged in Germany. There were introductions, welcome home speeches, hand shaking, and friendly conversation.

Across the room, I saw a face from long ago. On the barrack square each day, we drilled under the stern direction of a stern little disciplinarian whom we hated, yet in a way respected. I don't think anyone who drilled under his command ever forgot him. I know I didn't. Warrant Officer Mulcaughey.

He started across the floor, and when he stopped to talk to a WAAF officer, I walked over and stood close. I looked at his coat sleeve and recognized that he had remained a Warrant Officer. I now held the same rank. I recalled the times we forgot to stand to attention when he spoke to us, at which point he'd scream, "Don't you know who I am? Don't you know to stand to attention when I speak to you? Can't you see on my sleeve this badge of rank?" And he would hold his arm up close to our faces, showing his Warrant Officer's insignia. I smiled at the thought. Just then he turned to walk away, and we came face to face.

I surveyed this mighty little man: he was a disciplinarian from the sparkle of his cap badge and neatly pressed uniform to the highly polished boots. I thought of the five years that had passed since our first meeting, of how those years had been filled with experiences and personal contacts for which I will be forever grateful to the Creator of my destiny. I thought of how war, in its horrible and tragic way, seems to give something in return. The awful toll in misery, death, broken minds and bodies, is in some little way balanced by the discipline, comradeship, humour, lasting friendships, and love that somehow survives the chaos.

There was no recognition in his eyes. He must have put thousands of recruits through their paces during the past five years. I looked him straight in the eye, stood quickly to attention, and said smartly, "1006039, Aircraftman McMahon Second Class, No. 1 Mad Entry, Kirkham, June, 1940."

He looked blankly at me for a moment, then with a whoop of joy he put an arm around me and exclaimed, "I remember you crazy bunch of Scotch and Irish. You went off to Ireland on a two-day weekend pass, returned four days later, and got away without punishment."

"The luck of the Irish and a little bit of blarney," I said.

"Come with me," he said, and babbling like a little kid about the rough old days of 1940, he introduced me to a Group Captain saying, "This is one of the boys I passed through Kirkham in the dark days of 1940." Turning to me, he said, "And what did the lads think of me in those days?" I believe he asked the question because he knew the answer he would get if I was honest.

"We thought you were a rotten, pompous, little bastard."

He almost doubled over with laughter. He slapped my back and said, "You're right, you know? But you never forgot me, and I bet what I did to you on that barrack square helped to get you back here today." Looking at my arm he said, "I see we are equal rank now."

"Yes," I replied. "Now you can't make me stand to attention any more."

The Group Captain smiled and said, "The lad's got your number, Mulcaughey."

We had a long conversation, which was eventually interrupted by an announcement: "All ex-prisoners to form up in their travelling groups."

I bid Mulcaughey good-bye, and he wished me good luck. It was certainly a strange twist of fate—the disciplinary officer on my first Air Force station in 1940 turning up so unexpectedly in 1945 at the reception for returning prisoners of war. With his good wishes for the future still ringing in my ears, he walked away, this time strutting out of my life forever.

When our boisterous group eventually formed a creditable straight line, the welcoming committee was all but gone. A few stragglers were cleaning up. A number of tables had been left for other business, which included us. For the record, they wanted us to tell them about the loss of the aircraft, and, where applicable, the loss of life. Each man stepped forward, sat with an Air Force officer, and told his story. I told my story, but as I turned to leave, I heard a familiar voice call out from a nearby group. "Don't bullshit, Vickers." Turning quickly towards the speaker, I recognized an emaciated Mark Watson with little Bob Pierce by his side, looking no better. In a chair facing the officer was none other than Archie Vickers.

Soon there was another announcement: "Just one more hurdle, chaps—a quick check with our medical officers to ensure you're all okay to travel, then we'll have you on your way to billets for tonight. Tomorrow all Air Force personnel will go by train to Cosford Air Force Station, where the hospital people there will decide if you need a few days to fatten up before they send you home on leave. When you finish with your reports, line up at the entrances to the five partitioned-off areas and you will be processed quickly. This time it will not be necessary for you to stay in your travel groups. After your medical, proceed to the tarmac outside the hangar, where transportation will be waiting for you. Army on the right and Air Force to the left. Great to have you home again. Good luck and God bless you."

This announcement was greeted with a cheer from thankful hearts. I was among those first in the medical line-up. There was Archie Vickers, Mark Watson, little Bob Pierce, and Charlie Mawhinney and his pal Phil—my Obermassfeld buddies—and a variety of other personnel. As usual, Archie was full of news—some good, some bad. Markellie had not been seen anywhere and apparently had not turned up at any of the gathering points for return. Young Art Scott of the cleaning crew at Barrack 15A was dead of pneumonia, as was L. S. Maginis, editor of the hand-written news report, STIMNT. Both Art and Ross died at Gorlitz. "For sure those two are dead," said Archie, "Jock Martin and his mucker were seen in a jeep, and we think Sam Warnock and Zellbad got to the Russian lines and were taken east, and I wouldn't be surprised if the same thing happened to Montrose, McKitterick, and that swapover guy."

"Did you hear anything about Toad Hughes?" I asked.

"Arnold Hobbs and Toad Hughes were on one of the planes that continued to England when we landed at LeHavre." If Archie's information was correct, my friend Toad was safe, along with Arnold Hobbs. But what about my ex-mucker, Jimmy Grier? Archie couldn't help me on that one.

"Who's going in first?" Charlie asked. There were no volunteers immediately, so I said, "Why not yourself, Charlie?"

"Let someone else break the ice. It's been years since I dropped my slacks for a medical." With a chuckle, he added, "Guess I'm getting shy."

"For anybody whose been in Stalag three years, Charlie, you know that's a load of crap," said his pal Phil.

"Well, I'm not afraid to drop my slacks for any doc, so I'll go first," Archie said broadly. He sauntered through the space marked "entrance."

We waited for ten or fifteen minutes, and then he appeared solemnly at the exit. His head was down and he had a tight-lipped, crestfallen look about him. Slowly he approached us. We were immediately concerned, thinking the doc must quickly have diagnosed some incurable disease. When only a few feet separated us, Archie looked up, and his face broke into a great big grin. Then he burst into uncontrollable laughter, doubling up in the process of slapping his knee. "Who's next? Who's next?" he chortled.

I had volunteered to follow Archie. Now I wondered what had happened in there. Then it came flowing out, the words tumbling over each other, "It's a woman. It's a god damned woman doctor in there. And she's beautiful! I think they did it on purpose. It's a joke. Or maybe to check the reaction. How the hell do they expect a guy to keep things under control when a good-looking woman tells you to drop your drawers? I tell you, guys, it's impossible—for Archie Vickers, anyway. Don't they know that except for these last two days it's been years since we've seen a real live female? They must think we're very sick. Go on in, Paddy, she's calling 'next please.' Get on with it. I tell you, Mac, just think about something else when she gets to *that* inspection. Think about the march, the rotten guards, the starvation, the horrible nights—the cold wind, the snow, the ice. It might help you, though it didn't help me. Of course I'm still a very healthy young man." With a good-natured push, he helped me through the entrance. Archie was telling the truth. It was a woman doctor, and good looking, but she did not ask for an inspection of those private parts. Archie had made up the story and was delighted at the furtive looks and hesitation as each man took his turn. Charlie went in after me, but I did not spoil the joke. The others quickly caught on, and when each finished his medical, he came out smiling or laughing—adding fuel to the story with their own addition to the prank.

Next morning, sitting at a window table for an early breakfast, we saw in the small courtyard our faithful driver, standing beside his truck, waiting to take us to the station. Beyond him, out on the street, London bustled with life. At a bus stop stood a long queue of people, others hastening in different directions, going about their own business, while around them the ghosts of what once were stately buildings stood starkly silent on this April morning—reminders of other Aprils and hundreds of days and nights when the German *Luftwaffe* rained death from the skies, assisted later by V1 and V2 rockets. This was a time of liberation for these men and women, too; a time to rejoice, because the skies above now belonged to Allied planes and their own Royal Air Force.

Rebuffed

After a hurried breakfast we were off to the railroad station. We were like a class of kids getting out of school for summer recess. From a small platform wagon, a woman was selling tea and buns, or tea and "wads," as we used to call the buns. It was a very short time since breakfast, but who could resist tea and a wad on a British railway station? Our gang of a dozen happy, scruffy-looking returned prisoners surrounded the lady and her wagon. A number of people had obtained a few shillings at the reception centre, and it was sufficient to pay for the order. The lady immediately proceeded to close shop saying, "The train is leaving soon—I've no time to serve you." We knew the departure time was fifteen minutes away. She had lots of time.

"Look, lady," someone said, "I know we look a bit scruffy, but we're prisoners of war just liberated and returned yesterday from Germany." Ignoring the explanation, she said, "I'm not serving you lot," and with that she trundled her little wagon away down the platform and commenced to serve a couple of well-dressed businessmen. This was our first rebuff at the hands of a civilian who owed much to a multitude of not-so-scruffy airmen who had given their lives to ensure her freedom to say, "I'm not serving you lot."

Grumbling, we boarded the train. As usual, Archie Vickers led the pack, and now, five minutes before departure time, he was skipping down the corridor, checking for a compartment that would hold the majority of us. This end of the train was full, so following our leader we continued from coach to coach until space became more available. Then, as we passed joyfully into another coach, Archie cried out in delight. "In here!" he yelled, sliding open the compartment door with a bang. "Room for five in here, and the next compartment has only four people in it. Look at the beautiful material on these seats," exclaimed Archie, "and nice white clean towel things to rest your head on. I think they dressed these coaches up specially for us." We crowded in upon three startled but very well-dressed English gentlemen who had been quietly reading their morning papers.

One of the gentlemen asked, "Are you men sure this is where you should be?"

"We sure as hell are quite sure," Mark Watson said gruffly, "and thank God that we are here."

The gentleman lowered his brow at this remark and gave Mark a nasty look while the youngest of the three, probably in his early thirties and wearing a black jacket, black striped pants, and white shirt, glowered at us. He seemed very uncomfortable as he moved away as far as possible from Charlie.

Charlie was quick with his words, "Afraid you might get some disease if you sit too close?"

There was a stony-faced look from the young gentleman. The third gentleman wore a brown tweed jacket and a rough checked shirt, beige slacks, and highly polished brown boots. He looked different and I was certain he was suntanned. After Charlie's little speech, this gentleman's mouth twitched toward a smile, but he said nothing.

A minute later the door slid open and the conductor—a large, well-fed man stood before us with an exasperated look on his face. In a loud voice he said, "You people again! First I get a report that you hassled the tea lady. (I reported *that* to the Military Police, so you can expect to hear about it!) And now you're in a first class compartment. These compartments are not for the likes of you."

Shocked at this outburst, we were completely silenced for a moment. I saw the gentleman in the tweed jacket look up, raise an eyebrow, then continue to read his paper. The other two seemed pleased at the thought of us being ejected. The silence continued until the conductor shouted, "Out! Out, you untidy, dirty lot. You are a disgrace to whatever branch of the service you belong to." Immediately there was a chorus of unintelligible verbal abuse thrown in the conductor's direction. Archie Vickers' voice blasted above the rest: "Listen, you fat, over-fed bastard, there is no first class, second class, or third on Bomber Command. You don't sit on cushioned seats and read the newspaper when bombing Berlin. There's no lady on board selling tea and wads. And another thing, Hitler's prison camps don't have much food or water, or soap, and too often no hope, and it's just by the grace of God that this scruffy lot is sitting and staying in this here first class compartment on their way to an Air Force hospital where there are intelligent people who will look after us until we are fit enough to go home. So we ain't moving."

Archie received a round of applause for his great oratory, but the conductor was not impressed.

"I will have the Military Police here in two minutes. I will hold up the train until you are removed. You will all be charged with disturbing the peace and refusing to obey an official of the railroad. You are obstructing me in my duty."

The dark-suited ones nudged each other and nodded approval, now delighted at the thought of Military Police throwing us off the train. Charlie and his friend Phil were on their feet immediately the conductor mentioned Military Police. They grabbed hold of the conductor and propelled him out into the corridor.

"Don't come in again, you over-fed son of a bitch," shouted Charlie, "or next time you'll go out through the window."

The very agitated and desperate conductor made frantic efforts to attract the attention of four Military Police who were some distance away on the platform. The gentleman in the tweed jacket laid down his paper, and excused himself as he moved to the doorway and through into the corridor. We watched with great interest as he produced some identification from his wallet and showed it to the upset conductor. A short conversation followed, the tweed jacketed one doing the talking, while the conductor nodded his head and occasionally looked at us.

The train whistle blew and we moved slowly out of the station. The two men in the corridor seemed to have come to an agreement. The stranger returned to his seat and his paper. To us he said only three words, "It's okay, boys." After a final long, quizzical look at our scruffy lot, the conductor went about his business. We thanked our benefactor, but he would not be drawn into conversation. The other gentlemen did not look very happy at this turn of events.

The two dark-suited gentlemen got off the train on the outskirts of London. From his briefcase the tweed-coated gentlemen took numerous files and used the travelling time to study them, occasionally stopping to make notes.

There was little conversation during our journey, and as we neared Cosford more airmen boarded at each stop. With their new uniforms and schoolboy looks, they seemed so very young and naive. Way back in some other era, we had looked like that. Most of the time I would lay back with my head on what Archie called "nice clean towel things." I would close my eyes, listen to the clickety-clack of wheels on the metal rails, and keep repeating to myself, "It's true. The long trial is over."

We reached Cosford's small station and tumbled on to the platform. A large sign on the picket fence read, "Ex-Prisoners of War," and a red arrow indicated we should proceed down the steps. In case we did not see the sign, two Air Force Service Police stood nearby, immaculate in their blue uniforms, red arm bands, and white "blanco'd" belts, which indicated they were Air Force law keepers. I looked down over the picket fence and remembered that I had been here before, way back in 1941. I was here on an airframe course.

"Ex-prisoners this way, please." The tallest of the two SPs spoke firmly, but with a touch of kindness in his voice. "Welcome home, lads," he said, "you've done your job and we thank you. Please wait here until this crowd gets on their way."

For a few minutes we stood waiting, watched by those young schoolboyish recruits.

The war in Europe was almost over, but the Pacific Operation with Japan could take a long time. One of the Special Police stationed himself halfway down the wooden stairway—to help us, if necessary—but we stubbornly resisted any assistance. A short distance down, the steps turned at ninety degrees, just below the picket fence. Mark Watson nudged me and said, "Paddy, look up." I did so, and just above us, leaning over the fence, his briefcase tucked under his arm, and a crooked pipe gripped in his teeth, was the gentleman from the train. As we looked, he took the pipe from his mouth, exhaled, and the blue smoke drifted away in lazy circles. The gentleman in the tweed jacket and beige slacks, knowing we were staring at him, smiled and raised his pipe in salute.

Transportation was waiting at the bottom of the stairway and whisked us off to the hospital area of Cosford. We showered immediately, and afterwards dressed in an issue of hospital blues—light blue jacket and pants, white shirt and red tie.

"Now we're inmates again," chuckled Mark. We filled in cards they had given to each of us. At the top right hand corner was printed,

Reception Camp No. 106
R.A.F. Station Cosford
Nr. Wolverhampton

followed by message options:

I have arrived here

I am { well
      { in hospital

No visits allowed but I hope to be with you in a few days

I will { write   } as soon as possible
       { telegraph }

I wrote the date at the top left hand corner, scored out the IN HOSPITAL and the word TELEGRAPH, and signed the form. On the reverse side I filled in Alice's name and address and dropped the card in the mail box.

It was now the 12th day of April, 1945, and over the radio we heard the news that President Roosevelt had died at Warm Springs, Georgia. His Vice-President, Harry S. Truman, would be the new President of the United States of America. We had not heard newscasts for a long time, so it was wonderful to listen to numerous stations on the dial of the old Marconi radio in the common lounge. Later reports said that Hitler had toasted the health of America's new President with champagne.

We were also interested in General Patton's U.S. 3rd Army and the news that they were advancing towards the Rivers Elster and Weisse and were expected to cross those rivers in a couple of days. So those big Sherman tanks with the great white stars painted on them were still rolling across Germany, creating their own path to victory and liberating desperate prisoners of war.

The days at Obermassfeld had helped us on our way to recovery, but there were others—garnered in ones and twos from the treacherous roads of Germany—who had not yet had correct medical attention. There were cases of beriberi, and as we stripped and waited, this time for a thorough medical, I noticed that a number of the men around me were emaciated by hunger and fatigue. My own ribs were tight against my skin, and my stomach was a concave around my navel. I wondered if my health would be damaged for life.

When my turn came for a check-up, a robust, red-haired medical officer looked at me with a warm smile and said, "You look ready to meet the world."

"Are you a psychologist or a doctor?" I asked with a grin.

"Both," he replied quickly, "Maybe what I should say is, you're in better shape than most."

"I've already had medical attention." I told him about Obermassfeld. He seemed to know quite a bit about the great work being done by the prisoners who were in the medical profession before their capture.

"Now," he said, "hop up on this scale and we'll see how many Irish pounds you left in Germany. One hundred and ten pounds even," he exclaimed.

I had lost thirty-five pounds.

After a thorough medical, my jovial physician said, "We'll keep you here for a week or so to fatten you up a little, then you can go home to a well-deserved welcome."

I thanked him, returned to the dressing area, hastened to the washroom, looked in the mirror, then stood on a chair to see my skinny middle, but the mirror was too small to get a good view, so instead I inspected my face and shaved head. My face had that V-shaped look, with sunken cheeks that made my eyes look much bigger than normal. I thought to myself, I can't go home like this and meet Alice and all my friends. I must stay here until I look better. For a few moments my morale dropped a notch or two, then I thought, okay, the skin is stretched taut over my ribs, I weigh only 110 pounds, my big toenails are loose, black, and broken—but I'm clean, I'm in friendly hands, I'm free, and soon I'll be going home.

I buttoned the blue jacket of my hospital garb and went off to find Mark Watson, Charlie, and his friend Phil. I found them in the lounge area. Mark was trying to write a letter. When he finished, he suggested we go for a walk. Phil and Archie decided to accompany us, so it was a foursome in hospital garb that sauntered slowly around the grounds, absorbing the wonder of nature, spring flowers, and our own freedom.

Outside the administration building, a staff car pulled up almost beside us, and out stepped an Air Force officer. We moved aside to permit him access to the pathway. Rewarding us with a smile and a "thank you," he proceeded into the building. It was Phil who found his speech first as we stood rooted to the spot. "It's him again," volunteered Phil in a disbelieving voice.

"Of course it is," piped up Archie, "and I bet you didn't notice something else."

"And what might that be?" replied Phil, with a touch of sarcasm in his voice.

"He's a padre, he's a ruddy Air Force padre." Archie seemed quite shocked at his discovery.

It was our benefactor from the train—the one who had deflected the altercation with the train conductor. He was an Air Force padre travelling incognito, and first class coach, when we barged in to shatter the privacy.

"Strange he never came to see us," Archie quipped.

"You're not ready for the last rites," replied Mark, "and anyway, once in your company is enough, even for a padre."

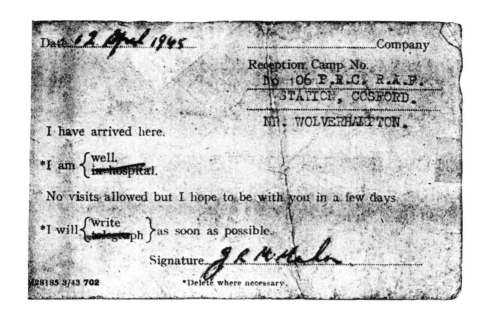

The "letter" I sent Alice from Wolverhampton didn't say much, but at least she would know I was alive.

CHAPTER 20

Journey to Remember

On the third day of May there was great news—we could go home on our "Journey to Remember." I had gained pounds, my cheeks had filled out just a little, and I looked much better. Our stay here had been longer than expected, but even with the extra time, I had been unable to get leads on Peter or Big Jock. They must have been taken to other centres. Someone volunteered information that the New Zealanders had been sent to their own receiving centres, so I presumed the Canadians would also have their own welcoming centre. But Big Jock should be around somewhere, unless he was processed immediately on arrival as fit to travel. In that case, he would have been home to consume numerous bowls of Midlothian oats in Bonnie Scotland a couple of weeks ago. Gnawing at my conscience was something about Australians, cigarettes, sausage meat, and my ex-mucker Jimmy Grier. Those Aussies were not the type to look after him, and I wondered, did Jimmy survive the rigours of that awful march?

It was a happy, yet sad farewell, with much back slapping, hand shaking and promises we knew deep down would never be kept—a reunion every year, a correspondence club to track our lives and if necessary help each other. What wonderful thoughts, and how terrific it would have been if they could come to pass, but life is not like that. Soon we would become the boys who came back. After that we would be veterans looking for work, and if lucky, we would marry, be happy, and bring up our own children and tell them stories about people we were with in the war. Then names would pop out from somewhere in our memories—names like Peter Chadwick, Nabber Giddens, Big Jock Martin, Farmer Ken Markellie, Archie Vickers, Kiwi Tim, Eddy Anderson, and maybe even *Unteroffizier* Kussel. If asked "what is a mucker?" I'd tell about Jimmy Grier and our two years of sharing food. I'd tell of the bombing mission on which my six flying companions lost their lives. As years passed by and we became older, we would make more wild promises to ourselves that correspondence must be renewed with those who were still alive, but the next day or the next week—or maybe within the hour—the cares and chores of daily living would take preference, so those wonderful thoughts of trying to find old comrades would be put back on hold until the priorities of the day were accomplished. And so the years would go by.

As I mused over these thoughts of the future, Archie Vickers and little Bob Pierce said their good-byes. They were catching an early train to the south of England. Mark Watson was next, and my friend from Obermassfeld, Charlie Mawhinney, and his pal Phil Wilson. They were all heading south.

"You're a real bunch of southerners," I said, "there's no one going north."

Then I was left alone to catch a train northward bound, whistling and clattering its way to Crewe Railway Junction, where I remembered there was always a hive of bustling humanity. It seemed that every train in England passed through Crewe. I would listen for the call I had heard so often when travelling home on leave, "All aboard for Carlisle, Dumphries, and the North, A-L-L A-B-O-A-R-D." This time when I heard it, I would sit back, close my eyes and know the train was not bound eastward across Germany to a prison camp, but to Scotland, to Ayrshire, and the port of Stranraer. And from there I'd travel across the sea to Ireland.

My instructions were to report to Wolverhampton Station Military Police or Air Force Service Police at the RTO's office, as all arrangements had been made to ensure my safety en route. Following instructions, I reported and was escorted by a congenial Military Policeman to a rail coach with a reserved compartment. A Red Cross sign on the window read WOUNDED, so no one was permitted to enter. At each main station, either Military Police or Air Force Service Police checked to make certain I was still on the train and asked if I needed anything. It was great to feel important and to be looked after in this way, but I would have preferred being with the crowd. In a way I felt a little bit like a prisoner, and anyway, I was not wounded. I was surprised at the attention I was getting, but guessed I was the only returning prisoner of war on this train.

I watched the English countryside roll by with no great distances between built-up areas. As the train rattled and whistled through these areas I saw numerous decorated streets with banners stretching from one side to the other, and on them large printed words WELCOME HOME TOM, BILL, HARRY, or the like. Many streets had platforms rigged up for some sort of presentation. In one small town, we passed the end of a decorated street where a band was playing on a makeshift platform. Union Jacks fluttered from the windows of the small row houses, and the banner that stretched across read WELCOME HOME HARRY HOLMES. On the platform stood important-looking civilians in suits.

I began to look forward to a sort of hero's welcome myself. After all, I would probably be the first returned prisoner of war in my neighbour-hood. Considering the circumstances—the only survivor of a seven-man Lancaster crew, two years in prison camp, and a trek across a fro-zen Germany—I could visualize a great welcome, complete with street banners, flags flying, neighbours shaking hands, and maybe a big crowd waiting for me at the railway station. Perhaps a reporter from the *Daily Press* would need pictures for his paper. I sat back, closed my eyes, and visualized this reception. Then I dozed off.

"Are you all right, sir?" The voice startled me awake. Seeing the uni-formed figure with the red Service Police arm band, I immediately came back to reality. This was a Corporal in my own Air Force Service Police.

"Yes, thank you," I said.

"Brought you something to eat and drink," he said, handing me a large mug of tea and two sandwiches wrapped in white paper.

"This is Carlisle. The train will be here for about fifteen minutes. I'll check with you again before it leaves." Then he was gone.

The corned beef sandwiches were good. The tea was strong, sweet, and coloured with canned milk, but very welcome. True to his word, the Service Policeman returned to retrieve the empty mug a few minutes before the train was due to leave. He wished me luck, holding the mug aloft. "Promised to return this to the tea lady." I smiled, thinking of this big man, a preserver of law and order, being hauled over the coals if he forgot to return the mug. I thought of the woman who would not serve us in the train station. I guess the tea ladies had a tough job.

A whistle blew and I thought our train was moving, but it was the one at the next platform. Slowly it seemed to slide away. Four late sailors ran for it. One opened a door and they all appeared to plunge into the compartment together. The last coach swaggered out and away, leaving the platform looking bare and out of place, as if someone had stolen part of it. There was a shrill whistle blast, the coach doors slammed shut, and above the noise and hiss of locomotive steam, loud voices shouted orders. Amid the roaring noise and the wild rush of the sailors, we slowly moved out.

As the locomotive laboured north, the daylight began to fade. I sat in the corner, alone with my thoughts, close to the window of this special coach compartment reserved for me only. I tried to visualize the future, and frightening questions scrawled across the blackboard of my mind: would Alice still be waiting for me? Maybe she had changed her mind and found someone else. If we were to get married, would I find a job with a decent salary? Where could we rent a house? The housing shortage was acute. Would she go to New Zealand or Australia with me, where better opportunities existed for our future?

There would be many stories about prisoners of war returning with broken health and mental illness. We heard, before leaving Cosford, that the Red Cross had sent letters home warning our families to be careful and not to rush us into regular every day life—to help us make a gradual transition, because a drastic change might be too much for us. Because of this, many wives and girlfriends would be wondering about the kind of man who would be returning to them.

"What a load of bullshit!" was Charlie Mawhinney's reaction when he heard about this Red Cross correspondence.

"I agree, Charlie," said Mark Watson. "I agree, and I say gradual transition be damned, the drastic change I'm looking for is a nice cozy nest with a beautiful blonde—about 38, 24, 36, with Betty Grable legs—and if I have a nervous breakdown, then she can look after me. I can instruct her on the kind of medicine I need to bring me back to health and give me a good mental outlook." He chuckled. "That's what we all need, fellas—a mental outlook of 38, 24, 36."

Things would never be the same without the Mark Watsons, the Archies, the Peters, the Jims and Taffys, the New Zealanders like Nabber, and all the others. I was going to miss the people with whom I'd shared the hardships, the fears, the tragedies, the laughter, the tears, the undying hopes, and especially the comradeship and friendship born of adversity. I knew that those contacts and experiences would help me live a completely different and richer life in the years ahead.

I settled down comfortably in the corner and tried to sort out my turbulent thoughts and emotions. Suddenly I realized we must have crossed the border to Scotland. I could see the Scottish hills of the Cheviot Range stretching up from Northumberland and across most of the Scotland/England border. From this side of the coach, looking west across the Solway Firth to the Irish Sea, I watched another sunset and reminded myself again: "I'm free, I'm alive, and I'll still be alive and free when the sun rises, and again when it sets tomorrow evening, and for all the mornings and evenings for the rest of my life."

Suddenly the train raced into the darkness of a tunnel. At the other end, the tracks turned westwards, as if trying to catch up with the sunset. Soon daylight bled into dusk and then darkness settled over the last few hours of another day of freedom. The dim compartment lights and the black cloak of night outside joined forces to reflect my image in the rail coach windows. I looked closely at this reflection and saw the sallow cheeks and the shaved head with its prickly growth of hair. For a moment I dreaded going home like this. Maybe if I had asked at the hospital they might have permitted me to stay another week, though one more week would make little difference to my hair growth.

Dumfries, Wigtown, Stranraer. Then a ferry boat across the Irish Sea to the port of Larne. From Larne there was a train journey of only twenty-four miles, which would terminate in Belfast's London Midland & Scottish Railway where, five years before, I had lined up with a dozen other new recruits on the way to a mysterious future.

I tried to quell my excitement as the train moved south. There was the town of Whitehead, where, at fourteen, I had delivered groceries. Then the little village station at Kilroot flitted by. I recalled the year I spent summer holidays with my family in that little seaside village. Often my brother and I would sit with other kids on the platform, waiting for the express train to rush through, pulled by the big steam locomotive named "Ben Madigan." Carrickfergus was next, with its old and famous castle, and where dungeons were still occasionally discovered.

Soon the "Journey to Remember" reached its final destination—the end of the line, York Street Railroad Terminus. The train slowed and the clickety-clack sound of its wheels seemed to soften as the coaches snaked their way to another track.

I was speaking with two Royal Air Force personnel and also looking earnestly beyond the black railing, searching for those faces I wanted to see, when I heard through the station's announcement system, "Will Warrant Officer McMahon report to the RTO immediately." The request was repeated several times and I knew why. At Dumfries I had joined that happy group of young people in another coach and also transferred my kit, so when the Military Police checked at Wigtown or Stranraer they had found my private Red Cross compartment empty. I had expected to be accosted on the ship from Stranraer to Ireland, because I knew there would be a slight panic somewhere when it was discovered that I had disappeared. I passed through the gate, looking everywhere, but found no familiar faces, only a very large army Military Police Corporal.

"Sir, let me carry your kit."

"Thanks," I said, "glad to be rid of the weight. Guess they're looking for me."

"Yes, sir," came the brisk reply, "they lost you at Dumfries and we were asked to check that you got here safely."

I chuckled and replied, "Maybe I lost them." I made a gesture to retrieve my kit bag and asked, "Would you be good enough to tell your superiors I'm here and I'm just fine."

"Sorry, sir, you have to check in at the office. They'll want to make sure it's you.

"How did you know?" I enquired.

"Just guessed, sir, just guessed." I thought sure, sure, not very hard to guess: the scrawny appearance, the shaved head, the sunken cheeks—all the earmarks of a returned prisoner.

"This way, sir." My military companion guided me through a number of people making a fuss over a very young airman dressed up in his new uniform. I stopped for a moment to survey the area, but there was no sign of friends.

"Please, sir, follow me." The MP was getting impatient. I was not used to all this *sir* business. Perhaps my mind was still programmed to Paddy Mac or Hi! Mucker. Then I spied my brother in the crowd. He waved to me and I shouted, "I'll be there in a minute." I entered the office and found a very unhappy looking Sergeant behind the desk.

"Warrant Officer McMahon?"

"Correct," I replied.

"You gave us the slip at Dumfries."

"Guess so, but I was in good company all the way."

He held out his hand, "Sir, can I look at your leave pass? I must confirm to my superiors that you are the right person." Quickly I cooperated, impatient to be on my way. I could see my brother waiting outside, so one person I wanted to see along with family and other friends must be close by. After scrutiny, my leave pass was returned, and with a forced smile, the Sergeant said, "Thank you, sir. Have a good rest, and good luck to you."

When I emerged from the transport office, my brother was skirting the family reunion of a young airwoman who wore officer rank. I knew by the quizzical look that he was thinking, "this is not the brother I said good-bye to."

With the most confident smile he could muster, he put out his hand and shook mine, "Welcome home!" he exclaimed. "Good to see you." He didn't lie and say I looked great.

"Can I take your kit bag?" he volunteered.

I would have appreciated not having to carry the weight, but my stubborn streak said, "Thanks, it's not heavy—no problem. Sure great to be home. Where's Alice? Where's Dad and the others?"

"Just me," he replied. "Alice is at her Mom and Dad's. Our Dad's at work and the others are at home. I got a few hours off work."

We emerged to the street. There was no welcoming crowd of friends—no banners—no daily press looking for a story or a picture.

Trying to hide my disappointment, I took a deep breath, hoisted my kit bag into the open trunk of an old Vauxhall Vanguard Taxi, then deposited myself in the front passenger seat next to the driver.

"Where do you want to go first?" I gave the driver Alice's address. On the way, my brother asked about prison camp. How were the conditions? What was the food like? How did they treat us? Was it very cold in winter? What were the chains like?

The taxi turned into Alice's street and stopped at number ninety-six. As I bounded out I heard my brother tell the driver to wait, and I noticed a few neighbours outside their front doors, trying to get a glimpse of the returned POW. Before I could knock on the door it opened, and there she was—as beautiful as ever—the girl I had left behind two years ago.

For a moment or two she stood and I knew what she saw was not the picture of me she had kept in her mind for such a long time, but the reality my brother had already seen when he met me at the station. She was looking at the skinny frame, the sunken cheeks, the shaven head, and the uniform sagging on my shoulders. Seconds ticked by like an eternity, I saw the tears welling in her blue eyes, then the outstretched arms. Soft words came to my ear. "Thank God you are safe." I WAS HOME AGAIN!

A little later, the taxi cab laboured up the last hill, turned right into our short street, and spluttered to a stop at the three-storey tenement house. With painstaking effort, the middle-aged, pot-bellied driver dragged himself from behind the wheel, opened the trunk, then stood waiting for me to lift out my kit bag, while my brother searched in his pockets for correct change.

I managed to swing the kit bag onto my shoulder. The short street was devoid of welcome home signs and there were no decorations. No Union Jack flew, not even from our own house, and I thought that surely they could have put out our old beat-up flag—it always flew for Orangemen's Day on July 12th and for Royal visits to the City, but not for Jack's homecoming. The street was silent—no neighbours at their doors or watching from behind curtains (there would have been for my funeral).

I let my brother carry the kit bag. The house was quiet and no sign of anyone, but I thought perhaps a crowd of people would be inside waiting, and I was sure there was a scout somewhere already giving the signal that I was here.

I took a quick look at the windows. There was no movement of curtains, nor did I spy anyone hiding behind them. Looking up at the attic, I thought, "That's my retreat. That's my hideaway if I need it." I opened the gate, took the short path in a few strides. I turned the handle, but the door was locked. I turned the bell three times and heard the rings echo down the hallway on the other side.

"The door should be open," said my brother. He stood on the top step, trying to balance my kit bag on his shoulder, but the way he was carrying it, three quarters of the weight threatened to overbalance him down the steps. I heard the *pad pad* of feet, then the lock bolt was pulled back and my sister greeted me with a joyful whoop. Then I was down the hall. I turned into the living room but there was no great unison cry of voices shouting, "Welcome home," just my stepmother greeting me warmly. My number two welcome home balloon had exploded in my face.

"Father will be home in a couple of hours. He's trying to get off early today. I've made some tea and baked a few things. Would you like tea now?"

"Yes, that would be great," I replied. Nothing in the room had changed: the table at the window, the couch against the wall, and on the shelf behind my father's place at the table, the old radio. The coal fire burned in the grate of the kitchenette fireplace, and in the centre among numerous trinkets spaced out on the mantelpiece, stood the Westminster chime clock which had been presented to my father in 1917, "with good wishes from the staff" engraved on the plaque.

Catching my young sister's eye, I asked, "Any boyfriends yet?"

"She's too young," came the quick retort from her mother. My sister, who was sixteen, did not reply.

"Thought you might have found a rich GI and then we could all move to America."

"She's not allowed to talk to those Yanks."

"Mother, the Americans have all gone to Europe or England."

"Oh, there's a few of them still around."

My brother broke into this escalating conversation. "I won't wait for tea. I got to get back to the office. See you later, Jack."

My stepmother served tea, home baked scones, and cake. I answered the same old questions regarding prison camp treatment, food, housing, and so on.

An hour later, after many cups of tea and too much cake, I heard my father's voice: "Have we got someone home?" He was a sentimental man and shed a few tears at my safe return. Then my brother returned with his wife Peggy and we all sat around drinking more tea (there were no alcoholic beverages permitted in this house). Then came another round of the same questions, but already I'd coined my replies.

I wanted to see Alice. I thought that there must be something going to happen later—a big surprise—maybe a room had been booked somewhere. Time passed, and everyone wanted to know if I'd brought back souvenirs. There was no great jubilation, no neighbours invited in, just a very solemn, thankful little group.

My father turned to me and said, "We give thanks to God our Lord and Master and we will never forget that He brought you safely home to us."

I agreed with him, but a thought flashed across my mind—would I cause a great disturbance if I said, "Do you know, Dad, that God is a woman?" But I decided not to rock the ship.

I brought out my souvenirs and said, "Take what you want. I don't care." But I had this dreadful urge to grab all of my gear, including those very few souvenirs, and get back on a train. I wanted once again to sit at a corner window and watch a glorious sunset. I wanted to go back to the first night of my Journey to Remember—all the excitement, anticipation, and expectation. I wanted to recapture that feeling when all alone in that special coach reserved for me I had watched the sunset and thought, "I'm free, I'm free, and I'll still be free when the sun rises and again when it sets tomorrow evening, and for all the mornings and evenings for the rest of my life." I wanted to do it over again—the train ride from Cosford to Scotland. I wanted to see again the welcome banners in the streets of Britain and I wanted to stand on the ship's deck just one more time and search the misty sea for my first glimpse of Ireland. I wanted to do it all again and maybe next time things would be different—perhaps this was only a rehearsal. If Alice had not been close by, I would have made my exit and set a new course to New Zealand or Australia.

After a reasonable time I excused myself, feeling certain that I had given more time than should be expected, considering my fiancée was waiting at her Mom's. I picked up my Air Force jacket from the old couch, and while buckling the belt, I looked up and said, "I'm going to Alice's home and I'm not sure what time I'll be back, but before I leave, I want to know if arrangements been made for my friends to visit? If so, I'll come back and bring Alice with me."

The reply I got was, "No special arrangements have been made, but maybe people will come to see you. Don't you think it's a good rest you need instead of going out?"

I continued, "Do most of my friends and relatives know I was coming home today?"

"All we could contact," and I wondered how many.

My brother interrupted, "Are you all right to walk, or will we get a taxi cab? Ritchie's, the Chemist at the corner, will allow me to use their phone."

I thanked him for his thoughtfulness and assured everyone I was okay, and also that I would not get lost, forget my name, or go berserk.

"If you're not home by 10:30, your father will be in bed. You know how early he has to rise in the mornings."

I spent a wonderful, carefree evening with the numerous friends who arrived to join in the welcome and laughter that filled the family room at Alice's home. She had baked a very large cake with the words "Welcome Home" on top and around it a red, white, and blue ribbon.

I did not make it home until a very long time after father had gone to bed.

During the next couple of days a number of relatives popped in to say "welcome home" and probably also to satisfy their curiosity regarding my health. I talked to a few neighbours, then one asked me in for a cup of tea. I learned that the neighbourhood had planned a big homecoming for me, but my parents had quashed the idea and requested there be no big welcome, so as a would-be organizer, this lady apologized on behalf of everyone. Possibly my parents' thinking was the Red Cross letter they received warning families that a sudden or drastic change might be too much for released prisoners. A quiet and slow return to civilian life was recommended. I thanked Mrs. McCandless for the tea and goodies she had served and asked her to thank all those who wanted to participate in a homecoming reception for me. When I said, "Guess that's life," she looked at me with expressive eyes, kissed my cheek, and said, "Is it?"

This sort of thinking on my parents' part prevailed when I was shot down. It was usual, especially in Saturday night's issue of the paper, to see a special area showing pictures of servicemen killed or missing in action. Mine never reached the paper. The same thing applied upon my return.

The next day, May 7th, the morning radio broadcast gave to the world this wonderful news: At 1:41 a.m. in General Eisenhower's headquarters at Rheims, France, the German representatives signed the unconditional surrender of all the German armed forces to the Allies. May 9th was declared Victory in Europe Day.

It was a wonderful, elated feeling when on the morning of victory day in Europe, crowds gathered and headed for the city centre to rejoice in the knowledge that the long six years of war in Europe were officially over. I had been visiting a friend and now waited for a trolley car that would take me close to home. Happily, I stood in a short line of people waiting patiently as one car went past without stopping because it was full. This morning I had not put on my uniform. Instead, I wore grey slacks, a white shirt and brown jacket, a brown tie, and my comfortable old black shoes—the same clothes I had worn that day in June, 1940, when I left home for England to put on the Royal Air Force uniform. This morning, in keeping with the news, I had reversed the situation and changed back to civilian attire. In civilian clothes I felt really free—no uniform, no Service Police or other MPs checking for leave passes. I had, by discarding my uniform, merged for a time into civilian life.

In the line-up for the trolley were a couple of young men in Air Force blue and an old sweat Navy sailor, his weather-beaten face showing the rigours of life at sea, and a few middle-aged ladies. An old gentleman, dressed smartly in a brown suit and carrying a walking stick, was first in line; on his jacket he proudly wore First World War medals. With the sailor was a lady I presumed to be his wife, and directly behind me the boys in blue were accompanied by two beautiful young ladies. The morning air was filled with laughter and happy chatter about the European war ending, and as the old gentleman listened to their jubilant conversation, he kept nodding his head in agreement. His eyes had a wistful look as he gazed over my shoulder at the two young couples. I caught the eye of the young lady close to me and said, "Isn't it great that it's all over in Europe?"

With a chilling look, she replied loudly and bitterly, "No thanks to you! What did you do since 1939? Look after all the girls when the *men* were away fighting and dying?"

The old sweat Navy man added his two bits by saying, "He probably made a hell of a lot of money and slept in clean sheets every night."

Immediately, all eyes were on me, and the looks I got from the old gentleman and the others in the line-up were looks of disdain. I had forgotten about my civilian attire, but I made no comment. A trolley car was fast approaching and I didn't feel like explaining that only this morning I had discarded the uniform that would have marked me as a member of the Royal Air Force flying crews. The crowded trolley car came to a halt, and when the old man made no attempt to move, I stepped off the curb. Before I could take another step, his walking stick shot out across my chest, "Our young heroes first, please. It's their day." Immediately the two Air Force personnel and their young ladies rushed aboard, followed by the sailor and his wife. The old man kept his stick across my chest muttering, "Now the others before us," until he and I were left. A thought crossed my mind—when I get on the trolley I'll produce my leave pass and show it to the old gentleman, tell him he made a mistake, that I was flying crew on Bomber Command, and watch his reaction. Looking at him in his nice brown suit and his 1914-1918 medals, I had second thoughts. I wouldn't tell him; he was enjoying this and felt so proud at his accomplishment. It would be something for him to tell his friends. This was his day, too.

I permitted him to board first. There was standing room only, but the young Air Force personnel and their girls moved close together to make room for the old gentleman. I stood alone in the centre aisle for a short time, until the conductor came down from the top deck and shouted from his platform, "Don't block the aisle. No standing. Please move to the rear platform."

With chuckles from the ladies and smirks on the faces of their menfolk, I moved unsteadily to the rear. I held onto the upright pole as the trolley car shuddered and shook its way towards my street corner.

"Next stop, please," I said to the conductor, who was writing up his ticket report. He automatically reached out, rang the bell, and continued his report. I hopped off before the trolley came to a standstill. As it moved off again I saw at the windows the young men in uniform, their girlfriends and the old gentleman, all with smiling faces, giving me the V for victory sign.

In the house, I quietly made my way up the three flights of stairs to my attic retreat, my hideaway. I needed it right now for a short time. I wanted to be alone. There was no sound from downstairs, so I don't think anyone heard me come in. Leaning my elbows on the old dresser, I looked out my favourite window.

I thought of the tea lady refusing to serve us at London station, and of the railway conductor who tried to evict us from the first-class coach compartment. I thought of the long, long trail I had covered to get here, and I thought about my mucker, Jimmy Grier, and all those who didn't make it, including the six who flew with me so very long ago. Once again I looked south across the slate rooftops beyond the city outskirts. Scrabo Tower's tall, slim structure was almost invisible—I could see only a small portion of the top. Then, looking east across the Irish Sea, I searched for "Paddy's Milestone," the big rock off Scotland's Ayrshire coast, but on this 9th day of May, 1945, it was shrouded in sea fog.

I spent an hour there with my thoughts, then went down to eat the evening meal with my sister, my father, and my stepmother. Afterwards I hastily washed, told my parents I was going out, and quickly made my way to Alice's home. We walked hand-in-hand to the city centre and joined in with the triumphant throng that jammed the grounds of the City Hall and overflowed down every street in its vicinity.

I wore my uniform.

✈

My return to Cosford was one week later. I was officially declared sound both physically and mentally, and was given another leave pass to return home for two weeks, after which time I was to report at 113 RTC Scarborough. This 113 RTC turned out to be a rest and recuperation centre for ex-prisoners of war and also a retraining centre for returning to civilian status.

I spent three months of summer convalescing, mostly at the holiday resort town of Scarborough, England. I was billeted close to the beach in a grand house owned by the film star Charles Laughton, who played the hunchback in *Hunchback of Notre Dame*.

Wearing my Air Force blue swim trunks, I'd often walk barefoot on the beach, stop, dig my toes into the soft sand at the water's edge, and look away out to where the blue sky and sea seemed to meet. I'd search the horizon, looking for answers to my future and hoping in that vast expanse of sea and sky I'd find the answers written there by some mysterious and powerful hand.

On the 25th day of August, 1945, at #104 Royal Air Force Dispersal Centre, Hednesford, Staffordshire, England, I received my release authorization. The effective date of release was the 15th day of November, 1945. I had eighty-two days leave with pay before once again becoming a civilian.

One afternoon late in September of that year, the sharp clang of the old spring-loaded door bell echoed down the long hallway. My sister answered its challenge, then immediately called, "Someone to see you, Jack."

The civilian standing there was smiling, his features strained, eyes uncertain behind the large glasses, despite the smile on his face. It was my lost mucker, Jimmy Grier. I answered those questioning eyes by hugging him and saying, "Great to see you, old buddy. I had fears you didn't make it."

Over numerous cups of tea, we swapped our stories. Apparently Jimmy's association with the Aussie combine was short-lived. Without mentioning the Australians or disclosing the reason, he volunteered the information that for many days he had struggled along on his own. At some point, he left the column, along with a couple of others, and decided to hide out in an old barn and wait for liberation. They almost froze and starved to death before the Allied forces arrived.

We talked for a long time about our life in prison camp, especially the inmates of Barrack 15A, and we swapped hopes and plans for our future. When Jimmy's leave terminated and he officially became a civilian, he would take up his old job at the bank. Thinking of the many months he spent studying in prison camp, I said, "With the knowledge you gleaned from those books on banking, it's a managership should be offered."

"True, true," he said. "Maybe like you, I'll plan to emigrate—better opportunities elsewhere."

"Good idea, Jimmy. Maybe we'll become Canucks or Kiwis."

Two hours later I walked with him down the steps to the iron gate. We shook hands and wished each other good luck for the years ahead. Watching him cross the street and walk away, my memory flashed a picture of the buttons at the bottom of his army greatcoat doing their little jig in front of me on the march. I waited, expecting him to wave before turning the corner, and felt a twinge of disappointment when he did not look back.

I never saw Jimmy Grier again.

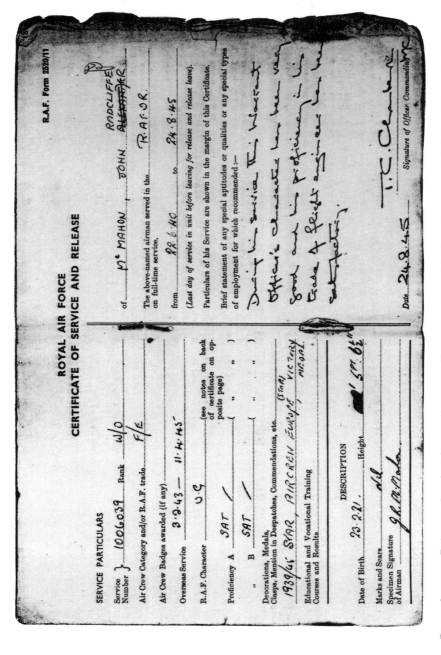

Pages from my Release, dated 15 November 1945. The note on the right hand page reads, "During his service this Warrant Officer's character has been very good and his proficiency in his trade of flight engineer has been satisfactory."

CHAPTER 21

Forty Years Later—1983

Have you at some period of your life tried to spin back your memory until the rewind process clicks to a stop at some designated time? Perhaps at the day you were married or the day your first child was born, or some other occasion of great happiness or sorrow. When we look back on our lives, each of us finds unresolved situations that call for our attention, but with the pressures of everyday life, we push them aside again, to be attended to when there is available time. From the day I exchanged my Air Force uniform for civilian attire, in 1945, I did just that.

Eleven months after returning from prison camp, I married the girl I had left behind, and seven years later migrated to Canada, to the beautiful and most westerly province of British Columbia. After thirty challenging years in the sales field, I retired in 1983.

My days of retirement were filled with all sorts of interesting endeavours, but from somewhere in my memory, unsolved situations from the past persisted in their claims for investigation. I could no longer claim the excuse of business pressures: I had no good reason to stuff those unsolved questions back into my memory bank. I decided to try and solve them.

In my mind were a number of unanswered questions—What happened to Peter, Big Jock, Taffy Mac, Nabber, Markellie, Eddy Anderson and the others? Did they return home safely? Did they achieve their goals in life and all those golden dreams of youth that were so full of expectation? There was a bigger question: Were they still alive and in good health, or had prison camp, the march, and life itself, finally taken their toll? Could I find the answers I was looking for?

All of these people would believe I was living in Ireland. Peter was the only Canadian; I would have to find Taffy Mac in Wales, Big Jock in Scotland, Farmer Markellie in Yorkshire, England, Nabber down under in New Zealand, and Crazy Anderson in Australia. And all may have pulled up roots and moved far afield.

Before I had the opportunity to set out looking for answers, two remarkable events emerged from my past to overshadow thoughts of finding my old buddies.

The night of February 2, 1943, when fate let me live and those brave Dutch people carried me into their home near the blazing wreck of our aircraft, I was in shock. I have always held vivid mental pictures of the room and its contents, but faces and names did not lodge in my memory, nor could I recall exactly where I was geographically. After forty years, it would be nearly impossible to find that crash site. For a long time I had talked about going back to Holland to find the graves of my flying comrades. I had written to the Commonwealth War Graves Commission in Ottawa, Canada, asking if they could give me their burial location. A prompt reply informed me that the burial plots were at Jonkerbos War Cemetery, near Nijmegen, Holland.

Early in 1983, with my son Jim, my brother Les and his son David, I planned a May visit to Holland. This decision prompted some dormant thoughts to life—could I find my Dutch benefactors? On a map of Holland I drew a circle, which according to the map's scale would be about thirty miles in diameter. I felt certain that somewhere within that circled area was the crash site...and my Dutch benefactors. Studying the map, I had a premonition that the area within the circle held secrets—forty-year-old secrets that would answer forty-year-old questions. And I had the strange feeling that coupled with those secrets would be other, extraordinary information. I was to embark on a "Voyage of Discovery."

With increasing excitement, I marked six places within the circle, wrote six similar letters, and added covering notes to postal authorities in each town and village. I requested that, if possible, the letters be translated into the Dutch language and displayed on their bulletin boards or similar information areas. A simple request: anyone remembering a survivor from a shot-down aircraft being carried into their home on the night of February 2, 1943, please reply or leave a message with the postal authorities.

It was a long shot, but something intuitive told me that somewhere in Holland, someone would read my appeal and spin back in their own memory to the night of February 2, 1943 and reveal the answers to my forty-year-old questions—and perhaps renew forty-year-old ties that never had a chance to begin.

During the last week of March I received important information, mailed from the Dutch town of Volkel:

> Dear Sir:
> We got your letter in which you asked about the place of your parachute landing in Nederland.
> We should like to have some more information about your crew and aircraft.

Then followed eleven questions. The letter finished with:

> You see, we have lots of questions. We hope you can help us with the answers so that we can help you.

I answered the questions by return mail and waited, wondering who put the questionnaire together. One question in particular, "Was your plane a Lancaster aircraft, letters A.L.-E., crash date February 2, 1943?" The date was right and the letters correct, except they were in the wrong sequence—it should have been E.A.-L.

Time was important now. Our foursome was flying from Los Angeles to Amsterdam on May 1. Two days prior to that, the reply letter came. Slowly I read the typed words. In precise and informative phrases, the writer stated,

> I think your aircraft crashed near a town named Kessel in the county of Limburg. We know there was a Lancaster crash February 2, 1943 with six killed and one survivor.

It was difficult to comprehend that I was reading a letter from a stranger in Holland recounting the most extraordinary night of my life. There was one sentence which I needed time to digest.

> I think your plane was shot down by Hauptmann Werner Streib, Commander of #1 Night Fighter Group, stationed at Venlo.

Now I had the almost unbelievable information that someone knew the name of the German night fighter pilot who shot us down!

The letter told me to contact a Mr. Willemsen upon my arrival in Holland. The letter ended,

> It was a pleasure to help you. If there is anything I can do for you, please ring me when you are in Holland. (Telephone number supplied.)
> Yours sincerely,
> H. Talen
> (Volkel Air Base)

I was re-reading the letter when my son Jim shouted, "Come on, Dad, don't keep us in suspense any longer. What does it say?"

I handed him the letter, then went out to the garden. It was a cool April day and I needed to be alone with my thoughts. I believed the mystery of the crash location had been solved, and along with it had come the bonus of the night fighter pilot's name. It was difficult to comprehend.

My thoughts were myriad, and excitement welled as I projected myself to the crash area. I could visualize finding the site and maybe the field I had parachuted to. Then, with strange emotions, I remembered the name of the German night fighter pilot, a Major Werner Streib, Commanding Officer of the *Luftwaffe* Venlo Air Base. I smiled at the thought—it took the Commanding Officer himself to shoot us down. Jacko and the rest of the crew would feel happier if they knew that, so perhaps someday, if our souls meet in the wild blue yonder, I'll tell them—or maybe they already know.

More questions poured into my head: Did Werner Streib survive the war? Was it possible that he was still alive? What feelings would I have if somewhere I met him, now that forty years had passed? Would I want to meet him? After all, by shooting down our aircraft, he killed my six comrades, so why would I wish to find out if he were alive and think about meeting him? I decided to make that decision when and if it confronted me further.

I was pursuing these thoughts when Jim, who had approached quietly, said, "Pretty interesting stuff, Dad. Do you think you'll ever find him, if he's alive?"

I turned around: "Do you think I should try?"

"That's up to you, Dad. Depends on how you feel?" The answer was the right one. It all depended on how I felt about this wartime enemy pilot named Streib and how I would feel if I discovered he was still alive.

Walking back to the house, I said to Jim, "Don't think I'll have to make that decision. If he survived all of his air battles, he probably died as a civilian—just another old veteran."

With a quizzical look, Jim hesitated for a moment before answering, "Dad, you don't think you're just another old veteran ready to die, so why should this man Streib be any different? If he is alive, you will find him."

This journey would indeed be "A Voyage of Discovery." I had the name of the *Luftwaffe* pilot involved. Was it possible that I could also find the Dutch people who came to my rescue so many years ago?

✈

May 1, 1983, arrived and our PanAm jet soared into the Californian sky above Los Angeles. Our Journey of Discovery had begun. Hours later we touched down at London, transferred to British European Airways, and crossed the English Channel to Amsterdam.

I climbed the stairs and looked into the rooms of Anne Frank's house: another tragedy of Gestapo terror. I found the waiting room at Amsterdam Station and the steps I had descended with German guards on my way to prison camp. And I was free to run or walk up and down those same steps.

The next morning, we returned to Amsterdam Station by taxi, boarded a train to Nijmegen, then journeyed by bus to Jonkerbos War Cemetery.

At the entrance I paused to read the inscription:

> 1939—1945
> THE LAND ON WHICH
> THIS CEMETERY STANDS
> IS THE GIFT OF
> THE DUTCH PEOPLE
> FOR THE
> PERPETUAL RESTING PLACE
> OF THE
> SAILORS, SOLDIERS

AND AIRMEN
WHO ARE
HONOURED HERE

We entered the grounds solemnly, found Row D, Plot 18, and six graves laid out in alphabetical order according to the first letter in their surnames. Approximately 2,000 young men were buried in this well-kept cemetery. There was an eerie feeling of respectful silence that hushed even our whispered comments. I had my own memories, my own thoughts of men I once knew, and their faces came back to mind so clearly. Jim broke the silence as he whispered, "Dad, do you feel they are here?"

"Yes," I said, "I can feel their presence."

I stood with three headstones on each side of me, and Jim whispered emotionally, "Dad, just one more stone and I wouldn't be here."

We stepped back and looked at the row of markers and at the flowers we had placed, and I thought, "Jim, Les, and David see cement headstones engraved with names, ranks, ages, and Air Force crests, but I see faces—young faces—five in their twenties and one just nineteen. My pals, my friends, my flying buddies of so many years ago. Just six members of a bomber crew among thousands in the graves that surrounded us."

After taking pictures, I was left alone to meditate and remember my friends in silence—just me and the six young faces from the past—faces that never had the chance to grow lined and old. I will always remember this experience. I remembered those aircrew days—the laughter, the comradeship, and the fears we all shared but seldom spoke of. I looked at the multitude of headstones that engulfed me and thought, "What a waste of young men's lives that we fail so miserably to maintain peace."

When I signed the visitors' register, I saw that Jim had written a few very touching words: "I feel privileged and extremely humble standing here today in the presence of over two thousand markers that represent only a small percentage of so many young men who a generation ago gave their lives so that I have freedom to come here and go where and when I please. I thank God that my Dad is alive and able to join me at this place of remembrance."

As we proceeded to the exit, I lagged behind my three companions and stopped for a last look, but I couldn't pinpoint those six markers among the multitude. Maybe that's how it should be, because over the course of the war years, we all shared the same mission. My six comrades had four decades ago left me to touch down right here and join the great multitude that formed this squadron, which was represented by the thousands of markers surrounding me.

✈

From the lobby of Hotel Etap, I dialed the telephone number I'd received in the Volkel letter. I was thrilled at the possibility of meeting Henk Talen.

A crisp, clear voice answered. For a moment I hesitated before telling him who I was, but then came the questions, "When can I meet you? Would you like to have dinner with me?" To my great disappointment, he declined both invitations and recommended I call Mr. Willemsen, whose address I had been given in the last letter. "My job with you is finished," he said. "I'm glad I could help. Now I can help someone else, so don't forget to contact Mr. Willemsen tomorrow."

I felt that I had been dismissed. At a loss for something to say, I spilled out a profuse thank you, but he cut in with his perfect English: "Mr. Willemsen has found the house and the people you wish to contact and also the crash site of your aircraft. I think we have found everything you are looking for. I must go now. Glad we were able to assist you."

I hung up the receiver, then stood for a minute looking at it. Jim was outside and knocked on the glass, then pushed open the folding doors. "What's the matter? Are you okay?"

"He doesn't want to see me."

"He's got to see us," came his reply.

"No he doesn't. And we don't need to see him, but we must contact Mr. Willemsen tomorrow morning."

Then, as the truth suddenly filtered into my brain, I almost shouted the news: "They have found the Dutch people who helped me forty years ago and the crash site and the house I was in!"

Jim's eyes widened in disbelief. We hugged each other before dashing upstairs to tell Les and David the fantastic news.

This called for a celebration. We descended to the hotel bar to drink a toast, first to those whose graves we had visited, secondly to the person named Henk Talen, then to the people who found the crash site. We toasted each other and we toasted Mr. Willemsen. We wondered what sort of person would answer to that name tomorrow, then drank a toast to tomorrow and to all tomorrows.

The morning came quickly, as is its habit after a late night of toasts, and of course our new European time said it was May 4th. With breakfast under our belts, each of us paid twenty-five gilders for our hotel rooms, crammed our belongings into the rented car, and headed for Venray.

When we arrived, I telephoned Mr. Willemsen at the Archives, but was unable to make contact. I had his address from Henk Talen's letter. We found the street and stopped at number 5801, where a lady was cutting the spring growth of new green grass. My three companions decided it was my day, so I was to break the ice. The lady smiled as I approached, and I felt sure she was expecting us.

"Does Mr. Willemsen live here?" I asked.

"Yes," she replied in perfect English, "he is my husband and is home for lunch."

I introduced myself, and with a delightful little whoop of joy, she invited all of us to come inside to a pleasant living room, where I met the man who had done so much to find answers to my forty-year-old questions.

Mr. Willemsen was more than sixty years of age, a strong and determined character. The handshake was firm as he greeted us. Then without undue fuss Mrs. Willemsen brought coffee and cookies. As we settled into comfortable chairs, I could hardly wait for this man to embark on his account of how he had found the Dutch family.

"You called Talen last night." It was a statement, yet a question.

"Yes," I answered, "but he didn't wish to see me, and that was disappointing and strange."

Wim, as his wife called him, looked steadfastly at me before replying, and for a moment I thought I had said the wrong thing.

"Talen is a busy man. He had other plans for last evening. He was meeting with someone who at one time had similar questions to yours for us to solve."

He hesitated for a moment, then bit into a cookie and washed it down with coffee. "Anyway, this problem of yours was in the area under my jurisdiction. It would have been a long way for Talen to come—over thirty-five kilometres."

Thirty-five kilometres would be a very short distance in North America, but Holland is a small country, and it was a long way for these people. Wim looked directly at me.

"The Giesberts are expecting you tomorrow. The old people are dead, but Coen, his younger sister Stein, and brother Jan are looking forward to seeing you. They live together in Heldenseweg."

My brain was working overtime, trying to digest and decipher these words. So now, after forty years, I had names. It was the Giesberts family who took me in that night and the village or area was called Heldenseweg.

"Coen is in poor health. The night you parachuted close to their house, I believe he was the one who helped you. He has a bad heart. His brother and sister are concerned, but all three are excited about you coming to see them, especially so because tomorrow, the 5th, is a holiday—our Liberation Day."

What a coincidence that I was to have this wonderful reunion tomorrow, their celebration day.

"How did you find them, and how do you know they are the right people?"

"I had proof, my friend. Otherwise I would not have confirmed my quest accomplished."

I felt that I'd been rebuked for asking the last part of my question.

Wim told, in matter-of-fact tones that belied his hard work and long hours, the story of how he found my people. He had scoured the area, knocking on doors in villages and throughout the countryside, always asking the same question: "Do you know of anyone who, on February 2nd, 1943, helped an Allied aircrew survivor?"

I don't know how many weary hours he spent, knocking on doors and asking his question. With that strong determination of his, he continued day after day until, in the area of Heldenseweg, not far from the town of Kessel, he knocked on another door. A frail man in his seventies answered. "Did you, or do you know of anyone who helped an Allied airman, survivor of a Lancaster aircrew, way back in February, 1943?" Expecting the same reply he'd heard for weeks, Wim was about to thank this person and continue his search.

Suddenly the man's eyes glowed with interest, then without explaining why, he said, "Can you wait for a minute or two until I find a book?"

Wim waited, not sure what to expect. The man returned with a book he had opened at a certain page. He held out a piece of paper and asked, "Are you looking for this man?"

The old gentleman had through the years made sure this scrap of paper was safe. He had the faith or the intuition to know that one day it would mean a great deal. My name was on that scrap of paper, and Coen

Giesberts had kept and guarded it for over forty years! Wim had found my brave Dutch family!

All four of us stared in silence as the story unfolded. Mary (Mrs. Willemsen) seemed accustomed to this sort of conversation, but showed interest as she stood by. Then Wim continued. "Coen Giesberts, his sister and brother, did not marry. They still live together, but in a new house, next to the one you were in."

"You were told that, according to our information, it was a *Luftwaffe* pilot named Streib who shot down your plane."

"Yes, that information was in the letter from Mr. Talen."

Fork still poised half way to his mouth, he had the look of someone participating in a play and had practised his lines to perfection. "Would you like to see a photograph of Major Streib?"

Instinctively my eyes traversed the room, looking at family pictures on the walls and other places. I could not understand why these people would have the photograph of a *Luftwaffe* officer. Quickly our host swallowed his pie. Then, from a book shelf nearby, he produced a volume printed in German, its title, *Der Zweite Weltkrieg Zwischen Rhein Und Maas* (*The Second World War Between the Rhine and Maas Rivers*).

He placed the book on the end table beside me, and opened it at page 126, and the picture of a *Luftwaffe* officer—a good looking man with strong features and a determined expression. His uniform showed the high honour awards of the Iron Cross and Oak Leaves. So this was Werner Streib, war-time Commander of Venlo *Luftwaffe* Night Fighter Base, the man who, according to my Dutch information, could be pilot of the enemy plane we met that night.

With my companions, I surveyed the picture, and conversation moved from his looks to the question of his character: What sort of a commander was he? He looked more than thirty. Was this the man who visited me in my cell at his air base? We could only guess at these and many other questions.

I was up early next morning. May 5, 1983—Holland's day to celebrate their liberation—was as bright as our spirits. Arrangements had been made to meet at Willemsen's by 9:30 a.m. After that, we were to proceed to the area of Heldenseweg for the reunion with "my people," the Giesberts.

We had a good breakfast, but on arrival at Willemsen's Mary insisted she serve coffee, cake and cookies, and so on. Eventually we left in two cars on our nostalgic trip. I was a passenger in Wim and Mary's car; Les, David and Jim followed in our rented one.

There was little conversation during the ride, but when Wim said we were almost there, my heart skipped a beat. I was on the threshold of rolling back the clock forty years and returning in daylight to see for myself the crash site and perhaps learn things I didn't know happened that wet February night in 1943.

"Just a few more minutes." His voice was low. Mary turned to me, her eyes alight as she said, "Exciting, isn't it?"

"More than that," I replied.

Although it was a dark night when I had walked this path, I remembered it as a narrow country road with a sharp curve before the house. Now we were driving on a straight, modern highway, yet Wim had said, "Just a few more minutes."

Wim said, "This is a new highway." Then he added, "They also straightened out the old one."

The car slowed and stopped beside other parked vehicles, and my three partners on this journey pulled in behind. Quickly we were out, standing on a narrow strip of road beside the new highway. It was my old country road—straightened out.

Waiting for us was a Mr. Co Van derGrient, representative of Kessel, the small town that was mentioned in Talen's letter. With him was his wife, Paula, and a Mr. Jan Int Zandt, who, with his wife Maria, spent many hours investigating World War II air crashes in Holland. Now our little company numbered nine. After introductions and handshakes, Mr. Van derGrient made a short welcome speech, then presented me with brochures and pictures of Kessel and the area.

After a few minutes of posing for the cameras, Wim said, "Let's take you in to meet once again with the Giesberts."

Pointing at the old home just a few yards away, he said, "That's the house you were in. We will visit there later."

I felt a shiver of excitement. I was to see once again the forty-year-old memory 'pictures' that were from inside that old house.

We proceeded up the path and into the Giesberts' new home to meet those helpers from so long ago. How does one feel after forty years, meeting again people who, by offering and giving their help, had risked horrible reprisals by their masters, the German occupation forces? I felt excitement and with it an overwhelming feeling of warmth, of joy at this reunion, and also great indebtedness. I could not repay their kindness.

Coen Giesberts, a young man of thirty-two when I parachuted almost into his back yard, was now seventy-two and troubled with heart problems. He was sitting in his chair, and when we came in, he rose unsteadily to greet me. I thought, "This is something that happens to few people." I clasped his hand and put my arm around him and wondered if he was thinking of his mother and father, the good people who were with him the last time we met. His younger sister Stein and brother Jan, both in their sixties, came forward to shake my hand. I presented this shy lady with flowers and gave her a hug.

They did not speak English, so we conversed through Wim and Mr. Co Van derGrient, but as we stood together with our hands joined, there was no need for speech. They knew I was here with a great thankfulness in my heart for their help when I needed it, and I knew that at this moment just being here, I had accomplished what seemed an impossibility. It was a happy reunion.

Coen rose from his chair and shakily walked to a cupboard. He produced the book that had held the scrap of paper for so many years. He found the paper with my name on it, and with a trembling hand, held it out for my inspection. It was only a page from a small notebook with the name 'MacMahon' written at the bottom, but what a central part it had played in bringing us all to this moment. Over coffee and Stein's cakes and pastry, we talked through our interpreters about the night they gave me help and shelter.

They said that the plane had exploded before hitting the ground and that the tail section was found a long way from the rest of the aircraft.

Next was a visit to the crash site. Coen insisted that he was able to go along. Bundling him up in a warm jacket and a winter scarf, along with his cane, we all moved by car to the field where our plane had crashed. Now it was ploughed to grow asparagus. We walked the ploughed furrows, searching for some small scrap of metal that might still be around.

I found one small piece.

Arrangements had been made for a visit to the old house. I was warned it had been changed—there had been a complete renovation.

I asked if I could go in by the front as I had forty years ago. I entered and immediately turned right. But it was not like the picture in my memory. I had the feeling that I was in a strange room, yet I knew I was in the big kitchen from 1943. Mentally, I started to reconstruct that room as it was. I asked questions, using Wim as interpreter.

"There was a window over there to my right."

"That's correct," she replied. "We moved it, as you can see."

A modern fireplace was installed where once stood the old light blue cook stove.

I thought of the young men who quickly left this room before the German Military Police entered. I knew at that time there was another exit. Now it was gone. The existence of a second door in 1943 was verified. It had become a casualty during renovations, so my memory was still good.

I took a few paces to the right and said, "The telephone was here on this wall, and to its left was a sculptured figure of Christ."

The answer to the telephone question was "Yes, now it is a desk phone," but regarding my sculpture query the young woman did not know and indicated that I should ask the Giesberts.

Now I could see the room as it was in February, 1943.

Upon my return to the Giesberts, I noticed a sculpture of Christ on a stand in the corner of the room. I asked, "Was this sculpture on the wall to the left of the phone in 1943 in the old house?"

"Yes," came the interpreted reply.

So another question in my mind was now cleared.

We spent an hour asking questions and listening to stories from the past, and then it was time to say good-bye. From her china cabinet, Stein presented me with a china cup and saucer, also a glass imprinted with a Dutch windmill. "For your lady," she said in English.

It was a touching farewell as Coen, with Stein's assistance, hobbled out to the old road. Both stood dejectedly by the roadside, waving their good-byes as we sped away. I watched as they continued to wave until distance faded them from my sight.

Then it was more farewells, first to the Van derGrients and then to those two wonderful people, Wim and Mary Willemsen. With promises to keep in contact, we returned to Nijmegen. Our day to remember was over, but the memories will live as long as I do.

The next day we returned by train to Amsterdam. From there the boat train whisked us off to the 'Hook of Holland,' where we embarked on the cross channel ferry *en route* to England.

All too quickly, we were flying west and changing our watches to regain the lost hours, but what wonderful events had taken place in a short time! I had stretched out into the unknown and reaped rewards that will last my lifetime and beyond, because I am certain my son will pass on the story of Wim and Mary Willemsen, Coen, Jan and Stein Giesberts, Jan and Maria Int Zandt, Kessel's Mr. Co van der Grient, his wife Paula, and all the happenings that culminated in a wonderful reunion that 5th day of May, 1983.

Soon I was home, sitting at my desk, trying to put down on paper my story, but something was still bothering me—it was a name connected with the *Luftwaffe*'s 1943 air base at Venlo, Holland—and the name belonged to its Commanding Officer—Major Werner Streib. Was he still alive?

In 1983, forty years after my first mission, I returned to look for the graves of my six young friends at Jonkerbos War Cemetary, near Nijmegan, Holland.

Flight Lieutenant R.A. Jackson, 27

Flight Sergeant H.M. Magder, 22

Sergeant A.J. Clover, 19

Flight Lieutenant E.J.F. Dunand, 25

Sergeant L.G. Alexander

Pilot Officer A.W. Lane

"Wim" Willemsen's determination and monumental energy helped me locate the Giesberts family.

L-R: Stein Giesberts, John McMahon, and Coen Giesberts at our reunion in the village of Heldenseweg, Holland, in 1983.

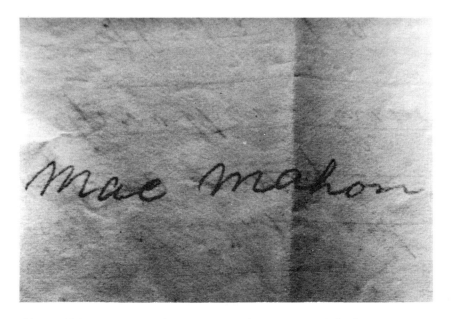

Above: This small scrap of paper, kept safe inside a book for forty years, helped Coen Giesberts make the connection between Wim Willemsen's questions and the night of 2 February 1943. **Below**: the house to which I was taken on the night of the crash.

Above: According to my Dutch friends, this was the point of impact. **Below**: Peet Segers was a twelve-year-old boy when he saw me parachute to a field near his home. He presented me with a rusted clip of .303 shells from our aircraft.

CHAPTER 22

My Second Quest

I recounted to many friends the events of my quest to Holland and wonderful reunion with the Giesberts family. For some time it became a conversation piece and often questions would be asked—and not about the Giesberts. Those questions were regarding a certain *Luftwaffe* pilot—dead or alive, no one knew: "Do you think this Werner Streib is still alive? Could he really be the pilot who shot down your plane? It's hard to believe. Would you want to find him? How could you prove it was him if you did find him?"

Others remarked with conviction: "I wouldn't want to find him," or, "Hope he was killed." Some rebuked my own ideas by saying, "You wouldn't think of trying to locate this man. After all, he killed your crew members."

A good friend volunteered his thoughts, "Finding this man would be a million-to-one chance anyway." He hesitated for a moment, then looked steadfastly at me before asking, "Where would you begin?"

"Where would I begin?" That question triggered my memory to H. Talen's letter, with its suggestion that the commanding officer of the Venlo Airbase night fighter group had shot us down, and the information that Wim Willemsem had confided. I had the answer to that question. I knew where to begin if I were to make the decision to look for this ex-enemy pilot, but I did not divulge my thoughts.

For a couple of months I wrestled with the thought of taking the first step to find more information about this man. My own feelings were that this *Luftwaffe* pilot was in wartime doing his job, defending his country from the stream of Allied bombers. To a German night fighter pilot it was an enemy aircraft loaded with bombs that he had to stop, and in so doing he must evade the stream of shells from that aircraft's gun turrets. By shooting down our aircraft he had killed my six comrades, but to him we were just another enemy aircraft. If I were to go in search of Werner Streib, my good friend's question would have to be answered—"Where would you start?" The answer would come from Wim Willemsen's confidential information.

The summer of 1984 raced quickly towards fall, and once again I sat at my faithful desk, weighing an important decision. It was September 13. My important decision was to start the ball of discovery rolling once more, my goal to find the ex-*Luftwaffe* pilot named Werner Streib. I felt certain the information gleaned from Wim Willemsen would give me a head start on this new venture.

I wrote a letter to Werner Streib. It was a simple run-down of my return to Holland and the information received concerning him. I mentioned some reports I had read regarding his war exploits and informed him of the date and time our plane was shot down. My question to him was did he recall or have a report in his log book of being involved in shooting down a Lancaster at 21:30 hours that second night of February, 1943.

It was October 17 before I took the step of writing a covering letter to tell the parties concerned I was trying to contact ex-*Luftwaffe* flyer Werner Streib, who in 1943 was a Commander of *Luftwaffe* air base at Venlo, Holland. I asked them to forward my letter to him if they had an address. My intuition said he was alive. After mailing the letter I had a strong feeling that I had embarked on another "Voyage of Discovery."

Wim knew that after the war Streib worked for the NATO organization, so I sent my letters to NATO Headquarters, Bonn, West Germany.

Impatiently I waited as the weeks passed, then in mid-November I received a short typed letter from the German Military Historical Research Department dated November 7. The typing was in German, but I understood the message. It was an answer to my 17.10.84 letter regarding, as they indicated, a Brigadier General Werner Streib (Retired); his address was given, and the information in my letter had been forwarded to him. Streib was alive, retired as a Brigadier General. Now the big question: Would he answer my letter?

This fuelled much discussion among family members and others, with replies such as, "Why should he answer? He has nothing to gain by doing so. He doesn't know who you are; you might have an axe to grind by tracing the man who killed your crew. For all he knows you might be of unsound mind with an ulterior motive like wanting to kill him."

Three weeks later there was a lone envelope in my mail, looking so important it appeared no other correspondence was permitted to share the box. Quickly I picked it up. There on the left hand top corner, below the *Luftpost* mark, was the name: W. Streib, and his address.

Did I now hold in my hand the answer to a question soon to be forty-two years old: "Who was the enemy pilot at the controls of the *Luftwaffe* night fighter plane that shot down our aircraft? Was I about to find that this man had caused the deaths of my six flying comrades? Carefully I opened this interesting envelope, and inside, in good English, was a typed nineteen-line letter dated Munich, 29.11.84. At the top left hand corner, above his address, was the name Werner Streib (Brigadier General, Retired).

He verified receiving my correspondence but said he had problems reading it because my letter was handwritten. Claiming that what he read was very interesting, his letter continued with the words:

Now to your question. In the night of 2 Feb., 1943 I shot down 2 aircraft. One Lancaster and one four-motor aircraft. This fact I take from a list which shows date and type of aircraft I shot down in WW II. Unfortunately I don't have a log book with more details.

His claim to the second plane he shot down that night as a 'four-motor aircraft' raised a question in my mind, as Bomber Command was equipped with Lancasters, Stirlings and Halifaxes, all four-motored aircraft. Streib could not say with certainty what type of aircraft he had shot down in the second instance that night. In his own printed words, the doubt was written in this way:

Maybe it was your Lancaster I met that night, but it also may be that some more Lancaster had been shot down in that night by other fighters.

The next paragraph was extremely interesting reading, and I realized this man must have been a top German flying ace:

I had 65 victories at night (+ 1 at day). I can't remember details to a special night and date, you may understand. On the other hand, it's long ago.

Then came two lines congratulating me on my escape by parachute, and he went on to say that one night he also had to bail out. Werner Streib finished his short correspondence with these thoughts:

> I wish you and your family much luck for the future, and us both more peaceful times than we had when we were young people.
> Enclosed you find foto from the time 40 years ago.
> Sincerely,
> Werner Streib

I then extracted from the envelope a glossy black and white print. There, staring out at me from that picture, was the 1943 Commander of Venlo's *Luftwaffe* night fighter Air Base. On the reverse side was written "To Mr. John McMahon with best wishes," the signature of Werner Streib, and dated November, 1984.

I replied to Werner Streib on December 29, telling what I recalled about Venlo Airbase, its guardhouse, the cell I was in for a number of days, and the high-ranking aircrew officer who ordered a pillow and mattress for me. I hoped it would jog his memory, because I was certain that he filled that role. There was no return letter this time. As I waited impatiently, the weeks changed to months.

My very special and almost impossible quest of finding Werner Streib was now just another old-hat story, and my question had not been answered beyond reasonable doubt, so I could not say 'yes' when asked, "Did you really find the pilot who shot down your plane?"

It was the middle of March, and I had tried to bury thoughts of the Streib episode. But then I received another letter. This time a new name appeared on an envelope below the West German *Luftpost* mark: Richard B. Spiro. This letter was from Kassel, West Germany, dated March 6, 1985. This new entry into my intriguing search introduced himself as a distant relative of Werner Streib, 1943 Commander of the Messerschmitt 110 Night Fighter Group Air Base at Venlo, Holland, and now retired NATO Brigadier General. The writer informed me that Werner Streib had asked him to translate my November 7th letter and write to me. As I read further into the third paragraph, startling information leapt out at me from the typed words as the writer looked back forty-two years and said:

But now back to the night of February 2/3, 1943. The night fighter group to which the Major Streib belonged gave every night fighter a silver cup for every enemy plane shot down. Naturally, Werner kept all these cups . . . 66 of them altogether. For the night of February 2/3 he has two such cups. One is engraved 'Lancaster,' but on the other only the date. Werner himself could only identify one Lancaster and of the other he shot down that night he only saw that it was a four-motor aircraft.

As I read the rest of Richard Spiro's narrative, my heart beat faster. The words were spelling out for me the answer to my forty-two-year-old question. The answer was in the fourth paragraph:

There is in Germany a Mr. Scholl who since years collects all data of night fighter activities, who sent to Werner a list of all Royal Air Force planes downed in the night of February 2/3, 1943:

LANCASTER 44 Squadron. Sergeant Herdon, Pilot
LANCASTER 50 Squadron. Pilot/Officer Power, Pilot
LANCASTER 49 Squadron. Flight/Lieutenant Jackson, Pilot
HALIFAX 102 Squadron. Flying/Officer Ross-Thompson, Pilot
STIRLING 7 Squadron. Squadron/Leader Smith, Pilot

Two of the Lancasters fell on Dutch territory, the third in Germany, and Scholl wrote further that Major Streib shot down:

2/3 Feb. 1943   1 Lancaster at 21:12 hrs over Eindhoven, 43rd plane downed by Streib

2/3 Feb. 1943   1 Lancaster at 21:30 hrs over Venlo, 44th plane downed by Streib

From all this, Werner says it can be concluded that one of these two was your plane, from which you escaped so miraculously.

284

Now I had the answer and the confirmation. It was *Luftwaffe* Major Werner Streib's aircraft we encountered at 19,000 feet in the night sky over Holland, and the time was 21:30 hours (9:30 p.m.) We did see a Lancaster go down at 21:12 hours (9:12 p.m.). So that was Streib's 43rd success, and thirteen minutes later we added to his collection of silver cups the one cup out of sixty-six that has only the date engraved. I wondered if he would now take it and have the word 'Lancaster' engraved on it.

I re-read this letter, trying to digest the fact my search was over. By his own endorsement of Mr. Scholl's report, this now ex-Brigadier General Streib is the *Luftwaffe* pilot I've been trying to locate. Once more I slowly read the last paragraph, hanging on to each word, making certain I missed nothing. There was a feeling of privacy about it, and for some unexplained reason I wanted to keep this information to myself for a while. I felt a great sense of achievement at my accomplishment and wondered how many shot-down aircrew had been able to trace the pilot of the enemy plane that stealthily crept in from the night, sprayed its lethal weapons, and swiftly disappeared in the darkness. I knew many people who had said to me, "It is an impossible quest." Now I held a piece of typed paper that proved I had once again accomplished the impossible.

Feeling it was time to share with others this latest correspondence, I read to my family this informative letter. They read it for themselves and in due course the news that Streib confirmed his involvement in downing our plane spread to interested friends and others.

There was a Christmas card from Werner Streib in 1984, but as the new year of 1985 sped by and brought us face-to-face with another December, only Richard Spiro and I continued with our exchange of letters. Correspondence with the 81-year-old Spiro had become a pleasure indeed. He fought on the Allied side in the South African regiment in the North African campaign against Rommel's Afrika Corp.

On the night of that first fateful mission, it would have been utterly inconceivable to me to think that I might one day contact the man who was to shoot us down that night.

Werner Streib in 1943, when he was Commander of Venlo Airbase, Holland. On the back of the photo that Streib sent to me were these words: "To Mr. John McMahon/With best regards/Werner Streib/29 Nov. 84"

EPILOGUE

December 1985 brought me new and interesting experiences. My son Jim booked a trip to New Zealand and I volunteered to join him. We flew on Friday, December 6, 1985, away from Canada's winter and into New Zealand's summer, this time on a different voyage of discovery, seeing New Zealand in our own way and in our own time slot, but I had an important person from my past to try and find. If he was alive I wanted to find him; if he was dead, I wanted to pay my respects. Before that crazy march from Stalag in January, 1945, I had collected home addresses of prison camp friends, so before leaving I searched out a few New Zealand ones, and of course the most important of all was my old buddy, Nabber Giddens. A forty-year-old address of his mother was not much to go on, but it was a start.

It was Saturday, December 14 when we arrived at Waihi on the east coast and asked directions to the forty-year-old address of the Giddens family.

I rang the doorbell on this hot December day. The window blinds were drawn and no one responded. I felt great disappointment. Forty years had passed; we had come from the other side of the world and found Nabber Giddens' family home, but there was no one to invite us in. At the house next door, I explained my desire to find an old prison-camp friend named Giddens. The gentleman expressed regret that it had taken me forty years to make this journey, because I had missed the opportunity of visiting with a grand old lady, Mrs. Giddens, who had died just one week ago at the age of eighty-four. I quickly asked the question, "Do you know her son who was in the Air Force? Is he alive?"

"Oh, Doug, he's alive, all right," came the encouraging reply. "Doug lives in Auckland. I've no idea where, but his sister lives close by."

Armed with street and number, we quickly found Doug's sister. After a pleasant visit, we left with Doug Giddens' address and telephone number safely tucked in my wallet.

Arriving at a friend's home in Auckland, I could hardly wait for the opportunity to use the telephone. When Nabber answered, I deliberately refrained from telling him who I was, but asked, "You are Doug Giddens, ex-Royal New Zealand Air Force?"

"Who is this?" he asked, but I followed up quickly with, "You were a prisoner of war in Stalag VIIIB and spent time in Barrack 15A?"

"Yes, I was in three different barracks, but most of the time in 15A. Who are you?" I smiled as his strong Kiwi accent showed signs of irritation.

"You slept in a top bunk?"

He confirmed this to be true and once again blurted out: "Who are you?"

Again I ignored his request. "Who slept in the bunk below you?"

"My memory is not so good," he replied.

"Was it Farmer Markellie?"

"Yes! Yes! That's right, Chubby Markellie."

"Who was in the top bunk to your right?"

"A crazy Australian named Eddy Anderson," he replied.

"Your memory's okay," I said. "Now to test it, who slept below Anderson?"

Immediately came the exclamation, "Paddy Mac! You're Paddy McMahon? Where are you? Are you coming to see me now? What about tonight?" There was a stream of New Zealand expressions mixed with a flood of recognition in his voice.

"My sister said a Canadian ex-prisoner from Stalag VIIIB was looking for me and that he'd slept in a bunk next to mine. She screwed up the pronunciation of your name. Someone told me you went back to Ireland and started a business."

"I did. I did, Nabber, but I'm a Canadian now."

He laughed and said, "Imagine, Paddy Mac a Canadian. You should have come down here and become a Kiwi. You always said you would. When are you coming to see me?"

"I'll come to see you this afternoon," I promised.

"Hope you won't be disappointed when you see the way I look," he said.

"Guess that could go for both of us," I replied.

Forty years plus creates havoc with the look of youth, and so it was that Jim and I visited Nabber Giddens and recorded on film the joy of meeting this old friend with whom I had shared experiences we wished to forget as well as ones we will always cherish. We spent a wonderful evening amid old pictures and old stories. The 'do-you-remembers' claimed many hours. A special bottle of red wine was unearthed from a secret place. Nabber said he had waited a long time for an occasion worthy of cracking it open.

When we said good-bye, both of us realized we were not twenty-two or twenty-three and that the odds were against another reunion. We hugged each other and vowed to keep the contact. We felt that for Nabber Giddens and Paddy Mac this might be the last farewell.

I had four addresses of other Stalag prisoners with me. Through enquiries, I discovered that three had died. Of the last name I learned nothing. One of those who died was Eric Johnston, the tenor-voiced prisoner who, at night when we were locked up and morale was at a low ebb, would sing the "Lord's Prayer" to silent inmates of Barrack 15A. He had been killed in a train accident. After surviving his plane crash, prison camp, and the march, "Eric was killed at work on the New Zealand railroad," my informant said.

We flew back home to Canada on January 12th. It was nice to be home. At the latter part of May, around the 22nd, I wrote to Richard Spiro and received a prompt three-page handwritten letter in return, dated June 9th. In his letter there was news that the Brigadier General had been in hospital and gone through surgery.

On July 3rd I received Spiro's second letter, dated June 23rd. It was straight and to the point, "This is a sad continuation of my last letter: Werner is dead." He then continued with the information that my former enemy night fighter pilot had died June 15th. My chance to meet face-to-face with this ex-*Luftwaffe* ace is gone, but always there will be the satisfaction of having found this man and corresponded with him, resulting in knowing a little about his personality.

When I think of this ex-enemy pilot I will always remember some information from Richard Spiro, so I can visualize the Brigadier General as a schoolboy in Pforzheim and as a young apprentice in a bank, his heart set on becoming a flyer. Years before the war he attained his great ambition to be a pilot. I guess Werner Streib's own words in that first letter to me are the ones we should all remember:

I wish you and your family much luck for the future, and us both more peaceful times than we had when we were young people.

POSTSCRIPT

Mr. Pete Segers (Heldenseweg Area Holland)

Mr. Segers was a boy of twelve when, on the night of February 2nd, 1943, he saw me landing by parachute in the ploughed field close to his home. He ran to tell his parents what he had seen, but the Giesberts got to me first.

When I visited Holland in 1987, Mr. Segers invited me to call at his home. I did so and he asked that I go with him to an outside barn. From a high crevice in the wall he produced a rusted clip holding eight 303 live ammunition shells used in the guns of the aircraft we were flying when shot down in 1943. He had kept these souvenirs in this hiding place for over a decade. He asked if I would accept them as a gift. I did.

Douglas Giddens

'Nabber' was a crew member of an aircraft shot down in the fall of 1942. He bailed out of the crippled aircraft over Germany. He was shocked to see that his descent was towards a river. He tried in vain to guide his parachute away from the water, but finally steeled himself for a dunking. Instead of hitting water, Nabber landed heavily on a wet German autobahn. Rain and the reflected moonlight had made the road look like water. Nabber's hard landing would cause him problems in later years.

When the march continued from Gorlitz, the struggling mass of humanity plodded westwards. Somehow Nabber made it to Muhlberg POW camp, where he was liberated by the American forces. Weeks later, when he was able to get around unaided, he was taken to the air base, where a multitude of liberated humanity waited for aircraft that would fly them to England.

Some time before he was shot down, Nabber had met Dorothy, a young English girl. They were able to continue correspondence through the erratic prison-camp mail. On his return, Nabber married Dorothy and took her to New Zealand. They had two sons. After a couple of adventures into the business world, Nabber decided to work for someone else. He gained employment with an aluminum manufacturing company. (Sometimes he must have thought about the wonderful plates and mugs he could have made with this product, and about the kind of cigarette prices he could have charged in Stalag).

The decades passed. Then Dorothy was struck down by a number of strokes and Nabber, assisted by government home help for a number of years, was able to care for her at home. Dorothy died in 1989.

In October, 1994, Nabber made his second visit to Canada. In Victoria, British Columbia, Alice and I met with Doug 'Nabber' Giddens and Betty, the lady who is now his 'Mucker.'

His parachute landing on the concrete autobahn so many years ago has cost Nabber hospital time on numerous occasions, and more than one artificial hip replacement. He is still in good physical condition and in great spirits. His sense of humour has not been dampened.

When our visit was over, we bid each other good-bye—not for all time, just for a while. At the hotel elevator, he echoed the words of almost fifty years ago, when military police guided us to separate aircraft. "Come to New Zealand, Paddy." Before the elevator doors closed my answer was, "I'll try, Nabber, I'll try."

Jimmy Grier

Jimmy Grier returned safely to Ireland sometime after I did. In my notes about returning home, I made mention of Jimmy's surprise visit to me. I gathered, from our conversation, that his association with the Aussies had not worked out very well.

For many days he had struggled along those horrible roads alone. At some point—he couldn't remember when or where—he left the column with some others and decided to hide in an old barn and wait for liberation. They almost froze and starved to death before Allied Forces arrived.

I said that when Jimmy left that day he did not turn to salute or wave a farewell at the street corner. I never saw him again, but I have in my possession part of a letter he wrote to me in 1946. He was going back to Germany in a civilian capacity with the occupation forces. That was my last communication with my mucker.

James W. Martin

A letter from James W. Martin dated August 9th, 1990 was my first contact with 'Big Jock' since those terrible February Days in 1945, when, weakened by dysentery, I faltered on the march and was left behind, my friends too weak themselves to help.

From Jock's letter:

You've had an interesting and eventful life moving about Canada—certainly a change from the time in Stalag when you used one of your precious letters to write to a certain Lord Nuffield in England and you got a reply sent to and received in prison camp. . . .

My time came on 23rd, February, 1945, when I took dysentery and marched for a further four days [and] got to a rest barn. Next day, sixty of us were loaded on two carts like sacks of rubbish and taken to a hospital at Stadtroda (POW Hospital) where we received as much help as one doctor could give and that was nil.

About thirty died at this place—one or two each night. After six weeks I was somewhat fitter, having built myself up slightly after the Americans liberated us. They finally passed thru, and by then I was able to walk around.

Four of us managed by certain means to obtain an Opel car to go with a stolen battery and petrol, and we set off westward for home. After a number of escapades—like breaking into a bonded warehouse—we filled the boot with booze and traded it to the Americans for jerry cans of petrol. (All's fair in love and war.) Eventually we arrived alive in the British Sector, and soon after they flew us to England. The rest was normal, re-hab center at Cosford, "bags of leave," over-eating and waiting to get out and into civvy street.

During his leave, Jock met a young "Land Army Girl" and they were married in December, 1945. Her name was Mary, and as Jock put it, "She was with me for forty-two years before the big 'C' finally won."

It is almost with a touch of pride at Mary's tenacity in holding on to life that he writes, "Cancer had a hell of a battle before it won."

Jock spent thirty years on the Edinburgh Police Force. His Scottish humour has remained with him. One paragraph in his letter reads:

On my own now, a seventy-year-old pensioner with Hiatis Hernia, Angina, and the slight remains of my first stroke, I still consider myself lucky to be where I am, and the in-built Mark 1 'Cranium Computer' given to me in 1920, albeit a bit rusty, still throws out a few memories.

All the best Paddy

Cheers

Jock

Peter Chadwick

It was sometime in February, 1945, during those awful days of the march, that I lost contact with Big Jock and Peter Chadwick. For many years there was a complete loss of communication. Almost ten years later, in Vancouver, British Columbia, I accidently met Peter at a car parking lot. He had been sitting in his car, and as I walked across the lot, he recognized me. He ran after me calling "Paddy Mac! Paddy Mac!" It sounded like an old prison-camp call. After warm greetings, we exchanged quick, condensed histories.

Peter had stayed in the Air Force and was stationed at the Vancouver base. He had the rank of Flight Lieutenant. I was working in a grocery chain store at the time and asked Peter if I should try to join up again. "A thirty-three-year-old Paddy Mac in the ranks again?" He laughed. "You'd have to stand at attention to people like me, and you wouldn't like that." My family became good friends with his, but he was transferred back east, and again we lost contact for a long time.

In August 1985 we had a wonderful visit from Peter and Bill (Taffy) McLean who came to see me and my family on Vancouver Island. Peter has, for a number of years, been retired from the Air Force and lives in eastern Canada. They have a number of grandchildren, and Peter, like many of us old war veterans, is writing his memoirs.

Mr. Wim Willemsen

Mr. William Willemsen, or Wim, as his wife Mary calls him, has some hair-raising stories of his own to tell. He was in the Dutch Underground during the war. Once, after an urgent phone message telling him to leave his home immediately, he escaped just before his home was surrounded and searched by German soldiers.

After hiding in a cemetery for a long time, he was able, with Underground help, to obtain false identity papers and so a new name.

He and his wife Mary live in Venray, Holland, where 'Wim' is in charge of the town archives.

The Giesberts

November 1994: At the Giesberts home in the little village area of Heldenseweg, Jan Giesberts lives alone. Coen died a few years ago and Stein, having suffered a number of strokes, is in hospital.

Jan is lonely, but each day—weather permitting—he rides his bicycle to the ferry that crosses the Maas River, then continues the journey to visit his sister at the hospital.

I keep in contact through a friend of the Giesberts, a Mr. Knippenberg, who lives in Kessel not too far from the Giesberts' home.

Bill 'Toad' Hughes

Toad's talent as cartoonist and artist had gained for him a nice little business, resulting in a reasonable income (in cigarettes, of course).

Being a non-smoker, I was able to purchase from Bill Hughes a number of unique cartoons. Now, more than fifty years later, it is an honour to include some of these in this book.

Perhaps if 'Toad' is still in the land of the living, he or someone who knows his whereabouts will contact me. I first made enquiries way back in 1987. My most recent efforts, in October, 1994, garnered a reply from the Royal British Legion in the area of his last known address. They have advertised and made personal investigations, but have not found him.

I am alive and well and living in British Columbia, Canada. On occasion, I take nostalgic journeys into the past by perusing my wartime memorabilia. Among those bits and pieces of times long past are two old letters. The reader will recall one of them—the letter written to my girlfriend and left on the bed of a buddy who wasn't flying that night. The request was, "If we don't come back, please mail it for me."

The letter was opened by censor number 2640. Strangely, not one word was blocked out. The last line on that letter read, "If we get shot down over enemy territory, I will walk back to you." Little did I know...

The second letter, mailed to me by Alice on February 1st, was curiously and intuitively mailed from Ireland to England by air mail for quick delivery, but arrived one day too late.

As war measures called for all incoming and outgoing mail to be censored, this letter was opened and officially sealed. Then, by AM (Air Ministry) instructions, it was stamped 'return to sender' because the would-be recipient was missing on an operational flight.

On the 25th day of August, 1945, I received my release authorization from the Royal Air Force. Officially, I became a civilian when I received my National Identity Card on the 5th day of September, 1945.

In Northern Ireland's capital city of Belfast, on March 12th, 1946, I married Alice. Soon after, I bought a grocery store in one of Belfast's working-class districts close to the dock area. Many of the residents were poor, but they were wonderful people.

With the will and initiative to make the venture pay, I hoped to produce my fortune before I turned fifty. It was not to be.

Almost seven years later, with strict food rationing still in place, I bailed out again. Not by parachute this time, but on the Canadian Pacific liner *Empress of France* bound for Canada. It was New Year's Eve, 1952.

Eventually I arrived by train in Alberta's capital city of Edmonton. It was another January 21st morning, with temperatures of forty below zero, but I was marching to a different drummer than the one I'd heard on January 21st, 1945, when, in similar weather, I had marched out of Stalag VIIIB toward a very uncertain future.

A job with a grocery chain enabled me to pay rent for an apartment and send for my wife and four-year-old daughter, Margaret. My son Jim was born in Edmonton a year before we all moved to the west coast of British Columbia.

After almost thirty years in the sales department of Kraft Foods, Ltd., I retired. Now my wife, son, daughter, and family all live on the west coast's well-known Saltspring Island. I have spent much time putting together my memoirs

At seventy-three, I like to go walking each morning—not around enclosures of barbed wire, but absorbing the fantastic scenery and filling my lungs with fresh sea air.

Even now, after many decades, I relish this life and my freedom. And I can still finish my walks with a hundred-yard dash to home.

As we were.

Alec MacKinlay

Paddy Mac

Nabber Giddens

Jimmy Grier

Big Jock Martin

The Stalag VIIIB propaganda photo

297